Timber-Framed Buildings of England

Timber-Framed Buildings of England

by

R. J. Brown

ROBERT HALE · LONDON

© *R J. Brown 1986*
First published in Great Britain 1986
Reprinted 1990
First paperback edition 1997
Reprinted 1998
Reprinted 2000

Robert Hale Limited
Clerkenwell House
Clerkenwell Green
London EC1R 0HT

ISBN 0-7090-6092-0

4   6   8   10   9   7   5   3

Printed in Great Britain by St Edmundsbury Press Limited
Bury St Edmunds, Suffolk and bound by
Woolnough Bookbinding Limited

Contents

Illustrations

Acknowledgements

In the preparation of this book I am greatly indebted to all the writers mentioned in the bibliography whose research over numerous years has made this book possible, and in addition to all those other authors of books and articles too numerous to mention who have assisted in some way in its production. In particular I would like to acknowledge the help given by the books and numerous articles of C. A. Hewett, especially on timber joints, and R. T. Mason, and to the important regional and technical reports by S. E. Rigold, F. W. B. Charles, N. W. Alcock, J. M. Fletcher, J. T. Smith and many others.

Also I would like to express my appreciation for the help and co-operation I have received from the staff of the following public libraries: Aylesbury, Birmingham, Brighton, Colchester, Chester, Exeter, Hereford, Lincoln, Liverpool, Manchester, Norwich and Shrewsbury.

In addition I would like to thank my wife for her continuing encouragement and assistance throughout and in particular for typing the typescript, my son David, from whose photographs the drawings were made and who prepared the index, and all those other people who over the years have assisted me in the production of this book.

Glossary

Arcade
: The structural members – posts and braces – which form the lateral division between the main span and its aisles.

Arcade-plate
: A horizontal member supported by the arcade posts tying them together and carrying the feet of the rafters of both the main and aisle roofs.

Arcade-post
: A vertical member, forming part of the arcade and supporting the arcade-plate.

Baluster
: A vertical member supporting the handrail.

Bargeboard
: A timber board, sometimes carved, fixed at the gable end and following the slope of the roof to mask the ends of the horizontal roof timbers.

Batten
: A small strip of wood used horizontally to hang or attach tiles, slates etc.

Binder
: A horizontal timber which unites the storey posts and which supports the bridging-joists.

Bolection moulding
: A raised moulding of bold outline of double curvature.

Boss
: A projecting ornament either square or round covering the intersection of the ribs in a panelled ceiling or roof.

Bower
: The women's apartment in a medieval house.

Bowtell
: A small roll moulding or bead.

Brace
: A diagonal timber, either straight or curved, to strengthen framework.

Bridging-joist
: Floor joist which supports ends of common joists, usually bridging the bays from one binding-joist to the next.

Cames
: Grooved bars of lead for joining small pieces of glass into a larger sheet.

15

Canopy	The projecting curved timber hood at the upper end of the medieval open hall.
Cant post	A post that converges upwards.
Cap, capital	The ornamental expanded top of a post or pillar designed to receive an arched superstructure as in a crown-post.
Casement	A window, of either metal or wood, which is hinged on one side, so opening inwards or outwards.
Catslide roof	A roof having the main slope extending uninterruptedly over an extension.
Chamfer	A splay, usually forty-five degrees, formed when the arris is cut away.
Cladding	A material covering the external face of the building but which is not structural.
Collar, collar beam	A horizontal timber placed above wall-plate level spanning between and tying together a pair of rafters.
Console	A decorative bracket usually in the form of an 'S'.
Corbel	A projection of stone or timber from the face of the wall for the support of a superincumbent weight.
Cove	A concave surface set at an angle generally between vertical and horizontal surfaces.
Cross-wing	A range at the end of and set at right-angles to the main range of a house.
Cusp	The projecting points separating the foils in tracery.
Damp-proof course	A horizontal layer of impervious material inserted in a wall to prevent rising damp.
Dormer	A window projecting vertically from a sloping roof and having a roof of its own.
Eaves	The horizontal overhang of a roof projecting beyond the face of a wall.
End girt/girth	Horizontal timber on end wall placed between

wall-plate and ground sill, shortening the studs.

Fascia

A horizontal board to conceal the ends of floor joists in jetty construction and end of rafters etc at roof level.

Fenestration

The arrangement of windows on the elevation of the external wall.

Firehood

A canopy of stone or timber and plaster over a fireplace to lead the smoke to the flue.

Foiled

In Gothic architecture cut into circles which may be grouped together in threes (trefoiled), fours (quatrefoiled), fives (cinquefoiled) etc.

Gable

The vertical triangular wall at the end of the roof, also applied to the wall at the end of a ridged roof.

Gauge

The part of a roofing slate or tile which is exposed to view.

Girt/girth

Horizontal timber placed between wall-plate and sill beam, which shortens and stiffens studs.

Heck

A short internal wall carrying the firehood, often with an entrance beside it.

Herringbone

Stones, bricks or tiles laid diagonally and sloping in opposite directions to form a zigzag pattern.

Hip

The sloping external intersection of two inclined roof surfaces.

Inglenook

The area under a large chimney or firehood.

Jamb

The vertical side of an opening for a door or window in a wall.

Jetty

The projection of an upper floor beyond the storey below on a timber-framed house.

Joist

One of several horizontal parallel timbers laid between walls or beams to carry flooring.

Jowl

The enlarged head of a timber post to carry a tie-beam.

Lath	A thin, narrow strip of wood used to provide a backing for plaster.
Light	The vertical opening of a window framed by mullions and/or jambs.
Lintel	A horizontal timber spanning an opening.
Lodged floor	A floor retained in place by its own weight.
Mortice	A socket cut in a piece of wood to receive a tenon.
Mullion	A vertical structural member sub-dividing a window.
Newel stair	A spiral stair with steps framed into a central vertical post.
Nogging	Brick used in the filling of panels between timber studwork.
Outshut	An extension of a building under a lean-to roof at either the rear or the end.
Ovolo moulding	A moulding of classical origin forming a quarter-round or semi-ellipse in section.
Plinth	The projecting base of a wall often with a splayed top.
Purlin	In roof construction, a longitudinal horizontal timber supporting the common rafters.
Rafter	One of several inclined timbers supporting the roof-covering.
Rendering	Cement or lime-plaster covering to external face of a wall.
Reredos	A stone wall at the back of a timber and plaster firehood.
Ridge	The apex of a roof, the ridge-piece being the horizontal longitudinal timber supporting the tops of the rafters.
Riser	Of a staircase, the vertical member of a step.
Sash	A glazed wooden window which slides up and down by means of a pulley.

Shutters	Timber boards between which semi-liquid material can be poured for building a wall.
Soffit	The underside of a lintel, beam or arch.
Solar	The principal chamber, usually at the upper end of the hall, in a medieval house.
Spandrel	The space between the curved or shaped head of an opening and a rectangular outer frame; the space between the curved brace and a tie-beam.
Spere	A wall usually at the lower end of the open hall and projecting from one or both sides of the hall to screen the entrances.
Spere-truss	A roof truss, with below the tie-beam two speres leaving a wide central opening into the hall from the cross-passage.
Stop	The feature at the end of a moulding or chamfer to transfer the batten to a square section.
Storey-post	A full-height wall post in a multi-storeyed timber building.
Strapwork	Flat interlaced decoration derived from strips of cut leather, popular in Tudor period.
String	Of a staircase, the raking side member carrying the treads and risers; closed string in which the treads and risers are housed, the open string in which the string is cut to the profile of the treads and risers.
Strut	In roof construction, a vertical or diagonal timber which does not support a longitudinal member.
Studs	The vertical members of a timber-framed house between the main posts.
Swag	An ornamental festoon of foliage etc which is fastened up at both ends and hangs down in the centre.
Tenon	The end of a piece of wood reduced in width in order to fit into a mortice of another piece of wood, thus making a joint.

Tie-beam	In roof construction, the main horizontal timber of a truss joining together the feet of the principal rafter at the wall-plate.
Torching	The filling-in with lime and hair mortar of the uneven space between the underside of tiles or slates on an unboarded or unfelted roof.
Tracery	The decorative pattern at the head of a Gothic window or opening, generally formed by the interlacing extension of the mullions.
Transom	A horizontal structural member subdividing a window.
Tread	Of a staircase, the horizontal member of a step.
Truss	A rigid framework spanning the building used to support the ridge, purlins etc that carries the common rafters.
Underbuilt	A wall added beneath a jetty.
Valley	The sloping internal junction of two inclined roof surfaces.
Wall-plate	A horizontal timber member at the top of the wall to receive the ends of the rafters, tie-beams etc.
Windbrace	A timber member often curved and set diagonally between the principal rafters and the side purlins to increase resistance to wind pressure and stiffen the roof structure longitudinally.
Winder stair	A stair turning continuously.
Yoke	A short horizontal timber joining the rafters together near the apex of the roof often supporting a ridge.

Introduction

Until some four hundred years ago, timber was the principal building material in England, with the possible exception of Cornwall, a county not well supplied with trees suitable for timber construction (even here, however, we can find some timber-framed houses, for instance at Launceston). Even in those areas, such as the Cotswolds and Derbyshire, where other materials, such as stone, were readily available, timber was preferred, for it was then plentiful, cheap and easy to handle, with the added advantage that every tree felled or woodland cleared provided additional land for cultivation.

Large parts of medieval England were covered with forests; over sixty genuine forests were recorded in the thirteenth century. Based on Gregory King's estimate that the acreage of woods and coppices in England in 1688 amounted to some three million acres, it seems likely, with the widespread depletion of the forests in the previous century for shipbuilding, fuel for iron-smelting, building and other uses, that at the commencement of the sixteenth century there were over four million acres of woodland. In some areas – for instance, in parts of the Midlands – so dense were the oak forests that early settlers avoided them.

The timber-framed buildings that survive today do not reflect the almost universal use of timber until about 1500, for only a small proportion of pre-1500 buildings have survived. Although timber was the principal building material used, it was not until the latter part of the sixteenth century that oak was used almost universally, for until that time 'men were content to dwell in houses built of sallow, willow, plum-tree, hardbeam and elm', with oak being restricted to the construction of 'churches, religious houses, princes' palaces, noblemen's lodgings and navigation'. These buildings of inferior timbers were rebuilt between the period 1550 and 1660 often in oak, but also in stone in those areas where it was available.

It is known that most buildings, except those of great importance, were in Saxon times of timber. Although many were of flimsy construction from light, unsquared timbers gathered from the waste, some of the hall-type houses revealed by excavation were of a more substantial nature. In all these cases the strength to resist wind-pressure was achieved by setting the posts upright in prepared pits in the ground, known as earthfoot construction. Because of this the damp to which the timber was subjected already reduced the life of these buildings to the length of time it took the principal posts to rot. From archaeological excavation, it is evident that these buildings were often repaired or rebuilt at least once a generation and that the irregular alignment and spacing of the upright in many buildings made it impracticable to form prefabricated framed buildings. It is this ability to form prefabricated buildings from halved or cleft timber with framed joints that distinguishes timber-framing from other systems of timber construction such as earthfoot construction or the use of whole logs.

These timber-framed buildings can be classified into two types: box-frame and cruck construction. Box-frame construction was by far the most common and comprised horizontal and vertical timber members jointed together to form a wall with the open panels infilled or with the entire wall covered with an appropriate cladding material. In cruck construction, pairs of inclined cruck blades are spaced at intervals along the building to collect the roof loads by means of ridge-beams, purlins and wall-plates to transmit the loads to the ground. The walls, which were non-structural, were often timber-framed but could be of any material. Within both groups are many variants: in box-frame there are the close studding, post-and-truss and interrupted sill, while in cruck construction there are, apart from true crucks, many forms within the family, the most important being the base-cruck and jointed cruck.

The distribution of cruck and box-frame construction differs (1). Full crucks, for instance, are to be found only in the Midlands, North and West. This form of construction is entirely absent from the south-eastern counties of Cambridgeshire, Essex, Kent, south Humberside, Lincolnshire, Norfolk, Suffolk and Sussex, with only isolated examples recorded in Surrey, Bedfordshire and Hertfordshire. It is also found only occasionally in the south-western counties of Devon, Dorset, Hampshire and Somerset. Clearly its scarcity in the south-western counties and absence from certain parts of East Anglia, Cambridgeshire and Lincolnshire can be attributed to the lack of suitable trees, but the reason for its absence from the other south-eastern counties – Essex, Kent and Sussex, where there were considerable forests – is not easily explained and several theories have been put forward. One is that the South and East were always influenced by the Continent, where this form of construction was never prevalent. This, coupled with the fact that the South-East was always more advanced socially and economically, being agriculturally richer than other parts of the country, suggests that this system was probably abandoned while still in use elsewhere. Even in areas where crucks survive, the distribution varies greatly, in both number and date of construction.

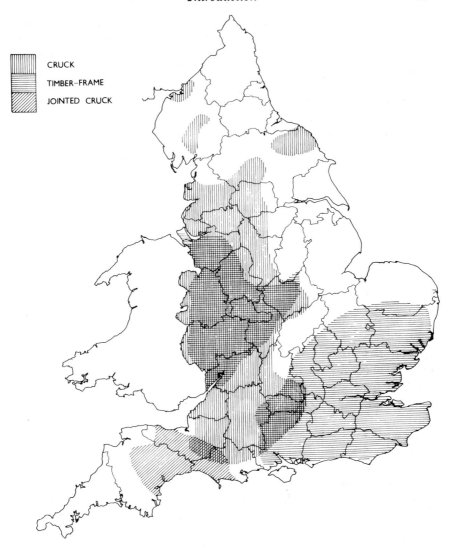

CRUCK

TIMBER-FRAME

JOINTED CRUCK

1. Main areas of cruck and box-frame construction

The social development of the country was not evenly spread, so that in one area, which was more prosperous, crucks were being replaced with other forms of construction, but in other areas they were still being built. Hence, while cruck construction was abandoned in most areas by 1700, in parts of Lancashire and Yorkshire cruck construction continued after this date. In Cumbria, around the Solway Firth, crucks, although of small scantling and not matching pairs, were still being used at the beginning of the nineteenth century.

Today more cruck-frames survive than is generally thought, for many have been incorporated within enlarged buildings, hidden beneath a cladding of brick, stone or mud or simply plastered over. This is particularly true in Cumbria, Derbyshire, Lancashire, Leicestershire and North Yorkshire, all with a relatively large number of cruck-framed buildings of which few are exposed. In Devon, Dorset, Somerset, Nottinghamshire and Northamptonshire, although all with fewer examples, the same applies. The county where most cruck buildings are to be found is Hereford & Worcester being particularly numerous in and around Weobley, Dilwyn, Eardisland, Pembridge and Eardisley. Other counties where cruck-framed buildings can best be observed are Shropshire (where they have even been incorporated in three churches, at Acton Round, Munslow and Stoke St Milborough), Staffordshire, Warwickshire and Cheshire. Many of these buildings can also be found in the northern part of Gloucestershire, in the area adjacent to Hereford & Worcester, in such villages as Ashleworth, Dymock and Sandhurst, while the Severn Valley is another area where a number survive. Cruck-framed buildings can also be observed in Berkshire and the adjacent areas of Oxfordshire, Wiltshire and Buckinghamshire. Ten cruck-framed buildings survive at Harwell, Oxfordshire, with Dell Cottage (2) and Le Carillon having been dated by the radiocarbon process as 1445 and 1425 respectively; cruck-frames can also be seen in the northern part of Wiltshire at Urchfont, Pewsey and Wilsford, and further west, at Lacock, there is another excellent example. Today crucks are to be found mainly on cottages and barns, so giving the popular belief that cruck construction was a humble form of construction. This is not so, for those examples surviving from the fourteenth and fifteenth centuries are of considerable standing with large scantlings with well-finished timbers, very different from those built in the sixteenth and seventeenth centuries.

Jointed crucks, the other form of cruck construction used in building, are restricted to a smaller area than the true cruck for they are found (except for a few isolated cases elsewhere, and then only in more important buildings) only in Devon, Dorset and Somerset. In the east and north of these counties they far outnumber true crucks but they are almost entirely absent from south Devon, with only one example being found in Cornwall. In Dorset and Somerset they are predominantly late medieval, while in Devon their use extended to the sixteenth century.

The distribution of base-crucks, though much fewer in number than true crucks, is much wider. They are widely dispersed from the north Midlands to the South, not only in those areas generally associated with true crucks but beyond its extreme eastern margin in the counties of Kent, Sussex, Cambridgeshire and Lincolnshire. They are com-

2. Dell Cottage, Harwell, Oxfordshire

pletely absent from northern England, an area where true crucks are
well represented. Like true crucks, they are not to be found in Essex
and East Anglia.

Box-frame construction of the various types is much more widely
dispersed than that of cruck construction. Today it can be found
mainly in the eastern counties, east of the limestone belt extending
northwards to central Norfolk and Cambridgeshire, and the counties
to the west of the limestone belt and north of the Severn estuary,
extending northwards to the east of the Pennines through Nottinghamshire to York and west of the Pennines into central Lancashire.
Within these broad areas the intensity of box-frame construction differs

greatly, but even where little timber-framing now survives it does not mean that it was not at one time the normal form of construction. Lancashire, for instance, is now generally regarded as a brick county but this is something new for even as late as the beginning of the eighteenth century brick buildings were rare, gaining popularity only because of the growing scarcity of wood. For many centuries timber was plentiful, and up to the end of the seventeenth century timber-framed buildings prevailed everywhere away from the Pennines, as far north as the River Ribble.

Outside these areas there are few counties which do not have at least some examples of timber-framing. These are to be found mainly in towns; in the South-West, in Devon and Cornwall (neither of which has a tradition of timber-framing), houses, sometimes of considerable size, are to be found within the towns. The timber houses at Launceston have already been mentioned; in Devon a few examples can still be found in Exeter and Dartmouth, while at Totnes there are many examples frequently clad with slate or plaster. Again in such places as the Cotswolds timber-framing can be found in towns and large villages, even occasionally in the countryside in those marginal areas which lie between the predominantly stone region and the timber ones. In the northern counties too, although box-framing is rare, it is not completely absent. In Cumbria, for instance, one can cite the guildhall at Carlisle, and the odd example at Kendal and Hawkhead. In Newcastle-upon-Tyne there still survive two or three examples, the most notable being Surtees House and 37 Sandhill.

The earliest surviving timber-framed buildings in England date from the thirteenth century, but these are rare, being of aisled construction, and occur only in the South-East, Essex and parts of Suffolk, although in Hereford & Worcester there is the occasional building of cruck construction, usually base-crucks which are of thirteenth-century date. The number of surviving examples increase from the fifteenth century until they reach their peak in the great period of rebuilding in the second half of the sixteenth century and the first half of the seventeenth. After the reign of Elizabeth, timber-framing began to be restricted to buildings of lesser importance and increasingly so until finally it was confined to cottages, farm buildings and non-domestic buildings.

The supply of home-grown timber had begun to decline in the sixteenth century, and by the beginning of the seventeenth century the continuing depletion of the country's oak forests forced the builders to exercise economies in the use of the remaining oaks. This growing shortage of timber was due only in part to the extravagant use of timber in house-building in the preceding centuries, partly to the widespread use of wood as a fuel not only for heating but also for use in the iron-working furnaces and forges, particularly in the Mayfield and Ashburnham areas of Sussex. In addition there was the ever-increasing demand for ships, for both the navy and the merchant fleet, started by Henry VIII and continued by Elizabeth. These factors, coupled with the failure to replant the felled trees, led to the depletion of the forests of the South and Midlands. Even by the end of Elizabeth's reign timber was becoming scarce, and it is reported that the price had risen by as much as twenty-five per cent in a few years. In 1608 John Norden deplored the lack of oak, elm and ash, which he called the 'three building trees'. The scarcity of oak was more acute in some areas than in others, particularly in the eastern coastal areas – for instance, in the Lincolnshire Fens where from the sixteenth and seventeenth centuries various species of timber, including poplar, lime and hornbeam, were often used. In the Breckland of Norfolk, the area around Thetford now covered with acres upon acres of fir plantations, a royal proclamation of 1604 ordained that all new houses must have their walls and window-frames constructed of brick or stone and that the cutting of trees for fuel must also cease. Therefore, in this area, as in other areas where timber was scarce, as timber-framed buildings decayed they were replaced by buildings constructed of other materials, until in some districts no timber buildings remained. During the Elizabethan and Jacobean periods oak was often taken from old buildings, which were for some reason being demolished, cut up into smaller sections and re-used, in the construction either of a larger building or of two or more smaller ones.

By the eighteenth century building in half-timber began to decline. The country's forests were so depleted that it became of increasing necessity to import softwood from the Baltic and Scandinavia, supplemented later, in the nineteenth century, with supplies from Canada and the United States. These softwoods, although easier to work than the traditional British hardwoods, were inferior in their structural capacity. Cottages and farm buildings using softwood framing continued to be built well into the nineteenth century, its use being fostered by the tax on bricks first imposed in 1784 and not abolished until 1850.

The structural use of timber was therefore in use for centuries, with surviving examples spanning some six centuries. During this long period of time, timber-framed buildings were affected not only by the various technical developments which occurred but by the many local traditions which influenced the appearance of these buildings from region to region.

Construction and Structural Details

Oak was the timber predominantly used in timber-framed construction, for its strength and resistance to rot were unrivalled, and if it was allowed to dry naturally, it actually improved and hardened with age. Of the other timbers, elm is most commonly met, for when grown in woodland conditions it grew taller than oak and was therefore sometimes preferred to oak for longitudinal members, such as collar-purlins, where a single continuous length was an advantage. It is, however, somewhat inferior to oak in that it is less resistant to damp and insect attack, yet it was frequently used in the construction of barns and other farm buildings in the seventeenth and eighteenth centuries. At Houchins Farm, Feering, Essex (3), a house built in the second half of the sixteenth century, both oak and elm were used, oak for those timbers under stress, such as tie-beams and binding joists, but elm for all secondary timbers, such as studs. Sweet chestnut was another timber sometimes used – Polsteads Farmhouse, Bures Hamlet, Essex, built about 1590, is one example – and when weathered even experts find it difficult to distinguish it from oak. Chestnut, although it does not attract beetle infestation, is less resistant to rot than oak. Other timbers known to be used were ash (one of John Norden's three 'building trees'), willow, hornbeam, black poplar and even plum.

In the eighteenth century, when many of Britain's forests were depleted, imported softwood was also used. Its use for flooring was, of course, widespread but in such places as Cambridgeshire, as well as in parts of the South-East, softwood began to replace oak as the traditional timber for wall-framing. An early example of the use of softwood in the structural frame was at the former White Horse Inn, in Castle Street, Cambridge, a seventeenth-century building. In Cambridgeshire it was not uncommon for oak and softwood to be used within the same building.

The oak was generally not seasoned, for timbers over about three inches thick took an extremely long time, and so the large scantlings required for structural purposes made it impracticable. In addition, when the oak was 'green', it was soft, allowing it to be cut and the joints made, but as the sap dried out, the timber hardened until eventually it was almost too hard to cut. Oak was, therefore, generally used within a year or so of felling, and this probably explains the warps

29

3. Houchins Farm, Feering, Essex

and twists to be seen on many old buildings. Even when oak has been fixed in a building for centuries, it will warp and twist, as if new, when cut up and used again. When oak was required to be seasoned, it was generally submerged in a running stream with butt-end upstream, the sap being flushed out.

Timbers from old buildings were often re-used, and it was common in Elizabethan and Jacobean periods, when so many of the timber-framed houses were built and rebuilt, to use timbers from old buildings. In the main these timbers were cut up and often used to construct two or more smaller buildings. These old timbers can usually be identified because of the position of redundant mortices, peg holes and marks, and this may have led to the widespread and persistent belief that many houses are built of old ships' timbers. There is nothing improbable about the idea, for up to about 1840 most ships were constructed of timber and at the end of their serviceable life were undoubtedly sold and broken up for their timbers, yet there is little evidence either 'documentary or practically' that the timbers were ever used in the construction of buildings. On closer examination the redundant mortices and peg holes can easily be explained.

The oaks were felled with a narrow axe, although a large tree was often cut around with a broad axe before the narrow axe was used on the heartwood. The larger trees were split into baulks by means of an axe and iron wedges, but for the smaller ones the baulks were often formed by roughly squaring the tree by means of an axe or adze. The baulks were then cut to length with a two-handled cross-cut saw, known as a 'twart-saw'. The length of these timbers was usually between ten and twenty feet, but lengths up to thirty feet were not uncommon, and very occasionally timbers up to fifty feet were used. The conversion of these timbers varied depending on their use within the building (4). The principal timbers (posts, wall-plates and main beams) were boxed heart and simply squared by means of an axe before finally being trimmed with an adze. For smaller timbers (the studs,

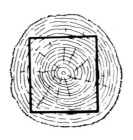 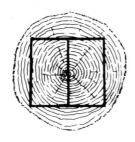 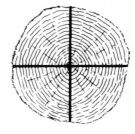

A. boxed heart   B. halved   C. quartered

4. Timber conversion

braces, rafters and joists), the squared baulks were generally halved or quartered.

The timber would be either hand-sawn or cleft and squared by means of an adze. At first the logs rested on a trestle with the top sawyer, who guided the saw, sometimes standing on the log, with the bottom sawyer, who pulled the saw, underneath. It was not until the sixteenth century that saw-pits first began to appear; the principle was the same, the top sawyer standing above the log, with the bottom sawyer pulling the saw from within the pit. For high-quality work the timber was usually sawn, for it gave a good straight face, but for less important work the timber was cleft – split along its length. Cleft timber has an advantage over sawn in that, as it follows the grain, it is more durable, minimizing the likelihood of splitting caused by cutting across the grain. Cleft timbers were widely used up to the seventeenth century, providing many of the small timbers such as wattle staves, laths and tile battens, as well as the larger timber. Early weatherboarding, known as 'clapboarding', was also cleft, the baulks being quartered and then split into wedge-shaped planks radially from the centre. Floorboards too were cleft. The disadvantage with cleft timber, particularly with timber of large scantlings, was that the length obtained depended greatly on the quality of the timber available, and from the eighteenth century onwards, with the shortage of suitable timber to be cleft and the increasing number of power-driven sawmills producing precision-cut timber, its use declined.

Recent research undertaken by Dr Oliver Rackham indicates that more trees were needed for construction than was at first realized. In an article in *Vernacular Architecture* he estimates that at Grundle House, Stanton, Suffolk, a slightly larger than average fifteenth-century house, with two cross-wings, 330 trees were used; a large number were small trees, about half of them less than nine inches in diameter, and even the larger trees rarely exceeded fifty years' growth, with only three exceeding eighteen inches diameter, the normal size of a mature oak. Similarly, the Royal Commission of Historical Monuments has found that, for a small three-bay, seventeenth-century, single-storey house at Swaffham Prior, Cambridgeshire, measuring some forty by 15½ feet on plan, about eighty oaks were used, varying in size from nine inches to eighteen inches in diameter.

Joints
With the timbers so prepared, it was necessary to cut the joints. The jointing system was, of course, of major importance in all timber-framed construction, the old carpenters bringing an astonishing degree of skill and ingenuity to the execution of their work. Joints were either mortice-and-tenon, half-lap or scarf.

The mortice-and-tenon was the most important and was the basis of all traditional framing (5). Generally these joints were of the unrefined type, but when beams were jointed into vertical posts, a hewn bracket or a housed soffit-shoulder or a ledge was provided for additional support. The tenons were cut with a hand-saw (a one-handled tool with a scimitar-like cutting edge) while the mortices were formed either with a chisel and mallet or more commonly with a series of holes bored by an auger, known in medieval times as a 'wymbyll', with the remaining wood being chopped away and trimmed with a 'twybyll', a thin iron bar, about three feet in length, with a central handle with one end of the bar pointed and the other end flattened and both ends sharpened.

Scarf-joints were used to join two beams together to form one continuous member – mainly purlins, wall-plates and sill-beams, and such ingenuity was needed to make it strong enough, especially for top plates, to prevent withdrawal and twisting. These often occurred near a main post, and unlike the mortice-and-tenon joints there were many different forms.

Lap-joints, although an important element in early medieval forms of construction, were later used in relatively few positions in timber-framed buildings, being almost entirely restricted to the joint between the collars and rafters in roof construction, and in cruck construction to the joints between the blades and the tie-beam and collar.

Extensive research undertaken by C. A. Hewett during the last twenty years or so has established that joints used in the construction of timber-framed buildings are an important criterion in their dating. At one time hardly any timber-framed buildings had been dated earlier than the fifteenth century, with the exception of aisled halls which were generally agreed to be fourteenth-century, and so the implications of Mr Hewett's views on datings were unacceptable to many experts.

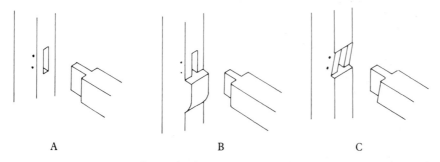

A. unrefined   B. with hewn-bracket
C. with housed soffit-shoulder or ledge

5. Mortice-and-tenon joints

However, subsequent dendrochronological and carbon-14 testing have proved him correct, and further researches by R. T. Mason in the Weald and S. E. Rigold at Steventon, Oxfordshire, have substantiated the original findings.

Lap-joints, (6) as previously mentioned, were important in medieval times, for at that time relatively few mortice-and-tenon joints were used, with many of the subsidiary members, such as scissor-braces, being inserted after the main frame had been assembled, and so a lapped joint was essential. The earliest of these lap-joints was the 'notched lap-joint' (6A), the notch designed to prevent withdrawal of the brace from the frame and roof-trusses. The bulk of these joints are to be found on buildings ascribed to the thirteenth century or earlier. Slightly later in date is what is known as the 'secret notched lap-joint' (6B), a slightly more refined joint with the notch hidden when the brace is in position. This type of joint has been dated by Mr Hewett about 1250 to 1300 or possibly a little later. The notched lap-joint was superseded by the mortice-and-tenon joint and lapped dovetail joint, the transition taking place in Essex, according to Mr Hewett, in about 1300.

More important as an aid to dating are the scarf-joints (7), of which there are many varieties and which varied considerably over the centuries. Among the earliest and simplest forms dating from the thirteenth and fourteenth centuries were the edge-halved scarfs with square vertical butts. More widely used, however, were the splayed scarfs, of which there were several varieties. The simplest of these was the through-splayed scarf, a joint known to have been in use in the twelfth and thirteenth centuries. More common were the splayed and

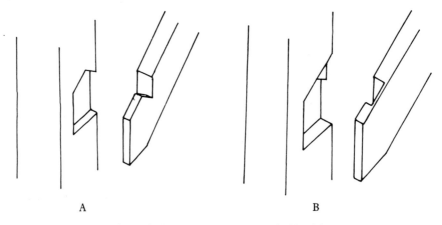

A   B

A. notched lap-joint   B. secret notched lap-joint

6. Lap joints

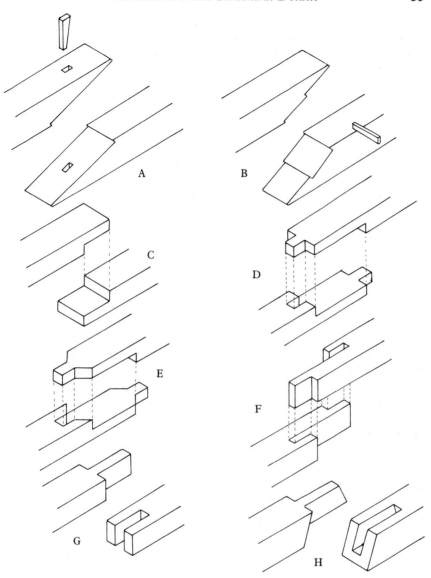

A. & B. splayed and tabled; C. lapped; D. edge-halved; E. edge-halved with sallied shoulders; F. faced-halved; G. & H. bridle.

7. Scarf joints

tabled scarfs – those in which there is a step in the middle of the plane of the joint – often with under squint-butts. The earliest versions of this joint, known in thirteenth- and fourteenth-century buildings, have either a wedge (feather or folding) driven between the tables to tighten it or a 'face-key' driven vertically through the joint. A highly refined scarf-joint was an elaboration on the simple splayed scarf in which the butt ends were bridled and pegged with a face-key driven vertically through the joint. It was a highly efficient joint, performing all the functions of the preceding types but requiring far less timber. It required, however, even more skill to make than most scarf-joints and generally indicates a mid-fourteenth-century date.

During the fifteenth and sixteenth centuries splayed scarfs were replaced by edge-halved scarf-joints, of which there were numerous and highly ingenious varieties. Both members were bridled onto each other, the bridle being pegged, the main variation being the abutting shoulders which were either 'sallied' (splayed) or birds-mouth, both of which indicate an early fifteenth-century date, after which all faces were cut square (this form continued in use until about 1650). In the latter part of the sixteenth century the face-halved and bladed scarf-joint began to appear. It differed fundamentally from all previous types, for the halving was in the vertical plane instead of the horizontal to produce face-halvings. It was never superseded, for, as it was cut almost entirely by a saw, it was cheap to produce, and it continued to be used well into the nineteenth century, especially in the construction of barns. Another scarf-joint was the bridle scarf, with square shoulders commonly used on wall-plates as well as sill-plates from the medieval period into the seventeenth century. During the eighteenth century the use of scarf-joints began to decline, with the timbers being jointed with iron plates and bolts, a technique commonly illustrated in the numerous textbooks of the period for builders and carpenters.

Another important joint is the complexed joint between the post, wall-plate and tie-beam known as the tie-beam lap-dovetailed joint (8). The tie-beam was secured to the wall-plate by a dovetail joint, generally of a lap-dovetail type, although sometimes they were of the bare-faced variety – that is, with a shoulder to one side only. In some instances, the lap-dovetail joint would open up, due to the strain, showing a gap, and to overcome this the shoulder of the joint was sometimes entrant, or housed. The post is secured to both the tie-beam and the wall-plate with a mortice-and-tenon joint. The joint was a very satisfactory one, used from the thirteenth until the nineteenth century with little variation.

To enable these lap-dovetailed joints to be undertaken satisfactorily, the maximum amount of timber was required so that the greatest rigidity in the joint could be achieved. This thickening out of the top

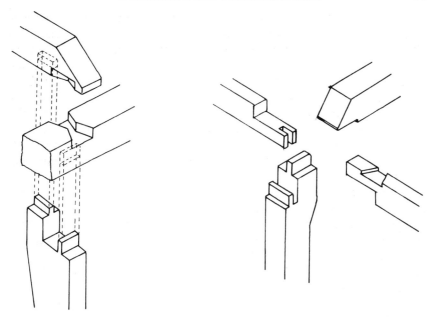

8. Tie-beam lap-dovetail joints

of the post is known as the 'jowl' and, though associated with the reversal of the trunk (that is, root uppermost, using the expanded growth of the tree's root), it has, like many other techniques, undergone many changes (9). Before about 1250, for instance, at The Bury, Clavering, Essex, the main post had no such swelling, after which time 'upstands' were built on top of the main posts, as at the Wheat Barn, Cressing Temple, Essex, and from this structural devise joints were subsequently developed. Jowls were first adopted in the thirteenth

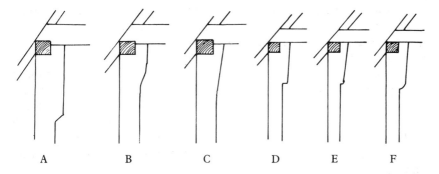

A   B   C   D   E   F

Typical jowls to main post. Types B & C most common; used between 1250 and 1700. Types D, E & F used between 1600 and 1900.

9. Jowls

century and were widely used until the middle of the sixteenth century at which time they were used not only at the top ends of posts but also, although to a lesser extent, on horizontal timbers. Towards the end of the sixteenth century the use of the feature declined, and by the eighteenth century it had generally been dispensed with altogether on domestic work, although its use continued in the construction of barns until the middle of the nineteenth century.

Most of these joints were secured with pointed heart-of-oak pegs, often referred to in medieval times as 'trashnails', driven into holes pre-drilled through the joints with the heads of the pegs left projecting. Iron bolts and nails were rarely used, for no carpenter would normally rely on such things as nails. In addition, iron was too expensive for general use and, moreover, if it had been, the tannic acid in the unseasoned oak would soon have corroded them unless they were galvanized, a process unknown prior to the eighteenth century although the dipping of bolts in tin was practised. The expense, however, of tinning prohibited its use in all but major buildings. In any case tightly fitted heart-of-oak pegs were as effective as untreated bolts and more so than nails. Wrought-iron straps, reinforcing joints, are frequently to be found on old timber-framed buildings, but these are nearly always of later date, added when joints opened due to unequal settlement or to the shrinking or twisting of the timber. It was not until the eighteenth century that much evidence existed of the use of nails but by this time softwood was frequently employed or if oak was used it was of such small scantlings that it could be more easily seasoned than before.

Before making any joints, the carpenter had to choose the face from which to work. This was known as the 'upper face' for when the timber was being framed on the ground, it was always uppermost. It was on this face that the carpenters' numerals and marks were cut and where the peg holes were drilled. This upper face was carefully selected and was generally the 'heart-face' (the face sawn from the heart-wood), the number of faces depending on whether a baulk was halved or quartered – one face when halved, two when quartered. In addition, baulks so halved or quartered were normally placed symmetrically in the building; for example four main posts quartered from one baulk would be placed at the four corners of one bay, or placed symmetrically within one frame, or when halved placed facing each other across a bay. The upper face also occupied special positions within the building; in the external walls it was always the external face, and internally it always faced the more important of the adjoining areas of the building; for instance, in the open hall the upper face always faced the dais.

All of this work was carried out at the carpenter's workshop or yard – the 'framynplace', the timbers being framed on the ground and the components incised on their upper face at the joints for assembling on site. These carpenters' numerals were based on a system of Roman numerals which, though not strictly Latin, were simple and effective (10). In Tudor times they were cut with a tool used for cutting straight lines, called a 'scribe', but in Jacobean times, when the marks were smaller, they were cut with a gouge or chisel. The system was based on various combinations of I, V and X with the Roman IV becoming IIII, and IX becoming VIIII, with the Vs often being inverted, while they also made one cross-cut do when X and V were used together or when two or more Xs were used. To assist in locating the various timbers for different parts of the building, carpenters' marks were added to the Roman numerals. These were a series of strokes, circles, segments etc, each mark denoting a particular section of the building. Sometimes a 'fleck' was provided on the final digit, indicating that this was to the right-hand side of the building as seen from the upper face. Again, in buildings of more than one storey, the timbers of the

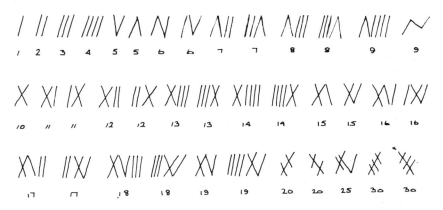

Examples of carpenters' numerals

Examples of carpenters' numerals with 'flecks'

Examples of carpenters' numerals with strokes indicating to which floors they relate

10. Carpenters' numerals and marks

wall-frame often had strokes cut above the numerals, indicating which floor they related to – one stroke for the first floor, two strokes for the second and so on. In some cases, as at the Ancient High House, Stafford, Arabics were used. These identification marks enabled workmen to sort the timbers easily prior to erection.

The erecting of the timbers on site differed between those of box-frame and cruck construction. The method employed in cruck building was rearing; that is, the components of each frame, previously prepared in the carpenter's yard, were jointed and pegged together to make a rigid frame which was then raised through ninety degrees, tenons on the bottom of the blades engaging with the mortices in the sill-beam. In addition, the longitudinal members – the wall-plate and purlins – were also used to locate each frame as it was raised. Although, according to L. F. Salzman in his book *Building in England Down to 1540*, there is evidence that for small buildings of box-frame construction a similar process was adopted (that is, that the end frames were assembled, pegged together and raised as a whole), in the majority of cases it appears that the building was erected timber by timber, the assembly proceeding in well-defined order, the joints being secured by oak pegs driven into the holes prepared in the yard and left slightly projecting. The hole in the outer wall of the mortice did not tie up with the hole in the tenon, which was drilled slightly nearer the shoulder of the tenon, so that when the peg was driven in for the first time the joint tightened.

There is evidence that these timbers were not at first permanently fixed during assembling and that plenty of play was left for easy insertion of beams, with the sills and posts not immediately pegged together but temporarily held by means of long wooden pins, shaped rather like tent-pegs, called 'hook pins', which could easily be loosened and withdrawn prior to driving in the oak pegs. In most cases all joints were pegged but in some buildings, for instance Synyards, Otham, Kent (11), only the main timbers were secured with pegs, the studs receiving no fixing.

Near the top of some posts, wedge-shaped depressions are to be found, and various views as to their purpose have been put forward. One is that they were used in the process of rearing the frame. Often, however, the position of these depressions is such as to make them impracticable for this purpose and, in any case, if this was normal practice, it would be found on all buildings, which is not the case; even when found, it is rarely on every post. F. W. B. Charles puts forward another explanation in that these depressions were used in conjunction with temporary props to hold the posts in a vertical position whilst the other timbers were assembled. Another and possibly the most likely explanation is that they were used in conjunction

11. Synyards, Otham, Kent

with temporary props to support the structure when repairs were undertaken, perhaps to the sill-beam or when the plinth walls had subsided. Often they appear to have been cut along after the building was constructed. Many, where they have been subsequently protected from the elements by some form of cladding, are still clean and crisply cut, contrasting with the weathered post in which they are to be found.

Bays
Timber-framing, whether of box-frame or cruck construction, consists of a system of bays, which are defined by pairs of posts tied together with a tie-beam – to form a cross-frame in the case of box-frame construction, or in cruck construction by a pair of crucks – and which are the points at which the roof loads are collected and transferred to the ground. The bays are connected laterally by wall-plates at eaves level and a sill-beam support on a dwarf brick or stone wall at ground level. Consequently the space between each post or cruck of the

external wall was non-load-bearing and could be of lighter construction. The length of these bays varied considerably from as little as five feet up to between eighteen and twenty feet, determined to some extent by the length of timber available, and formed a close relationship with the overall plan of the building. In a house this relationship is evident enough, the bays corresponding with the desired length of the room, with the short bays generally indicating the position of the cross-passage, smoke bay or chimneystack. Some rooms were of two-bay length, and this is particularly true of the medieval open-hall divided by an open truss, but even then the bays were not necessarily equal in length, the upper bay generally being longer than the other.

Box-Frame Construction

We have seen earlier that the transition from earthfoot timber-framed structures to sill-mounted structures and therefore a permanent framed building of box-frame construction occurred in England between about 1150 and 1250. As the name implies, box-frame construction consists of a box-like framework in which the roof load is distributed along the supporting walls, unlike cruck construction in which the walls are normally non-load-bearing and are, like the roof timbers, supported directly by the crucks from the ground. Box-framed buildings are based on the use of a pair of posts held together at the top by tie-beams and connected laterally at the top by wall-plates (on which the feet of the common rafters are supported) and at the bottom by the sill-beam. Further lateral support is generally provided by a girth or girt, a horizontal member placed about half-way between the wall-plate and sill-beam which also supports the first-floor joists. These basic components, together with various angle braces, form the frame, and the studs (secondary vertical timbers framed between the sill-beam, girth and wall-plate) and any other horizontal member only serve to reduce the overall size of the panels. The sill-beams are supported on a low plinth wall, to provide a level foundation for the building as well as to raise the structure clear of the earth.

Although the above members form the basic elements of all box-framed buildings in England, there is a great variety of forms not only in wall-framing but also in decorative styles, with many features subject to regional variations which changed with time, with one often intermingling with others to form hybrid patterns.

(12) The characteristic feature of medieval timber wall framing is the use of very large open rectangular panels (12A), in which the long sides, usually measuring some six or seven feet, are formed by the main posts, wall-plates, girths and sill-beams with the absence of common studs and with the main variation being the types of bracing used. A further characteristic is the free use of halvings, rather than

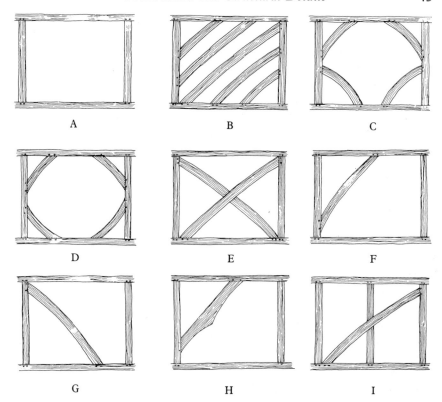

A. square open panel; B. herringbone pattern; C. scalloped; D. circular; E. cross-bracing; F. arch-brace; G. tension-brace; H. arch-bracing cusped; I. tension-brace with panel divided by one stud found in Kent and referred to as Kentish framing.

12. Wall framing – medieval

or in addition to the mortice-and-tenon joint universally used later, made necessary perhaps by the thickness of the braces. A further characteristic early feature is the use of 'dragon ties' joining the wall-plates on two adjoining walls to triangulate the framing on the horizontal plane.

At first the framework had no angle bracing, the only certain example being at Tiptofts Manor, Wimbish, Essex. All other examples of medieval large framing are braced, for angle bracing was essential for the stability of the frame and a fundamental part of timber-framed construction, although it must be said that they were not always used on all walls. Sometimes multiple braces were used diagonally within one panel to form a herringbone pattern often decorative rather than structural (12B). Decorative bracing sometimes in the form of serpentine or ogee-bracing was also introduced. Cross-bracing was also used

13. 39, The Causeway, Steventon, Oxfordshire

and still survives on the gables at the Merchant Adventurers' Hall, York, and on the cross-wing to a contemporary cruck hall at 39–43 The Causeway, Steventon, Oxfordshire (13), a house probably dating from the mid-fourteenth century. However, by far the most common form was angle-bracing, of which there are two basic types: 'arch-braces' (12F) which rise from the post to the girth or wall-plate, and 'tension-braces' (12G), which run down from the post to the sill-beam or girth. The arch-brace is possibly the earlier of the two, but by the early mid-fifteenth century the tension-brace gradually became dominant throughout the country, although never completely replacing the arch-brace in some areas. The arch-brace is to be found mainly in the Midlands and West, the tension-brace in the East and South-East, with a mixture of the two in the east Midlands counties of Bedfordshire and Buckinghamshire – the arch-brace predominantly to the west of these counties, and the tension-brace to the east.

In Kent, such is the widespread use of the tension-brace on the cross-wings of Wealden houses that it is often referred to as Kentish framing, and it is frequently used in conjunction with open panels. Although most common in Kent, it can be found in other parts of the South-East as well as East Anglia and may occur in conjunction with close studding. In eastern England the tension-brace is far more common than one would at first suspect, for with close studding the braces are visible only on the inside, being concealed externally by halving them behind the studs. A variant to the normal tension-brace is to be found in Essex and Suffolk, where often it does not reach down to the girth but stops at a stud, into which it is framed. This of course destroyed the principle of tension-bracing. An early example can be found at Baythorne Hall, Birdbrook, Essex, built about 1360, where it was used in conjunction with normal tension-bracing. It can also be found on several aisled barns in Essex of an early date as well as in later houses in both Essex and Suffolk. Occasionally both arch- and tension-braces were used in one panel to form either a scalloped (12C) or circular pattern. Most of these braces were curved and sometimes cusped (12D), especially in the West. Possibly the best example can be seen on the church at Hartley Wespall, Hampshire.

Another and perhaps lesser known form of stiffening a timber-framed building was by the introduction of straight braces between the main post and the girth or wall-plate. Although there are some early examples, they are generally associated with those timber-framed buildings built towards the end of the sixteenth and throughout the seventeenth century. The distribution is similar to that of the arch-brace, which it replaced, with the exception that it is also to be found in Lancashire and West Yorkshire, where the arch-brace was never a feature.

Although large framing was the commonest form before about 1450, small framing, in which the frame was divided into small squares or near squares by horizontal and vertical members, also appeared at an early date particularly in the West (for instance, at Lower Brockhampton Manor and Amberley Court, Marden, Hereford & Worcester) and in the North-West. Close-studding is another form of early framing.

Later timber wall framing can be classified into three separate schools or traditions of carpentry: the eastern school, with close studding forming tall, narrow panels; the western school, where the studs instead of rising from a sill-beam rise from a sill framed between the main posts; and the northern school of carpentry, which differs greatly from the other two, having a distinctive style of its own which did not spread outside the North.

Except for the northern school, these techniques are in no way restricted to these regions. Close studding is concentrated in East Anglia and may, although there is no real evidence, have originated there, for there are examples of close studding dating from before the middle of the fifteenth century to be found in other parts of the country. One early example is the guildhall at Leicester, which retains its original close-studded side walls. By the middle of the fifteenth century it had spread into most towns, and in the following two centuries it was used in many buildings of high social status throughout the country. The use of square panels first appeared in the West, particularly in Hereford & Worcester, Shropshire and Gloucestershire, during the fifteenth century, and it spread throughout the following two centuries northwards into Cheshire and eastwards towards Kent but never into East Anglia, where close studding persisted unchallenged until well into the seventeenth century, when, with the need to economize, the studs were set wider and wider apart.

In close studding (14) the studs were storey height, framed into the sill-beam at ground level, the girth at the upper-floor level and the wall-plates at roof level. Until the middle of the sixteenth century these studs were placed at intervals approximately equal to their own width, often six inches or so wide, spaced six inches apart, and although closely spaced studs continued to be employed well into the first quarter of the seventeenth century, on some houses by then the spacing had become wider – as much as two feet or more. This was probably due more to the lack of timber and consequently the cost of close studding than to any desire to change the overall visual effect. Close studding was not merely a form of timber framing but a decorative form, and the extensive use of studs which had no structural use made this type of framing the most expensive – so expensive that it was often restricted to the prime elevation, with more widely spaced or open

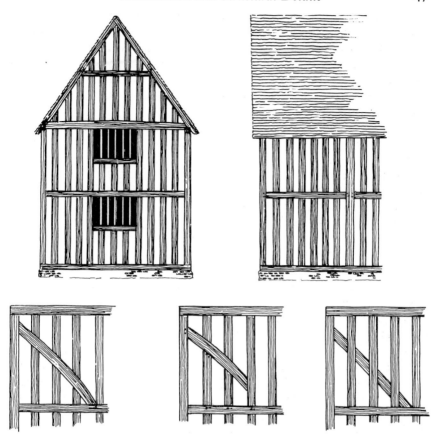

14. Wall framing – eastern school

square panels being found elsewhere. In order to achieve the overall effect of uniformity, the main posts, though of larger scantling than the studs, would have the same external width as the studs, therefore showing externally no obvious division into bays as with other forms of box-frame construction. In addition, as we have seen earlier, in order not to affect the overall close-studded appearance, internal tension-braces were introduced of smaller depth than the studs and halved over the inside face of the intervening studs and concealed externally with plaster. Later, tension-braces of the same scantling as the studs were used, with the studs being cut and framed into the braces. In Cambridgeshire studs were almost always of smaller section and spaced wider apart than those in the neighbouring counties of Suffolk and Essex.

This form of construction was used extensively in eastern England in the late fifteenth and sixteenth centuries, but, due to the popularity of cladding buildings with plaster in the sixteenth and seventeenth centuries, much is no longer visible. Such is the abundance of timber-framed buildings, particularly in Essex and Suffolk, that there are still plenty to be seen, especially in the villages where there has been a tendency in recent years to remove the plaster. Similarly, in the South-East there is much hidden behind plaster, tiles, weatherboarding and Georgian brickwork, yet there is still plenty to be seen.

The characteristic feature of the western school is the use of plain rectangular panels, more or less equal in size (15). This was achieved

15. Wall framing – western school

by the introduction of a horizontal rail to divide the storey height with widely spaced studs being introduced between this rail and the sill-beam, girth or wall-plate. To increase stability, diagonal arch-bracings were introduced between the posts and wall-plate, but from the middle of the sixteenth century these tended to become straight. This form of construction is predominantly a western feature, and those which date from before the middle of the fifteenth century are to be found mainly in this area and are of high social standing. Later its use spread to all buildings, with the exception of the very large. The main concentration is to be found in the Welsh Marches and West Midlands yet, it is by no means exclusive to these areas, extending from Lancashire down into Kent with a large number to be found south of the Thames in Wessex.

A variant form of square-panelling, in which the height of each storey is divided into three or sometimes four or more panels and not two, also began to appear in the sixteenth century. Generally this was achieved in a way slightly different from those with two, the studs being storey height with the horizontal rail being framed between them to form smaller square panels. This form of framing is often referred to as close panelling to differentiate from the former large rectangular panels. Once again the main concentration is in the West, perhaps being more popular in Shropshire than elsewhere, and to a lesser extent in Kent and Sussex.

By the seventeenth century, the vast majority of buildings, with the exception of those in East Anglia, were formed with open rectangular panels. However, these were often irregular in size and perhaps reflected the decline in suitable timbers more than anything else.

Close studding was also employed, but unlike the eastern school, in which the timbers ran the full storey height, the western school has an uninterrupted middle rail. Also, because these studs had no structural importance, it was not unusual for boards rather than studs to be used to give the desired effect. Close studding with a middle rail first appeared around the middle of the fifteenth century, but only in the sixteenth century did it become common, remaining so well into the seventeenth century in the West, long after its disuse in the South-East. Buildings where close studding is employed throughout can be found, but more common is the combination of close timbering and square panels. Often this comprised close studding to the ground floor, with the upper floor formed of square panels; in some houses the front of the hall range is close timbered throughout, while the cross-wing has close studding below and square panels above. Sometimes this combination of close studding and square panelling denotes a house of two builds. Although the employment of close studding with a middle rail is to be found mainly in the West, it is to be found

RJBKOWN '84

16. Manor House, Berrington, Shropshire

elsewhere in the country (one notable example being Prinkhams, Chiddingstone, Kent). These somewhat rare examples in the South-East are not to be confused with the widespread practice in the region of applying a narrow moulded timber to the close-studded framework which also serves as a continuous window sill, as at Old Bell Farm, Harrietsham, Kent.

A feature of many of the timber-framed buildings is the use of decorative framing (17), none of which had a structural role, within the panels formed by the studs and horizontal rails. In the sixteenth and seventeenth centuries and when the panels were fairly large, diagonal strutting, often in the form of a herringbone pattern, was popular. It is absent in the East, rare in the South-East but can be found over much of the West Midlands, Welsh Marches and South Lancashire. It appears in such famous houses as Speke Hall, Merseyside, Little Moreton Hall, Cheshire, and Pitchford Hall, Shropshire, as well as on numerous smaller houses in many of the towns and villages along the Welsh border. During the second half of the sixteenth century, when close panelling became popular, the motifs within the panels became more elaborate. The effect was achieved by the use of short, curved timbers elaborately cut to form quadrant braces. The concave-sided diamond shape, which was often enriched by shaping

17. Wall framing – decorative patterns

each timber with cusps on both sides, was a common design followed for the next thirty or forty years by all manner of shaped infillings as they became more and more elaborate. Concave lozenges, cusped, concave-sided lozenges, stars, crosses, quatrefoils and many other highly decorative shapes were all found. A variant form, widely used in Cheshire and Lancashire, was the sunk quatrefoil intended to be filled with plaster.

Early in the seventeenth century studs of the same outline as stair balusters and panels with round-headed arches were also employed. Wavy braces, used singularly or symmetrically to form a pattern, often used in conjunction with close studding, are also to be found in many parts of the country. Decorative framing can be found mainly in the West, in Cheshire and in some of the larger houses in southern Lancashire, with the highest concentration being in Shropshire and Hereford & Worcester. Again this form of decoration is not to be found in East Anglia and Essex, with the exception of a solitary panel found on a house at Eltisley. There are, however, scattered examples in the East Midlands – for instance, in Bedfordshire, as well as in the South and South-East, in Kent, Surrey and Sussex; there is also an isolated example at Taunton.

Like close studding, these decorative motifs were generally restricted to the front or more important elevation. One excellent example of this is Sweet Briar Hall, Nantwich, Cheshire (18). Later, in the seventeenth century, decoration became more restrained, with timber more sparingly used in larger squares with the more universal adoption of long, straight tension-braces.

The northern school of carpentry (19) differs from the others in that, instead of the main posts being framed into the sill-beam, they rest on large stone foundations, known as 'stylobates', with sill-beams framed into them at ground-floor level – a feature known as 'the interrupted sill'. The walls are framed with closely spaced studs arranged in two rows of unequal height framed into a horizontal rail spanning the main posts. Curved arch-braces are provided between the main posts and the wall-plate. A feature often seen in the northern school and in particular in parts of Yorkshire is the use of parallel diagonal bracing. This 'herringbone-work' often differs from that found elsewhere in the country for it is not confined to small panels but replaces two or three studs to form a large, bold pattern. Panelled diagonal bracing is a feature of many gabled walls in which the central panel has vertical studs with a central window, and the panels on either

18. Sweet Briar Hall, Nantwich, Cheshire

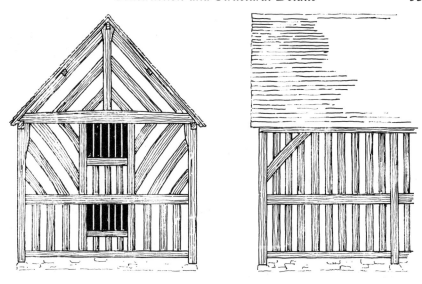

19. Wall framing – northern school

side have diagonal bracing, as at Bay Hall, Birkby, and Elland New Hall. Often the gable has similar parallel diagonal bracing set at the opposite angle to those on the floor below. At Wormold's Hall, Almondbury (20), the spaces between the studs are filled in with diagonal braces to form a herringbone or chevron pattern, another frequent feature. It can also be seen at Gunthwaite Barn, although here the studs are set wider apart and the panels are almost square. A large number of timber-framed buildings in the North were cased in stone in the seventeenth and eighteenth centuries and later in brick, so few can be recognized from the exterior, and even in those buildings where the frame is exposed, the ground floor has often been rebuilt in brick or stone.

So far, the timber-framing under review has been mainly of a substantial nature, generally constructed of oak. Even from the sixteenth century, however, timber-framed buildings using slight and inferior timbers were constructed. In the Lincolnshire Wold timber-framed houses and cottages were built in the latter part of the seventeenth and the early part of the eighteenth century, using a very slender frame with the studs rarely having intermediate rails; the only cross rail was one fixed to the inside of the frame to support the floor joists. The panels therefore were of considerable size, and they were covered with thin staves fixed to the outside of the frame, with daub carried across the outer face of the timbers to protect them. Some of these cottages, known as 'mud-and-stud', still exist here and there in villages

20. Wormald's Hall, Almondbury, Yorkshire

– for example, Coningsby, Somersby (21) and Thimbleby (22). A
similar form of construction is found on the Lancashire Plain, known
as 'clam-staff-and-daub'. Here, unlike the mud-and-stud buildings of
Lincolnshire, which always incorporated a frame, the houses are
generally of cruck construction, the walls being of clay stiffened with
thin studs morticed to the wall-plate and sill (23).

The size and quality of the timber used decreased for several reasons.
Obviously the decline of suitable timbers and their increase in price
had some bearing, but improved techniques in carpentry and the
availability of suitable cladding materials – plaster, weatherboarding
and tile-hanging – also contributed. Although many buildings, particularly in the South-East and East Anglia, are clad, there are some
examples in the South, West and Midlands built in the eighteenth
century, and some, such as the semi-detached cottages at Ampthill,
Bedfordshire, from the nineteenth century, which have their timbers

21. Woodman's Cottage, Somersby, Lincolnshire

22. Mud-and-stud cottage, Thimbleby, Lincolnshire

23. Cottage, Formby, Lancashire

exposed. The timbers used were slight and straight but the construction was similar to that of earlier buildings, though the sparing use of timber gives a somewhat different visual effect.

Often these timbers came from demolished buildings, which were cut up to provide timbers of smaller scantlings for re-use, but by the eighteenth and nineteenth centuries, with the availability of imported softwood of uniform section and the manufacture of cheap machine-made nails, oak was no longer regarded as a necessity, and the elaborate joinery techniques of earlier timber-framed buildings were no longer required.

The walls, constructed of softwood, comprised studs of approximately the same section spaced about eighteen inches apart to form one continuous load-bearing wall. Sill-plates and wall-plates were used in a manner similar to box-frame construction with intermediate noggings introduced for greater stability. Window and door openings were simply formed in the studwork, an extra large or a double stud being introduced at each side, with a large timber over them to form a lintel. As previously mentioned, joints were generally omitted, the timbers being nailed together. Houses using this method were quick and cheap to erect, particularly when clad with weatherboarding. Examples survive in ever-increasing numbers from the seventeenth century onwards, ranging in social stature from the small, detached farmhouse through many groups of semi-detached houses to the numerous rows of humble terraces. The majority are plain, but some have simple classical architectural details while others hide behind a brick façade. They can be found throughout the South-East – in Kent, Sussex and Surrey, principally in the Weald, and in a number of the London boroughs (24). They are also to be found in Essex, Suffolk and particularly Cambridgeshire, in the villages of Fen Ditton, Lode (25) and Swaffham Bulbeck, which has a number of terraces of single-storey cottages with attics, framed in softwood and plastered, built in the first quarter of the nineteenth century.

24. Cottage, Epsom, Surrey

25. Cottage, Lode, Cambridgeshire

Upper Floor and Jetty Construction

In a timber-framed building the construction of the upper floors comprises floor joists spanned either across the building or along the building from bay to bay. When the span was too great, one or sometimes two bridging-beams were introduced to reduce it, with the joists jointed into them. (26) At first these floors were 'lodged' – that is, the joists were not fixed to the framing at all, relying solely on their own weight and gravity to hold them in position, in addition to which they usually spanned a short distance. When the span was of some length, the joists were usually supported on a longitudinal bridging-beam which itself could be supported by a 'samson post' with bolsters and braces. Most of these floors are to be found within masonry walls – for instance, at Little Chesterford Manor, Essex, but at 39–43 The Causeway, Steventon, Oxfordshire (13), there is a rare example of a lodged floor within a timber-framed house, the ends of the joists being supported on side girths. However, by about 1300 the floor joists were jointed to the bridging-beam, at first by a simple mortice-and-tenon placed centrally in the depth of the joist. Improvements in these

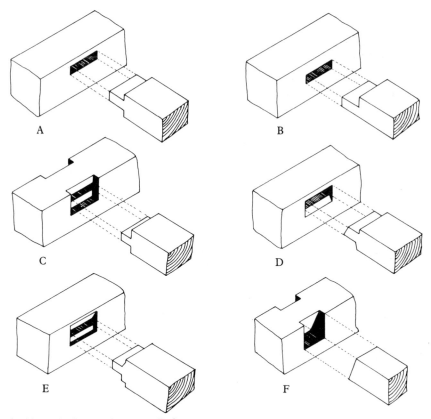

A. thirteenth–fourteenth century; B. fourteenth century; C. & D. fifteenth century; E. sixteenth century; F. seventeenth–eighteenth century.

26. Typical joints between bridging floor and joists

joints from the fourteenth century onwards included the soffit tenon, structurally the best of all the types, often with diminished haunches above the tenon to prevent winding. This was also achieved by housing the shoulders in various ways. Generally those of the seventeenth century, although having additional features, were structurally inferior, and by the beginning of the eighteenth century floor joists were commonly slotted into position – cogging – which was both quick and easy.

Generally the bridging-beams spanned between bays with the joists spanning between them and the front or rear wall. Medieval floor joists were heavy timbers, about eight inches by five inches deep, and were laid on their side (that is, with broad side horizontal), and it was not until the sixteenth century that they gradually began to be reduced in size, perhaps to five inches by four, while at the same time being spaced further apart. It was not, however, until the beginning of the seventeenth century that the practice of placing floor joists on their broad side was universally superseded by the improved carpentry technique of placing them on their narrow sides. This led to the introduction of floors with beams and joists of the same depth designed for the then fashionable plastered ceilings which could then be uninterrupted by the beams. The ends of the joists either sat on or more commonly framed into the girth; on poorer-quality buildings they sat on a ledge pegged to the inside of the frame. The bridging-beams, however, were almost always tenoned, sometimes double-tenoned for extra strength, into the girth of the cross-frame or external wall. This was not always the case, for the floor in the fourteenth-century cross-wing at Baythorne Hall, Birdbrook, Essex, is supported on four samson posts placed in the side walls, so relieving the walls of the weight of the floors.

Bridging-beams, the largest timbers (rarely less than twelve inches square) in any building, always acquired some form of decoration. The plain chamfer was the basis of many of these mouldings, but during the seventeenth century the ovolo moulding with many varieties of stopped ends became popular. In high-quality timber-framed buildings of the sixteenth and seventeenth centuries there are sometimes two parallel bridging beams to each bay, sometimes with heavy transverse beams to form a square pattern to give a coffered ceiling. These beams were usually richly carved or moulded (27).

One of the outstanding features of some timber-framed buildings is jettying – the projection of an upper storey beyond the one below.

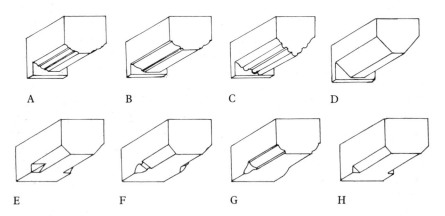

A   B   C   D

E   F   G   H

A., B. & C. moulded beams fifteenth and sixteenth-century date; D. late sixteenth – early seventeenth century; E. mid-seventeenth century; F. early seventeenth century; G. late sixteenth – early seventeenth century; H. seventeenth – early eighteenth century.

27. Ceiling beams – mouldings

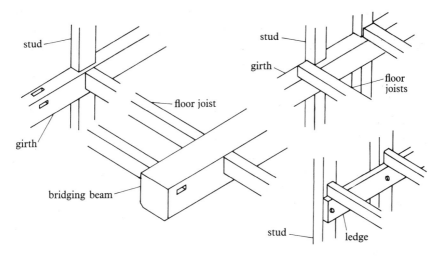

28. Upper floor construction

(The word comes from the French *jeté*, meaning something thrown out.) Jettying can occur on one or more sides and even on occasion on all four sides and on more than one storey, projecting in some cases as much as four feet. When jettying was to one side only, the construction was simple, for all that was required was for the floor joist to cantilever over the wall below and rest on the 'summer', the beam situated at the back of the overhang (29). When the overhang was on two adjacent sides, the process was a little more complex (29B). It was necessary to change the direction of the floor joists, and to enable this to be undertaken one of the floor joists was replaced by a larger one to which was framed another horizontal beam, called the 'dragon-beam', which ran diagonally to the corner of the floor. Into this beam the ends of the floor joists were framed, each pair set at right-angles, although sometimes the last few were framed at a slight angle. Towards its end the dragon-beam was supported by and framed into a massive corner or dragon-post, usually finely carved, which often had a curved bracket to support the outer end of the dragon-beam. The best area to see these carved dragon-posts is undoubtedly East Anglia. Some excellent examples can be seen at the Moyses Hall Museum at Bury St Edmunds, but many examples can be seen *in situ* – for instance, a house in Northgate Street, Ipswich.

To support the jetty along its length, additional curved brackets, occasionally carved and springing from moulded shafts, were sometimes provided framed to the studs and floor joists. Scrolled console-brackets were also frequently used, however, as these were cut from a solid piece of timber as distinct from a curved timber which were

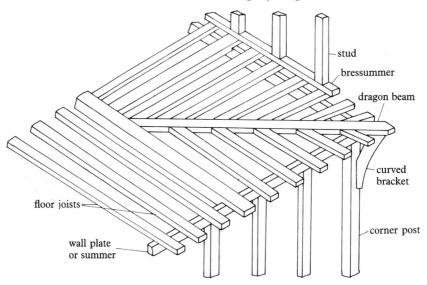

B. general layout showing arrangement at corner

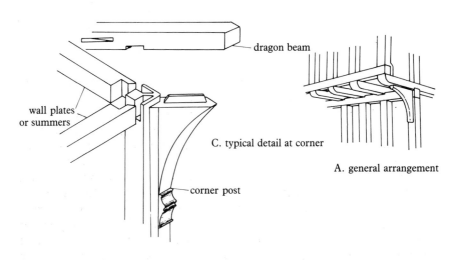

C. typical detail at corner

A. general arrangement

29. Jetty construction – 1

generally weaker. This weakness was perhaps realized, for by the middle of the seventeenth century they were occasionally banded with iron. On many of the timber-framed houses of northern England a plastered cove was constructed below the projection (30). A rare feature is the 'hewn-jetty' in which the end post extends the full height of the building with the lower part – the ground floor – being reduced in width to form the jetty (31A). Although this eased the jointing problem

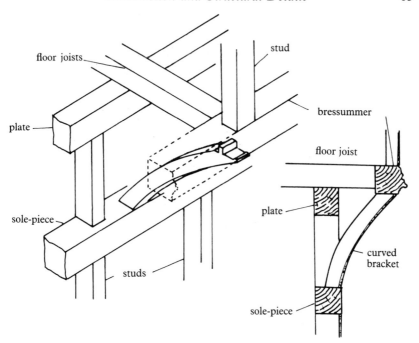

30. Plastered cove construction

at this point, the jetty provided was of a very limited projection, rarely more than a few inches.

Once the floor joists were in position, the framing of the next storey could continue, with a bressummer laid along their ends. In some instances, and this is particularly true of some utilitarian buildings, the ends of the projecting floor joists were left square, as at the Hanseatic Warehouse, King's Lynn, Norfolk, but generally the ends were shaped into a quarter-round and left exposed (31B). In some buildings the ends of the timbers were framed into the bressummer rather than supporting it from beneath (31C). This was a popular feature from the sixteenth century onwards. An alternative method used in concealing the ends of the floor joists, also popular in the sixteenth and seventeenth centuries, was to provide a fascia (31D). Both fascias and bressummers were either moulded or richly carved. Fascias are today rare, for once decayed they were not replaced. An excellent carved example still survives at the house previously mentioned in Northgate Street, Ipswich.

Jettying was first introduced in the thirteenth century – Tiptofts Manor, Wimbish, Essex, being of this date – and remained popular until the latter part of the sixteenth century, when its use began to decline, although it still continued to be used in the seventeenth

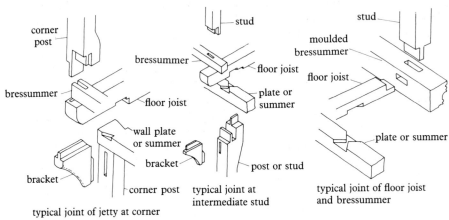

corner post

bressummer

bracket

typical joint of jetty at corner

stud

bressummer

floor joist

wall plate or summer

bracket

corner post

typical joint at intermediate stud

plate or summer

post or stud

stud

moulded bressummer

floor joist

plate or summer

typical joint of floor joist and bressummer

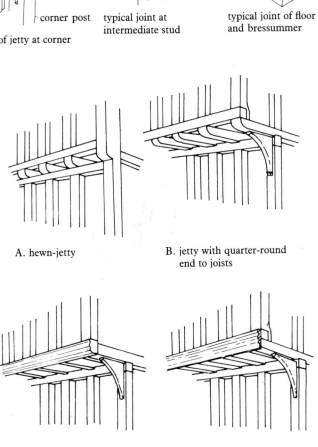

A. hewn-jetty

B. jetty with quarter-round end to joists

C. jetty with joists framed to bressummer

D. jetty with ends of joists concealed by fascia

31. Jetty construction – 2

century. In most of the houses built in the fourteenth and fifteenth centuries jettied upper floors were confined to the end bays or cross-wings flanking the open hall. Generally this was to the front, but sometimes, especially in the Wealden houses, the jettying returns along the ends and even on occasion at the rear as well. Towards the end of the fifteenth century, when the open hall had generally been abandoned in the South-East and eastern England and houses began to be constructed with two storeys throughout, it became possible to extend this overhanging upper floor the full length of the building. These continuous jettied houses are perhaps more numerous in towns and villages than in the countryside, but there are a good number of farmhouses with this form of construction to be found. This is especially true in the South-East and in particular in Kent.

Jettying was not only restricted to the first floor, for where there was a second storey this too was often jettied like the floor below. It is a feature of many gable-fronted town houses throughout England, as well as many of the gable cross-wings or houses built not only in eastern England but also in the West Midlands. These jettied cross-wings must not be confused with projecting gables, a common feature, especially with moulded bressummers, at the beginning of the seventeenth century. Less common is the use of the continuous jetty at both first and second floors. So popular was the continuous jetty in the South-East that it is not uncommon for the central recess between the jettied end bays of a Wealden house to be filled in to form a continuous jettied front when the open hall was divided horizontally.

The widespread use of jettying has caused much speculation, and at least four explanations could account for it.

One is that it increased the floor area of the building – from ten to twenty per cent per floor for an average two-foot projection – without increasing the land on which it sat, which was undoubtedly desirable in towns but not in the depths of the country where there was no shortage of land. This can be explained by the desire of country builders to follow the fashion of towns.

Another reason often given is the need to protect the building from damp. There were, of course, no gutters or downpipes in those days, and on buildings without jetties much of the rainwater would, on windy days, pour off the roof and be blown back onto the face of the building. It is obvious that a building constructed of timber with wattle-and-daub infilling would not last long if incessantly soaked by rainwater, and jetties would certainly help to protect the wall beneath.

The other two reasons are both structural. It has been suggested that jettying was used to overcome the problem of obtaining posts long enough to run the full height of the building, for with jetties it was necessary to have posts of only one storey height and certainly it alleviated the difficult joint of the three mortices from three directions at one point at the junction of the studs and floor joist with the bressummer. Another structural reason given is that the weight of the walls and roofs transferred to the cantilevered end of the floor joists counteracted the possible main-span deflection of the floor joists caused by the weight of the furniture, particularly as these were placed on their broadside. This, however, seems unlikely, for although in some cases the projection was as much as four feet, often – particularly in the fifteenth century – the projection was only moderate, rarely more than two feet, having little cantilever effect.

All or any of the explanations could be why jettying was used, although it could be, as Alex Clifton-Taylor put it, that '. . . men who could afford to pay for it could not resist a feature so charming . . .'.

Cruck Construction

The characteristic feature of a cruck building is that the weight of the roof, and often that of the walls as well, is carried on a series of transverse trusses, each formed of two inclined timbers which rise from the ground and meet at the apex, tied together by a collar or tie-beam to form an A-frame (32). This frame then serves as a roof

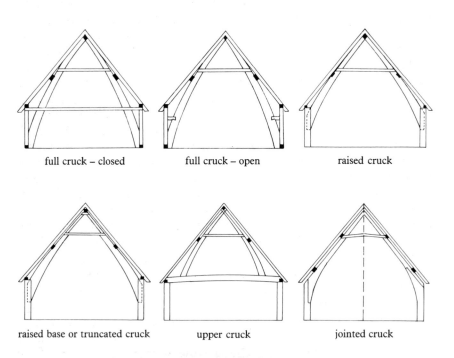

full cruck – closed   full cruck – open   raised cruck

raised base or truncated cruck   upper cruck   jointed cruck

32. Cruck types

truss to support the purlins and ridge-beam. Consequently the vertical walls have no structural importance, and when constructed of timber they depend greatly on the crucks for both support and stability.

The inclined timbers of the cruck frame, known as 'blades', were cut from trees which had, whenever possible, a natural curve, or from the trunk of one tree split in two along its length to ensure a symmetrical arch. The blades varied in shape according to the curvature of the tree and could be nearly straight, smoothly curved or elbowed. The ends of the blades were either supported on a stylobat or framed into a sill-beam. At the apex, however, a variety of methods were used to secure the blades, and N. W. Alcock in his book *A Catalogue of Cruck Buildings* gives distribution maps of the six main methods. The most common forms are not jointed at the apex but held together either by a yoke situated at the top on which the ridge-beam sits or, somewhat lower, by a collar with the blades butting against the ridge-beam. In other cases they are either simply butted, halved or crossed. Between each cruck frame ran the ridge-beams and purlins which supported the common rafters. When the external walls were of timber, the tie-beams were extended until their ends were directly above the base of the blades, and vertical posts were introduced, pegged to the base of the blades and to the end of the tie-beams. Wall-plates running between each cruck frame were fixed to the end of the tie-beams, and the panel between each post was filled in with studs and horizontal members. Often, however, in order to obtain more headroom the tie-beam was omitted, and in these cases the wall-plate and vertical post were tied back to the cruck by means of a 'cruck-spur'.

The above briefly describes the 'true' or 'full' cruck, but there are several other forms of cruck construction which, although not full crucks, are obviously related, some more than others, to the cruck family. First there is the 'raised' cruck which is similar to the full cruck in all respects except that, instead of starting at ground level, it starts some way up a solid wall; it has been defined by R. A. Cordingley as a truss in which the feet of the blades are raised at least five feet above ground level. In fact, full crucks are often referred to as raised crucks because the starting-point of the cruck, being concealed within the wall, is uncertain. With the 'base' cruck the blades, although rising from the ground, are truncated well below the apex and are tied together at the head with a tie-beam or collar which supports the roof structure. In the raised base or truncated cruck only the middle – the curved part of the cruck – is used, while in the 'upper' cruck the blades rise to the apex from a tie-beam at or near eaves level. Another form of cruck construction is the 'jointed' or 'scarfed' cruck where a vertical post is jointed to an inclined blade to obtain a cruck-like form (34).

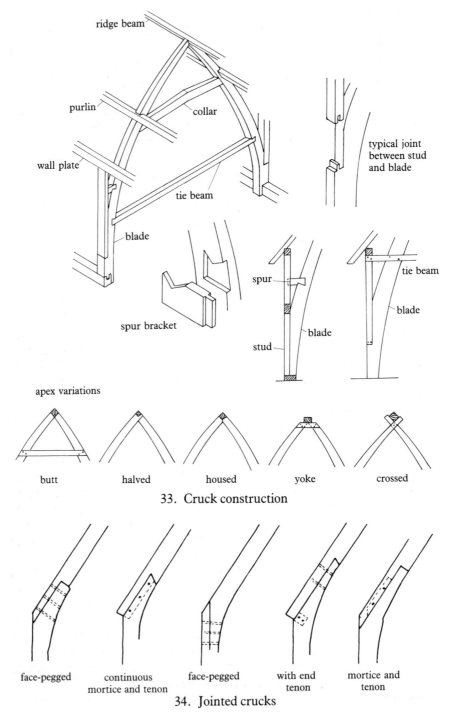

ridge beam

purlin

collar

wall plate

tie beam

blade

typical joint
between stud
and blade

spur bracket

spur

stud

blade

tie beam

blade

apex variations

| butt | halved | housed | yoke | crossed |

33. Cruck construction

face-pegged

continuous
mortice and tenon

face-pegged

with end
tenon

mortice and
tenon

34. Jointed crucks

Roof Types

The roof of any building, and of a timber-framed one more perhaps than others, is archaeologically the most important feature, for it is generally the least altered part. There are a considerable variety of roof types (35), and R. A. Cordingley in his *British Historical Roof Types and their Members: A Classification* divides them into eight major groups subdivided into seventy-five classifications which are again subdivided to make nearly eight hundred variants, although some have only minor differences. Many of these roof types are, however, unsuited to timber-framed buildings. Essentially two types of roofs were used in timber-framed construction: single-framed roofs, which consist entirely of transverse members such as rafters, which are not tied together longitudinally, the weight of the roof being transferred equally along the external wall frame, and double-framed roofs, in which ridge beams and purlins are employed, transferring most of the roof load onto trusses which are supported on principal wall-posts.

The simplest and earliest forms of single-rafter roofs have no longitudinal members above the wall-plate, the pairs of common rafters, spaced between one and two feet apart, meeting at the apex of the roof and held apart and gaining its longitudinal stiffening solely by the roof-coverings. Slightly more elaborate are the close-coupled rafter-roof types in which the pairs of common rafters are tied together at their base by a tie-beam, and the collar-rafter roof, in which the common rafters are secured at mid-point by a horizontal collar-beam.

All these ties prevented the feet of the common rafters from splaying out, causing the roof to collapse, but there was still a degree of instability. To remedy this, the passing-brace roof was designed, and to provide lateral stability long, slender timbers running parallel to the rafters were engaged by means of halved-lapped joints to all the horizontal and vertical members they passed. This method, commonly employed on aisled construction, was a typical feature of the thirteenth and fourteenth centuries. Also used at this time was scissor-bracing in which the pairs of rafters were linked by braces crossing one another in their passage in the centre line of the roof. In aisled construction both passing-braces and scissor-bracing were often used in the same building, as at Purton Green Farm, Stansfield, Suffolk. Needless to say, these single-rafter roofs were still subject to structural failure, mainly from racking, in which the common rafters, although being kept parallel by the roof-battens, incline from the vertical. To overcome this, in the thirteenth century diagonal bracing, fitted into trenches cut into the outer faces of common rafters, often formed into a saltire-cross, was fitted between each bay. The single-rafter roof form was one generally used in most timber-framed buildings in the twelfth

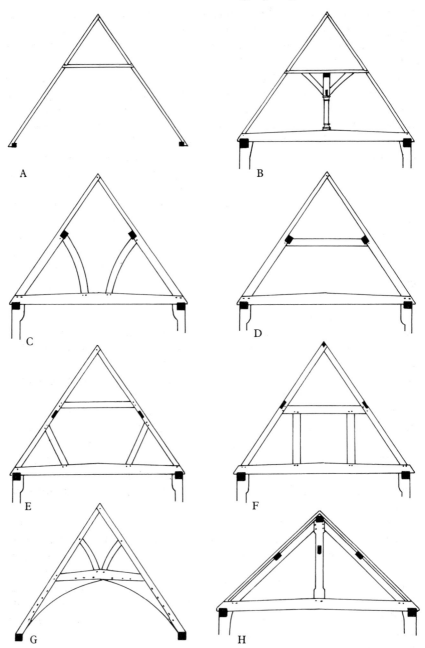

A. single-framed; B. crown-post; C. & D. clasped-purlin; E. butt-purlin; F. through or trenched purlin; G. arch-braced collar-beam; H. king-post

35. Roof types

and thirteenth centuries but seems unlikely to have persisted, in other than poor buildings long since disappeared, after about 1400.

To overcome the longitudinal collapse of rafters, a collar-purlin was introduced (36), running the whole length of the building and placed immediately below the collars and supported along its length at each bay division by crown-posts and at its end by a king-stud. The crown-post or king-stud is framed into a tie-beam at the bottom and the collar-purlin at the top, thus supporting the collars along its entire length and so the pairs of common rafters and hence the roof load. The collar-purlin was rarely fixed to the collars but restrained by friction, therefore removing any tendency for the longitudinal collapse of the rafters. The crown-posts too required braces to prevent lateral movement, while longitudinal braces were added to triangulate the roof.

It is the arrangement of these braces and the size and shape of the crown-post itself that are the main variants of crown-post/collar-purlin roof construction. The most common form of bracing was that in which the crown-post was braced four ways at head, twice to the collar-purlin and to either side of the collar. Others were braced only at the head longitudinally to the collar-purlin, while others had in addition braces at the bottom between crown-post and tie-beam. The most important braces were at the head of the crown-posts, for they prevented the sideways movement of the collar-purlin as well as providing longitudinal stability by triangulating the roof structure. Yet there are crown-posts which are braced only at the foot of the tie-beam, and others with no bracing whatsoever, a feature of Berkshire and Wiltshire. In some instances the crown-post is carried up beyond the collar-purlin to the apex of the roof, as a king-post. At Tiptofts Manor, Wimbish, Essex, the crown-posts appear to have been intended as king-posts but they are truncated and fail to reach the rafters' apex. Braces were generally curved but straight ones were also used, although they became less common in later years.

There is an almost infinite variety of crown-post designs, varying in length of shaft as well as shape and decoration. The length can vary from as little as a foot to seven feet or more depending on the span, pitch and collar-beam height. Generally, however, they were between five and six feet high. In many houses built before the middle of the fourteenth century they were either square in cross section or chamfered to form an octagonal shaft. Bases and caps were rare, although those that were chamfered did produce a simplified base and cap when the chamfer was stopped. Later, in most houses, particularly in the central open trusses of the halls or solar chambers, the crown-posts were decorated, with the cap and base moulded and the post itself shaped, usually octagonal in section, but chamfered, rebated and

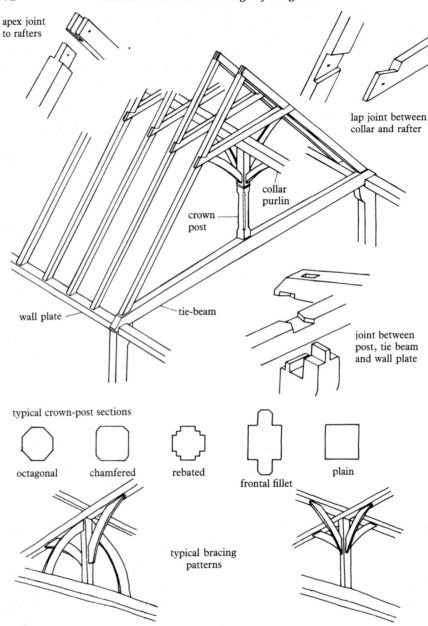

apex joint
to rafters

lap joint between
collar and rafter

collar
purlin

crown
post

joint between
post, tie beam
and wall plate

wall plate

tie-beam

typical crown-post sections

octagonal   chamfered   rebated

frontal fillet

plain

typical bracing
patterns

36. Crown-post roofs

cruciform sections are all to be found. Unfortunately none of these features or the length or number of braces has any dating significance, and many of the features can be found in buildings of similar age. In less exposed positions within the house, in barns and later in humbler buildings, crown-posts without decoration are to be found. The heads, at the junction of the collar-purlin, also varied, generally taking the form of a jowl, sometimes, as at Tiptofts and Southchurch Hall, near Southend, and in several town houses in York, as a double jowl with the collar-purlin let in.

The crown-post roof belongs predominantly to the South-East and East Anglia, but it can be found on high-status medieval buildings in most parts of the country, particularly in towns. In York, for instance, almost all roof trusses erected from the early fourteenth to the early sixteenth century have a crown-post. Crown-post roofs first appeared in the thirteenth century (that at Manor Farm, Bourn, Cambridgeshire (37) in about 1260 and the large roof at St Mary's Hospital, Chichester, West Sussex, built about 1280 being some of the earliest) and continued to be built until about 1500, after which their use declined rapidly,

37. Manor Farm, Bourn, Cambridgeshire

their place being taken in the South-East and eastern England by side-purlin roofs. This generally occurred with the abandonment of the open hall; the roof, no longer requiring to be exposed, lost its decorative function, and at the same time there came a desire to utilize the roof space by forming an attic. The crown-post and collar-purlin were obviously a hindrance and by the middle of the sixteenth century had generally been replaced by a roof with side purlins (38). At first the side purlins were butted and mortice-and-tenoned into the principal rafter which formed part of a roof truss. Alternatively, instead of a mortice-and-tenoned joint to the principal rafter, a through splayed-scarf or a through halved-scarf joint was used. These roof-trusses comprised a tie-beam, two principal rafters and a collar-beam, the collar-beam generally being supported off the tie-beam by a central strut, similar to the crown-post but now devoid of its collar-purlins

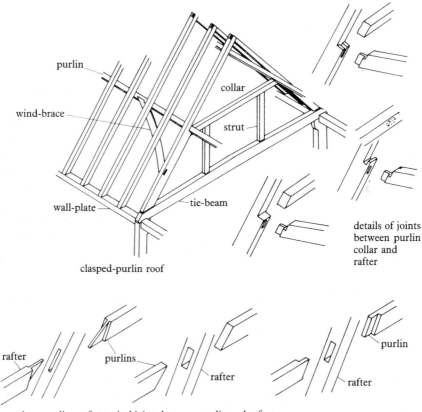

purlin

collar

wind-brace

strut

wall-plate

tie-beam

clasped-purlin roof

details of joints between purlin collar and rafter

rafter   purlins

rafter

purlin

rafter

butt-purlin roof – typical joints between purlin and rafters

38. Butt-purlin and clasped-purlin roof

and known as a lower king-strut. This type of roof truss was soon superseded by the queen-strut roof with through-purlins clasped at the angles between principal rafter and collar. Occasionally a tenon was provided at the cut-back of the principal rafter engaging a mortice in the underside of the purlin.

The feature of these two roof types is that the principal rafters are in the same plane as the common rafters and are, in most cases, only slightly larger in section. When the purlins are clasped at the back of the principal rafter, that section of the rafter from this point to the ridge is often reduced in depth to that of the common rafters. In addition windbraces between the principal rafters and purlins were also introduced to increase stability. Side-purlin roofs were economical in both timber and labour in that they no longer required collars to all the common rafters, and at the same time the area between the trusses was open and unimpeded.

Clasped purlin roofs with queen-struts remained the most popular of the two and, although found here and there throughout the medieval period (the earliest example of a type of clasped purlin being at the Wheat Barn, Cressing Temple, Essex, of about 1250), it was not until early in the sixteenth century that they became universally adopted in lowland England; then they continued to be used until the beginning of the nineteenth century. Towards the end of this period the queen-struts tended to be set at an angle rather than vertically. In the transitional period between the use of the crown-post and side-purlin roofs, complex hybrid roofs using both old and new methods were built, one fine example being the roof of the granary at Rookwood Hall, Abbess Roding, Essex, where crown-posts and collar-purlins were used in addition to side purlins with windbraces. Although butt-purlins were found in high-quality medieval carpentry in highland England – for instance, in Hereford & Worcester and Shropshire, it was not until the sixteenth century that they were generally adopted as an alternative to clasped purlins in much of southern and eastern England. The purlins could be either tenoned to the principal rafter on line or staggered, a method which appears to be somewhat later in date.

The crown-post and butt-purlin roofs belonged predominantly to the South-East and eastern England. In the North it was the king-post truss (39), in which a stout post, the king-post, rises from the tie-beam to support the ridge-piece, with the principal rafters rising from tie-beam to ridge being framed to the tie-beam and the side of the king-post. Between each principal rafter run the purlins, trenched partly or wholly into them to support the common rafters. In addition the principal rafters were sometimes supported by struts off the tie-beam. Variations within this general arrangement were not as numerous as in crown-post construction, the main variation being

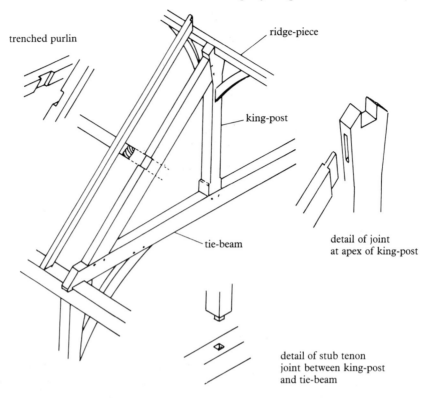

trenched purlin

ridge-piece

king-post

tie-beam

detail of joint
at apex of king-post

detail of stub tenon
joint between king-post
and tie-beam

39. King-post roofs

number and shape of the struts. These may comprise king-strutting,
twin-angle strutting, curved angle-braces or queen-strutting. Apart
from a few decorated examples, particularly in Lancashire, king-post
roofs were plain and unpretentious. Generally the posts themselves
were sturdy, usually about eight inches or more in section, compared
with the more slender crown-post. The height of the posts varied from
about five feet up to eight feet, although generally they were somewhere
between the two, probably six to seven feet. The top of the posts was
often provided with a double jowl to take the principal rafters.
Although there are a few timber-framed buildings with king-post
trusses in other areas, they are common in the North in medieval and
post-medieval buildings and, unlike the crown-post trusses of the
South, were widely adopted in the rest of the country in the eighteenth
and nineteenth centuries.

Another, and perhaps the most ornamental open roof used in
medieval secular buildings, was the arch-braced collar-beam roof truss
(40). In this roof truss the tie-beam was eliminated and a collar-beam

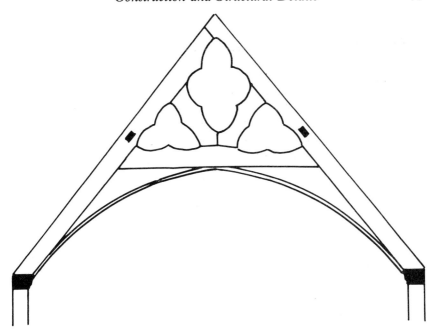

40. Arch-braced collar-beam roof

provided at high level, supported with arch-braces framed either into the underside of the principal rafter and down onto the main post or directly to the main post at the bottom and at the top into the underside of the collar, often so formed to make an impressive Gothic arch. Side purlins, sometimes trenched but more often tenoned into the principal rafters, supported the common rafters. The area above the collar-beam was often filled with tracery. Usually this took the form of bold trefoils or quatrefoils frequently formed by two raking struts between the collar and principal rafters, foiled or finely cusped, and forming, with equally foiled or cusped principals and collar, a decorative panel. In addition the windbraces, of which there may be one or two tiers, were similarly foiled or cusped. Due to the absence of any tie-beams, there was only limited restraint to any overturning movement which in turn tended to cause sheer stresses in the truss-joints, as surviving examples show. The arch-braced collar-beam roof truss was the standard medieval truss for open roofs in western England and may have been influenced by the cruck construction, as suggested by the number of fourteenth-century base crucks with an arch-braced collar. These decorations are to be found in many of the domestic roofs of Hereford & Worcester of the fourteenth and fifteenth centuries. One of the finest examples is undoubtedly to be seen at Amberley Court, where the main truss is arch-braced with a central quatrefoil and flanking trefoils, with the intermediate trusses having a higher foiled collar with the rafters cusped below.

In many ways cruck and king-post roofs were similar in that they both employed ridge-pieces and side purlins laid on or trenched into the crucks or principal rafters. In the West and Midlands during the sixteenth century, when the use of cruck construction began to dwindle, and in the North, when the use of the medieval king-post declined, the trusses that succeeded them continued to adopt this same trenched or through purlin technique (41). With this type of roof the principal rafters are of a much larger scantling and in a lower plane than the common rafters, with the purlins trenched into their upper face onto which the common rafters sit. Also, more often than not, the roof incorporated a ridge-piece, a feature not normally employed in the clasp- and butt-purlin roofs of the South-East and East.

In all forms of roof construction, with the exception of cruck and arch-braced, the trusses are built off a tie-beam, preventing any outward movement of the principal rafters. However, there were buildings in which the tie-beam was often in an inconvenient position. To overcome this problem, several methods were adopted. One was to eliminate the central part of the tie-beam, the end being framed into a post which rose from the main cross-beam at floor level to the underside of the principal rafter or collar-beam. This system was

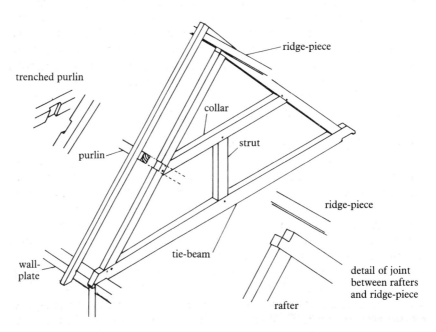

41. Through or trenched purlin roofs

generally adopted in trenched-purlin roofs. In clasped- or butt-purlin roofs a similar method was used, but the post was replaced by a diagonal member, introduced from the main post to the principal rafter, into which the remaining length of the tie-beam was framed. Finally there was the use of upper crucks which rose from first-floor cross-beam level but which did not always continue to the ridge, being held together by a collar.

From the seventeenth century onwards the development of the double-pile house provided the carpenter with another problem to overcome. With the increased depth of these houses and when the roof covering required a steep pitch, the resultant roof would have been of excessive height. To overcome this, two identical roofs were placed side by side to form an 'M' roof with a valley gutter between. The disadvantage of this roof type was that it divided the roof space into two, needing two separate accesses, both small with little headroom. A roof was, however, devised in which the valley wall was raised and the purlin forming the valley was supported on a tie-beam strutted off ceiling beams. The result was to provide a single attic with reasonable headroom over much of its area.

From the eighteenth century imported softwood replaced oak as the predominant timber used in roof construction and marked the end of traditional roof carpentry. Carpentry techniques became progressively simpler, with nails, bolts and metal straps often replacing the elaborate joints formerly employed based on the many contemporary pattern books which became available during the eighteenth century. The trusses used were often adaptations of old ones; the king-post truss, found almost exclusively in northern England up to the seventeenth century, was adopted in many parts of the country and can be found in many of the timber-framed farm buildings erected with softwood in the nineteenth century in lowland England.

Aisled and Quasi-Aisled Construction

A roof could span only a limited width, usually about eighteen feet and rarely more than twenty feet, without increasing the size of the timbers so much that it would become both impracticable and uneconomical. In order to increase the roof span and therefore the floor area, aisled construction was used, dividing the structure into a central nave with side aisles (42). This was achieved by the introduction of timber posts, known as 'arcade-posts', which supported the 'arcade-plate', a longitudinal plate running between each post for the full length of the building. The arcade-plate supported the common rafters which ran from the ridge of the main roof over the aisle to the wall-plate of the external wall. To increase rigidity, a tie-beam was introduced, spanning the building and sitting on top of the arcade-beam above the

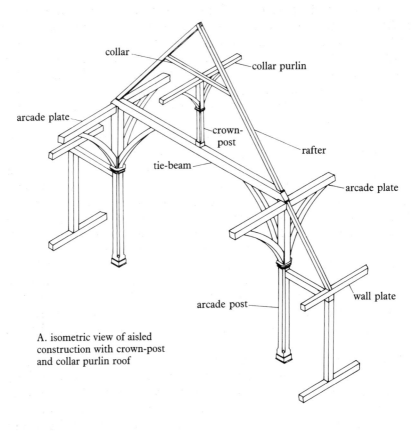

collar

collar purlin

arcade plate

crown-post

rafter

tie-beam

arcade plate

arcade post

wall plate

A. isometric view of aisled
construction with crown-post
and collar purlin roof

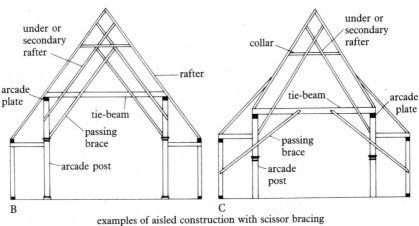

under or
secondary
rafter

rafter

arcade
plate

tie-beam

passing
brace

arcade post

B

collar

under or
secondary
rafter

tie-beam

arcade
plate

passing
brace

arcade
post

C

examples of aisled construction with scissor bracing

42. Aisled construction

post into which the principal rafters were framed. These rafters were further strengthened by a collar at high level. Stability could be further increased by the introduction of straight braces between the arcade-post and the beam, or later with curved braces between the arcade-post and -beam and arcade-post and tie-beam. To secure the external wall of the aisle and prevent its being forced out by the thrust of the rafter, a tie-beam was introduced between the wall-plate and the arcade-post.

In early aisled buildings, as we have seen previously, transverse rigidity was obtained by the introduction of passing and scissor-bracing, comprising ties fixed to the face of the main structure extending from either the external wall posts or the arcade-posts to a point high on the principal rafter on the opposite side. These timbers are often referred to as under or secondary rafters. In addition, duplicate passing-braces, extending from either the external wall post or the arcade-post to the tie-beam or to the under rafters, were on occasions provided, while elsewhere longitudinal stability was obtained by the introduction of a collar-purlin and crown-posts. This became the standard form of construction for aisled houses built in the fourteenth century. One feature of these early aisled buildings was the free use of lapped joints instead of or in addition to mortice-and-tenon joints.

Most aisled houses, with the exception of those in Yorkshire around Halifax, were built before 1400, but so suitable and economical was aisling that, long after it was abandoned for domestic work, it continued to be used in the construction of barns. Throughout the lowland zone, in the counties of Kent, Essex, Sussex, Surrey, Hampshire, Berkshire, Buckinghamshire, Suffolk, Norfolk and Cambridgeshire, barns of aisled construction can be found, and in Kent and East Anglia they continued to be built well into the eighteenth century and in some cases even into the nineteenth century.

Aisled construction when used for barns differed slightly from that used in domestic buildings, the main variation being the introduction of a post-sill securely fixed back to the sill-beam of the external wall; into these post-sills the arcade-posts were framed and reared (43). In addition shores were introduced between the post-sills and the arcade-posts – a feature more common in the medieval barns of the South-East, and in particular Kent, than elsewhere. As aisled barns continued to be constructed long after aisled construction had been abandoned for domestic buildings, roof construction continued to develop. The earliest aisled barns incorporated passing and scissor-bracing and later crown-posts and collar-purlins in much the same way as domestic buildings but later various types of side-purlin roofs became common.

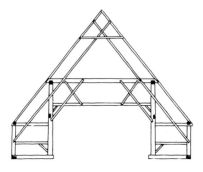

13th-century Essex barn (based on
wheat barn Temple Cressing).

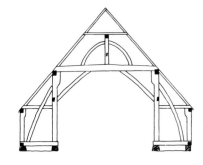

15th-century Kent barn (based on
Court Lodge, Brook).

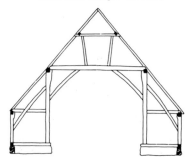

17th-century Essex barn (based on
Gatehouse Farm, Abbess Roding).

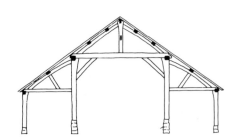

16th-century Yorkshire barn (based on East
Riddlesden Hall, Keighley).

43. Aisled construction – Barns

Although aisling provided a greater floor area, in dwellings the
arcade-posts caused an obstruction, and the problem was to overcome
this yet still maintain the overall span and support the arcade-beams.
One solution was the use of the base cruck which enabled the arcade-
plate to be supported from the external wall (44). As mentioned earlier,
the base cruck, an adaptation of the true cruck, was truncated and did
not extend above the arcade-plate. The two blades were tied together
at their top by a collar-beam supported at the top of the base cruck
and was secured by various methods. The most common device was
the introduction of a second collar-beam, with the arcade plate being
clamped between the two. Another was to introduce subsidiary framing
in the spandrel between the base cruck and the arch-brace to cradle
the plate. A third and simpler method sometimes used was for the
arcade-plate to be notched or tenoned into the top of the base cruck.
In houses the timbers are large and heavily moulded, with the moulding
of the arch-braces continuing down the cruck itself. Like aisled construction, base crucks were also used in barns, although they are to be

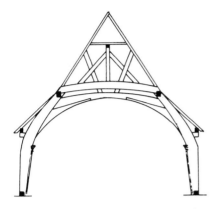

West Bromwich Old Hall, West Midlands.

Amberley Court, Hereford and Worcester.

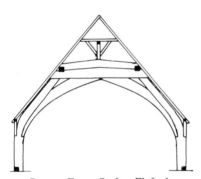

Rectory Farm, Grafton Flyford,
Hereford and Worcester.

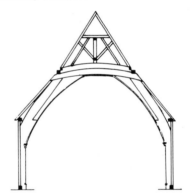

Manor Farm, Wasperton, Warwickshire.

Showing some of the methods used to support the plate.

44. Base-cruck construction

found mainly in the South-West – Gloucestershire and Somerset having the most.

As we have seen, the base cruck was never adopted in eastern England, and here raised aisles were used to provide the required unobstructed floor space. It was a comparatively simple method in which the arcade-posts supported off the ground floor were omitted and replaced with shorter arcade-posts complete with capitals and bases supported on a tie-beam spanning the full width of the building (45). The tie-beam was low – only some six feet, as at Gatehouse Farm, Felsted – supported at its ends on large, curved braces joining wall posts to tie-beam. Above the tie-beam two or sometimes three posts complete with braces and with moulded base and capitals supported the arcade-plate or purlin and an upper tie-beam. Above, supported

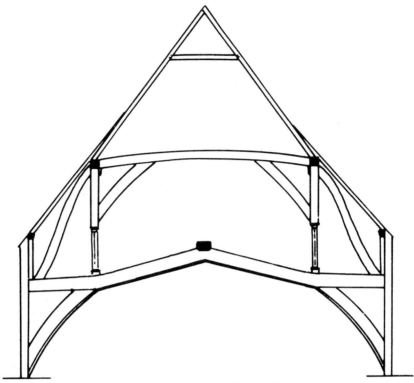

Based on Gatehouse Farm, Felsted, Essex.

45. Raised aisle construction

off this tie-beam, was usually a collar-purlin and crown-post. This simple device freed the floor, it is true, but only by substituting a structure which lacked headroom and so destroying the overall effect of height obtained within an aisled hall.

Another method of clearing the hall was to place the whole aisled structure on hammer-beams (46). The function of the hammer-posts was to carry the arcade-plate on purlins as in aisled construction, the end of its supporting beam supported on large curved braces framed into the main posts. It seems likely that hammer-beam trusses were, like raised-aisle construction, derivative from aisled construction, the lower, inconvenient part of the arcade-posts being removed and the truncated top part of the post supported on brackets. Hammer-beam construction was not widely used, for such a roof is alien to timber-framed structure, needing masonry walls to resist the excessive thrust. In some cases they alternated with a tie-beam and crown-post, alleviating some of the outward thrust on the external timber walls, as at Great Dixter, Northiam, East Sussex.

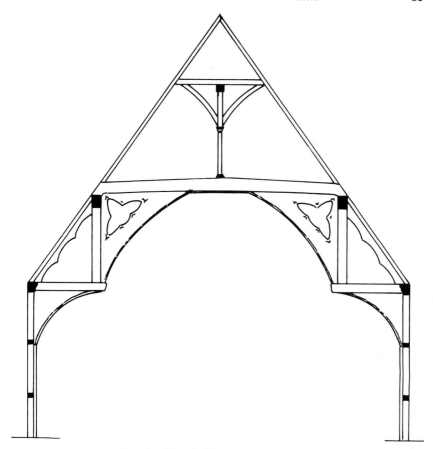

Based on Tiptofts Manor, Wimbish, Essex.

46. Hammer-beam construction

Wattle-and-Daub

By far the most common and the earliest form of infilling that is known is wattle-and-daub (47). This comprised an interwoven timber background fixed between the studs (the wattle) onto which was put a layer of wet clay mixed with straw or hair (the daub).

Many local variations are to be found in the construction of the wattle. When the panels were square, or nearly so, it was usual to have upright staves, usually of hazel, cleft chestnut or oak, which were pointed at one end to fit into holes in the underside of the horizontal member, forming the top of the panel, and chisel-shaped at the other end so that they could be slid and wedged into grooves in the lower horizontal member. In some instances grooves were provided on both the top and bottom horizontal members so that the staves could be

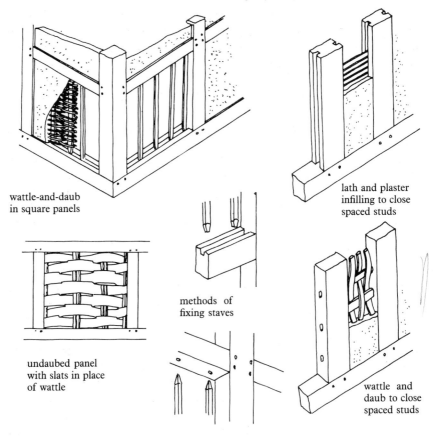

wattle-and-daub
in square panels

lath and plaster
infilling to close
spaced studs

undaubed panel
with slats in place
of wattle

methods of
fixing staves

wattle and
daub to close
spaced studs

47. Wattle-and-daub

easily fitted. The staves were generally spaced at about ten or twelve inches apart, although it is not uncommon for them to be spaced up to eighteen inches apart. Between these staves were interwoven pliable withies or wands, usually unbarked hazel or ash sticks, to form a hurdle or basket-like panel. In better-class work riven oak or sometimes beech laths replaced the hazel or ash wands. When the studs were spaced close together, other methods for forming the wattle were employed. Often only uprights were used, usually fixed in a similar way as staves but it is not uncommon for them to be merely wedged in position. Sometimes, where the panel was tall, short cross-pieces were wedged between the studs on which were tied the uprights. The material used for tying these upright staves varied greatly: tendrils of wild clematis, tough bramble strands, green willow withies, string formed of twisted grass and thin strips of leather have all been discovered. Alternatively, the uprights could be omitted and horizontal sticks, or in better-class work riven oak laths, were used, being slotted into grooves in each of the studs. In East Anglia during the sixteenth century, when the studs began to be placed further apart, stout cross-pieces were fixed horizontally between and sprung into V-shaped grooves in the studs. In all these methods, the wattle was constructed and inserted without the use of nails.

It was to this rough panel that the daub was applied. As previously mentioned, the daub consisted of wet clay or mud well mixed or pugged with the addition of water and tempered with chopped straw or cow-hair, and in addition cow-dung was added. As little water as possible was used, thus avoiding excessive shrinkage, and where available lime was added to increase the overall strength. In 1530 Palsgrave stated that, 'Daubing may be clay onely, with lime plaster or lome that is tempered with heare or straw.' The daub so mixed was thrown onto both sides of the wattle simultaneously by two men, one on the inside of the wall and the other on the outside so as to fill in the interstices between the wattle. The first layer was left to dry before successive layers were applied to reach the overall thickness required. Although the daub set hard, it needed protection from the elements, for once wet it soon deteriorated. The daub was therefore generally treated with limewash or an earth ochre wash to give it some protection. Later, a thin coat of plaster – a mixture of lime, sand and cow-hair – was commonly employed. At the Clergy House, Alfriston, Sussex, the daub is covered both inside and out with quicklime and tallow. If properly protected and maintained, daub will last indefinitely.

Not all wattle was covered by daub, for where, as in the case of barns, ventilation was of more importance than a completely weatherproof building, the daub was omitted. These undaubed panels varied from those of ordinary wattle: the upright staves remained, although they were usually increased in number to form groups of two or three, and the pliable withies interwoven between them were replaced by thin, narrow oak slats. The width of these slats varied in different locations from as little as an inch or two up to seven inches, as at Bridge Sollers, Hereford & Worcester, although the usual width was between three and four inches. The pattern of the weave also varied, and in some instances the slats were notched and fitted into the slats at the top and bottom as one passed the other. This type of wattle panel was a feature of many of the barns in Hereford & Worcester and Shropshire but sadly today much has been replaced with brick-nogging.

Brick-Nogging and Other Solid Infillings
The use of brick as an infilling of the open panels (48) is a common enough feature and is to be found in all those areas where timber-

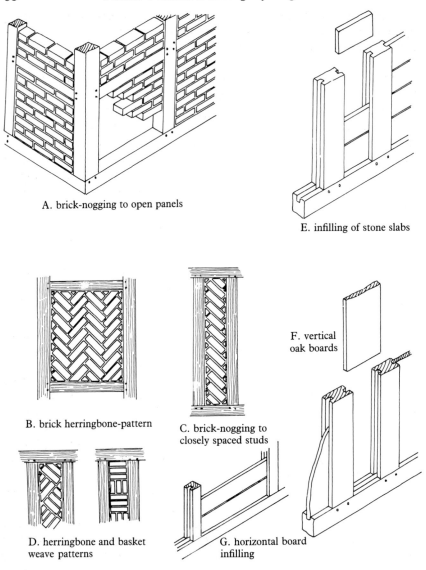

A. brick-nogging to open panels

E. infilling of stone slabs

B. brick herringbone-pattern

C. brick-nogging to closely spaced studs

F. vertical oak boards

D. herringbone and basket weave patterns

G. horizontal board infilling

48. Brick-nogging and other solid infillings

framed buildings survive. Brick-nogging, as this type of construction is known, is an old-established practice, although when it was first introduced is unknown. One early example of its use can be seen at Tilbury-juxta-Clare church, Essex, where a late fifteenth-century wall-painting portrays a scene of a man holding a horse, standing in front of a timber-framed house showing clearly its brick-nogging.

Certainly by the beginning of the sixteenth century it was gaining popularity in the South-East and eastern England but there is little evidence of its widespread use prior to the seventeenth century. With the change-over taking place at different times in different locations – Warwickshire, for instance, was much earlier than Hereford & Worcester – in some parts of the country wattle-and-daub continued in common use until the end of the eighteenth century.

Why bricks gained popularity is unknown, for early bricks were more porous than wattle-and-daub, encouraging dampness; the widely disparate rates of expansion and contraction between timber and bricks caused cracking and insecure panels, and the excessive weight imposed on the frame often caused many structural problems at a later date. The main reason was at first undoubtedly one of fashion, for bricks in Tudor times were of a high social standing, but later it is more likely that the old specialized craft of daubing began to decline as more and more timber-framed buildings were being clad with weatherboarding and tiles. Much of the brick-nogging seen today is the replacement of earlier defective wattle and daub infilling but by the seventeenth century, when the production of bricks became more widespread and cheaper, it was used not only for this but also in the construction of new buildings, and it is often impossible to decide whether it is original infilling or a later replacement. Much is Victorian but here again it could be a replacement of earlier defective brickwork.

The bricks were generally laid in horizontal courses in stretcher bond, although it is not uncommon to find them laid in a haphazard manner with little or no pattern. The most attractive is herringbone-pattern (48B), although its use is usually restricted to larger buildings and is particularly suited to narrow panels, for the bricks tend to be forced onto the frame by the weight of the brickwork. Other variations include oblique courses (48C), particularly when the studs are very closely spaced, and basket-weave pattern, formed with horizontal and vertical brickwork, while a combination of both horizontal courses and herringbone pattern is frequently found. Most of the brickwork laid in some kind of pattern was left untreated but most of the plain brickwork in Hereford & Worcester, Shropshire and Cheshire was treated with limewash, while in the South-East and eastern England the brickwork was often recessed and plastered.

Brick was not the only solid material used for infill panels: many local materials were employed. Local building-stone – for instance in Surrey and Sussex, flint, chalk and sandstone were all frequently used. The Old Shop, Bignor, West Sussex (49), clearly shows the variety of materials employed, including flint, plaster and bricks laid in both horizontal course and herringbone pattern. In Suffolk and Norfolk, although flint and chalk were available, clay lump – blocks formed of

49. 'The Old Shop', Bignor, West Sussex

clay mixed with straw or grass and left to dry but not fired – was
sometimes used, as at Ufford Hall, Fressingfield, Suffolk.

In those areas, where the stone could be easily split into thin slabs,
these two were used (48E). The studs needed to be spaced close
together and have grooves in their side into which the slab could
be fitted horizontally, one above the other. In west Yorkshire and
sometimes in Lancashire, sandstone flags were used in this way, while
in south Yorkshire, C. F. Innocent observed thin slithers of stone,
known locally as 'grey slates', frequently employed. Similarly, in
Coventry sandstone slabs have been discovered in a number of
sixteenth-century buildings and still retained at Cheylesmore Manor,
while in Stamford, Lincolnshire, slates from nearby Collyweston,
usually eight or so inches wide, were also popular. These stones and
slates were generally plastered both sides. Oak boards were used in a
similar manner, set vertically when the studs were close together (48F),
as in the early fourteenth-century granary at Grange Farm, Little
Dunmow, Essex, and the late fifteenth-century house by the churchyard at Penshurst, Kent, or horizontally one above the other where
the studs were spaced wider apart. Horizontal board infilling was a
feature of many timber-framed barns (48G), particularly in the North
and West, but few examples still remain for when decayed they

could not be replaced. Some still remain in the upper panels of the timber-framed barn at Home Farm, Hodnet, Shropshire, built in 1619; the lower panels and gables have later brick infilling. In all these forms of construction it would have been necessary for them to be inserted at the same time as the frame was erected and not, like wattle-and-daub, brick-nogging and local stone, inserted afterwards.

External Plastering
The external plastering of timber-framed buildings began in the sixteenth century and by the latter part of the seventeenth and throughout the eighteenth century had become common practice in eastern England and the South-East, coinciding with the improvement in the quality of plaster and the availability of timber laths (50). Like other cladding materials it was introduced to provide greater comfort for the inhabitants of the buildings.

The consistency of the plaster varied considerably and depended greatly on local traditions and customs. Ideally it was a mixture of slaked lime and coarse sand (normally in the proportion of three to six times the quantity of sand as lime) to which was added a variety of materials: chopped straw, cow-hair, scrapped from the hide, cleaned of dust and finely teased, horse-hair and even feathers were all used to bind the stuff together and increase the strength. In addition road scrapings and fresh cow-dung were often added, and stable urine. One or more of these admixes were introduced into the basic lime-and-sand

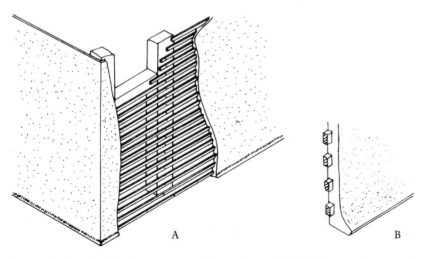

A. isometric view showing plaster and riven timber laths; B. detail of plaster and lath showing bellmouth

50. External plastering

plaster, water added, the ingredients beaten, carefully mixed and blended to produce a thick plaster which, when laid, was described by Professor Lethaby as 'tough as leather'.

This plaster was generally applied to the face of the riven timber laths closely spaced and nailed to the face of the studwork, the plaster worked in between the laths to form a key. For the best work the plaster was floated on, in at least two coats the first coat being 'picked' or 'roughened up' before becoming set as a key for subsequent coats. When applied to an old timber-framed building, the infilling of wattle-and-daub was generally removed and, as with new buildings, the plaster and lath finish was applied to the internal face as well. In these cases it was not uncommon to fill the void between the two faces with chaff to improve insulation. In some cases it has been found that the wattle-and-daub infilling has been retained, with the plaster being applied directly to the face of the daub and timberwork, both of which had been simply hacked to produce a key. Occasionally the laths were omitted, the cross-pieces of wattle being carried across and nailed to the external face of the studs, with vertical staves set between the studs with the cross-pieces tied to them. Onto this was applied a layer of daub, a thick coat internally and on the outside a thin coat keyed to the wattle and extending over the entire face, onto which the plaster was applied.

The plastering of timber-framed buildings was generally confined to the eastern part of the country, in Suffolk and in the surrounding counties of Cambridgeshire, Essex, Hertfordshire, Norfolk and further westwards into southern Bedfordshire. Within this area it can be seen at its best in the villages of Suffolk and Essex (51). In Suffolk, in such delectable villages as Boxford, Kersey, Clare, Nayland, Hartest and Cavendish, not much timber-framing is exposed yet nearly all the houses are of timber. Similarly in Essex, in Finchingfield, Great Bardfield, Wethersfield and Manuden, among others, most of the buildings are timber-framed yet few of the timbers are exposed, most being plastered. This is also true in the southern and western parts of Cambridgeshire – for instance, the houses around the green at Barring-ton (52), and the village of Linton, and in Hertfordshire particularly in the north-east of the county, in Ashwell, for example. The use of plaster was not restricted to eastern England for it was used fairly frequently in Kent, particularly to the north of the county, as well as to some extent in Surrey and Sussex.

Plaster was probably more widely used than is evident today. The Georgians did not like exposed timbers, but the use of plaster fell into their concept of domestic architecture and there is evidence of its use in many of the towns in Hereford & Worcester, Shropshire and Warwickshire. Clifton-Taylor in *Six English Towns* gives one such

51. Plastered and jettied houses, Debenham, Suffolk

52. Cottages at Barrington, Cambridgeshire

example in Broad Street, Ludlow, where a photograph of about 1900 shows nearly all the buildings on the east side plastered, whereas today they are all black and white in the customary western style. Even in eastern England there is a growing desire to strip away the old plaster to expose the underlying timbers. Lavenham, that most resplendent of all Suffolk's wool towns, is one such example. Thirty years ago there were few houses that had their timbers exposed; today there are many. The removal of the plaster is often unfortunate, for in many cases the underlying timbers are of poor quality and were never intended to be exposed. In addition, even where those timbers were originally meant to be exposed, the subsequent plastering process, which necessitated the driving-in of numerous nails to secure the laths or the hacking of the timber faces, has disfigured the face of the exposed timbers. This can often be seen, especially where the timbers are left untreated, as is the custom in eastern England.

Stone was a popular material throughout the Georgian period, and during this time and in particular from the latter part of the eighteenth century there was a desire to simulate stone in other materials. On timber-framed buildings this was generally carried out in plaster or stucco. Plaster was by far the most pleasing, the joints being recessed and moulded to produce the rusticated effect, which can be a little curious, particularly when the house is jettied as at King's School

53. King's School shop, Canterbury, Kent

shop, Canterbury (53), and at the gate house near the castle in
Colchester, Essex. With stucco the joints were usually lined, a feature
widely used on the half-timbered houses in Stamford, Lincolnshire.

Tile-Hanging

Tile-hanging (54) first appeared in England in the South-East towards
the end of the seventeenth century, and it remained popular throughout
the next century and well into the second half of the nineteenth

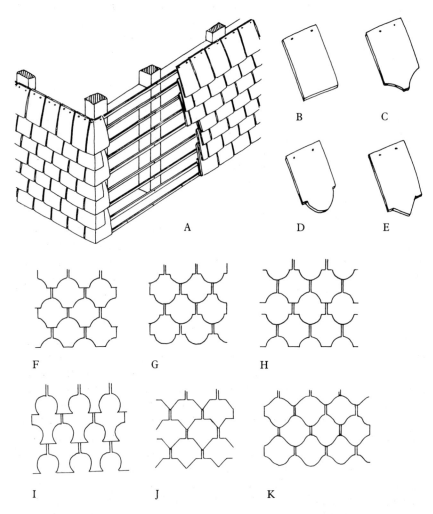

A. isometric view showing plain tiles hung on laths; B. plain tile; C. hammer-head tiles; D.
fish-scale tile; E. arrow-head tile; F., G., H., I., J. & K. various tile patterns

54. Tile-hanging

century, when machine-made tiles became readily available. Like older cladding materials, they were first introduced on timber-framed buildings as a method of weatherproofing existing buildings to provide greater comfort for their inhabitants, but they were so popular and cheap that they were also employed on new timber-framed buildings, especially the many slight timber-framed cottages built towards the end of the eighteenth and early part of the nineteenth century in the South-East.

It is in the South-East that most tile-hanging is to be found, especially in Kent, Surrey and Sussex, spreading to a limited extent into the adjoining counties of Hampshire, Berkshire and Oxfordshire, where its use is often restricted to the gable. Why it was not used elsewhere to any great extent, for instance in Essex and Suffolk, where tiles comparable to those in the South-East were produced, can only be explained by local traditions, taste and, in these areas, a preference for plaster. So it is in the South-East, especially the Weald, that tile-hanging is mainly to be found. In Kent one can cite such villages as Goudhurst, Biddenden, Tenterden, Yalding and Chiddingstone, in Surrey, Alford, Chiddingfold, Brook, Newdigate and Witley – probably the most typical of all Surrey villages in its proportion of tile-hanging, brick and half-timber, and in Sussex one sees it from Burwash, in the east, to Fernhurst in the west, and especially in the villages to the north, close to the Surrey border, such as Plaistow, Loxwood, Lurgashall, Northchapel and Rusper. Tile-hanging is found not only in these and many more villages throughout the South-East but also in the countryside, where it was used to clad many of the old farmhouses and even on occasion farm buildings, such as Peper Harow granary.

Plain tiles were at first used for tile-hanging and were in size, shape and construction the same as those used for roofing, though some were manufactured slightly thinner. Peg tiles were manufactured with two holes at the top, into which the pegs could be fitted which hooked over the battens. It was not until about 1890 that tiles were produced with nibs cast on the back as well as nail holes, the weight of the tile being carried on these nibs and secured by nails. Although as early as 1477 the size of the tiles was laid down as $10\frac{1}{2}$ by $6\frac{1}{2}$ inches, there were many local variations. Those from Kent were made to a size of nine by six while in Sussex the width was usually $6\frac{3}{4}$ inches. Being handmade, the tiles varied slightly in size, shape, colour and texture and had a slight camber both ways, producing a wall-covering of exquisite charm. Later, in the second half of the nineteenth century, these handmade tiles were replaced by machine tiles which, being of the same size, shape and texture, cannot compare with earlier, handmade ones. When applied to timber-framed buildings, horizontal riven timber battens, usually oak but later softwood, were fixed to the external face of the studs set about four inches apart, to which were hung the tiles, first by the means of oak, willow or hazel pegs, later by iron nails. The tiles were so hung as to give a triple lap (each tile lapping two others) and were generally bedded solid in lime hair mortar to make a secure and waterproof wall. Special tiles were manufactured for corners and jambs but often at these positions vertical timber battens were used. Occasionally the vertical joints were filled with mortar, spoiling the overall appearance, and fortunately most were left open, giving an attractive overall appearance. When tile-hanging was restricted to the upper floor, especially with exposed timber below, a triangular timber was provided at the lower edge of the tiling onto which the battens were fixed to throw any water running down the face of the tiles away from the wall below.

In towns and villages, tile-hanging was generally restricted to the upper floor, as it was frequently in rural areas too, but here it is not uncommon for a whole front, or one side or even on occasion the whole building, to be clad. When it was applied to an existing framed building which had a jettied upper floor, the opportunity was often taken to underbuild the jetty with a new brick wall flush with the tile-hanging above. The modernization of such buildings was completed by the insertion of new sash windows, to replace the earlier mullioned ones, and a new entrance door, making these old buildings from the outside at least almost indistinguishable from later buildings.

It is perhaps the colour of the tiles of the South-East that adds much to the delightful appearance of tile-hanging, and especially the clays of the Weald, which produced the beautiful terra-cotta tiles which have over the years mellowed and toned down yet still retain their soft, glowing red. Unlike roof tiles, which often remain damp long after rain has ceased encouraging the growth of lichen and moss, tiles hung vertically soon dry out and tend to retain their natural colour.

The plain rectangular tile was the type most commonly employed but patterned tiles of considerable variation of design were frequently used to give decorative effects. On occasion plain tiles of differing colour or texture were used in a variety of diaper patterns. To obtain a different texture, the tiles were dabbed with the bristle of a stiff brush before being fired, producing a rough surface which weathered faster than ordinary tiles and so, after a while, produced a pattern. More frequent was the use of purpose-made, shaped tiles. The fish-scale or scallop tile was one of the earliest and most popular, but a variety – the V, the arrowhead and the various forms of hammerheads – were all used. These ornamental tiles could be used individually, which often gives a pleasant effect, or in a combination of two types (fish-scales and Vs were a popular feature, as were fish-scales and curved hammerheads) which can look equally effective, or a combination with plain tiles – a few courses of plain tiles alternating with a few courses of ornamental tiles. While patterned tile-hanging is by no means rare in either Kent or Sussex, it is in Surrey that perhaps most occur, as at Ewhurst (55), Hascombe, Haslemere and Witley. In all these counties, however, most decorative tile-hanging belongs to the Victorian period.

Slate-Hanging

Slate-hanging was often employed as a cladding material in Cornwall, Devon and to a lesser extent in the North-West. Here, however, it was generally employed to give added protection to stone walls, for the use of timber framing in these areas, as we have seen earlier, is rare. Needless to say, there are examples to be found in the towns and villages of the South-West. One notable place is Totnes, Devon, which has quite a number of timber-framed houses of Tudor origin, and these, together with a good many later ones which are also timber-framed, have been subsequently hung with slates quarried locally. Outside Devon perhaps the most famous example of slate-hanging is the group of old houses at Dunster, Somerset, known as The Nunnery. The ground floor is of red sandstone, while the upper two floors are timber-framed and hung with slates. Again, in Cumbria slate hanging was used on occasion, one example being the timber-framed porch at Fell Foot Farm, Little Langdale. The slate-cladding of timber-framed buildings is generally restricted to houses but on occasion it can be found on farm buildings, particularly some of the granaries in Cornwall.

Unlike clay tiles, slates were supplied in a variety of lengths and widths, but they were generally cut much smaller than those used for roofing. The slates were holed and nailed to battens fixed horizontally to the face of the studs. They were fixed either single-lap, each slate lapping the slate below, or double-lap, each slate lapping two slates below, depending on the position and exposure. Most slate-hanging is plain, but often, particularly in the nineteenth century, it was cut along the bottom edge to form a pattern – a fish-scale pattern was popular. Sometimes the slates were arranged in a diamond pattern, as at The Nunnery, where such a pattern was fixed between windows to the upper floor. Totnes has a number of examples of polychrome slate-hanging, generally of contrasting colours in simple horizontal bands. A good deal in Totnes is painted, as it is in Launceston (160) and in some cases in Cumbria.

Mathematical Tiles

The mathematical tile or brick tile as it is sometimes known was another material used to clad timber-framed buildings (56). These

55. Cottages, Ewhurst, Surrey

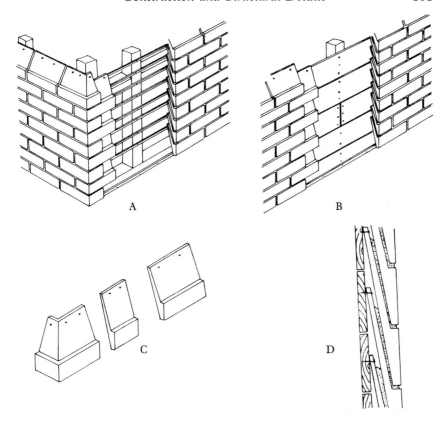

A. isometric view showing tiles fixed to battens; B. isometric view showing tiles fixed to boarding; C. typical mathematical tiles; D. section through tiles showing methods of bedding.

56. Mathematical tiles

imitation shaped brick tiles have the exposed face generally made to brick dimensions to give the appearance of brickwork. To fix them to a timber-framed structure one of two methods was employed, depending on the type of backing. Where the infilling was of wattle-and-daub, the usual practice was to cover the entire building with horizontal softwood boards onto which the tiles were nailed and bedded in lime putty. Where the infilling was brick nogging, the boards could be omitted and the tiles were bedded onto the face of the wall with plenty of lime putty and secured in addition, where possible, with nails. These tiles could also be fixed to battens nailed to the face of the walls, but this is much less common than was originally thought. In addition to being bedded, they were also pointed in mortar, so preserving the illusion of brickwork. The tiles were made in both headers and stretchers – although it was common to use headers only, as can be seen in many of the houses in Lewes and, for instance, on the rear elevation of Guildford House, High Street, Guildford, Surrey.

When well constructed, these mathematical tiles are practically indistinguishable from the true brickwork they intend to resemble. This illusion is often dispelled, however, for frequently their use was restricted to the main elevation, with the side and rear walls covered with tiles or other cladding material, often finished with only a vertical batten at the corners. Corners were always a problem, it seems, and Nathaniel Lloyd in his *A History of English Brickwork* mentions the use of rusticated timber blocks painted to represent stone quoins at the external angles. Special corner bricks were not made until the end of the 1700s and were rarely used, being more common in Surrey than in Kent and Sussex. Other 'tell-tale' features are the lack of arches over the windows, the widespread use of header bond, and the setting of the window frames flush with the wall and lined with a thin timber batten like the corners.

Although generally restricted to the front elevation there are rare examples of these tiles being used on side elevations as well; however, there appears to be only one example in which all four façades are clad, and that is Spring House, Ewell, Surrey, built about 1730, where not only all three floors of this timber-framed house were clad but also the parapet as well.

Exactly when these tiles were introduced is unknown, but it is evident that they appeared before the introduction of the Brick Tax in 1784, the avoidance of which is often suggested as the reason for their popularity in the eighteenth and nineteenth century. Recent research, however, has shown that these tiles were taxed as well as bricks from the commencement, although the tax on bricks was increased twice after 1794 while that on mathematical tiles remained unchanged. Moreover, the tax on tiles ceased in 1833, while on bricks it continued until 1850. One earlier example of their use is Helmingham Hall, Suffolk, when between 1745 and 1760 the old timber-framed building was modernized by the underbuilding of the first-floor jetties and by the battening out and hanging of mathematical tiles to the upper floor.

Although found on occasions elsewhere in the country, most are in the South-East, where there was a long tradition in the production of excellent tiles and bricks. However, why they never gained popularity elsewhere – for instance, in Essex and Suffolk, where bricks and tiles of equal quality were produced – has never been satisfactorily explained. Most are to be found in Kent and East Sussex, especially in the southern and coastal towns of these counties – Canterbury, Hythe, Tenterden, Lewes, Rye and Brighton – but they have been seen in Surrey and Suffolk and also in Hampshire, Wiltshire, Berkshire,

Cambridgeshire and Norfolk. Generally they are to be found in towns, rarely in rural areas.

Although usually these mathematical tiles were made of local clay and were therefore similar in texture and colour to local bricks, this was not always the case. Black tiles, often glazed (particularly around Brighton), were also manufactured. Sometimes two different colour tones were employed, as at Cotterlings, Ditchling, Sussex, where black tiles were used with red tile dressings. In some instances, however – and this is particularly true of the black-glazed mathematical tiles of Brighton – they were used to face an existing brickwall.

Weatherboarding

Weatherboarding, sometimes known by its American name of clapboarding, is yet another method of cladding a timber-framed building to render it both water- and draught-proof (57). Its use in preference

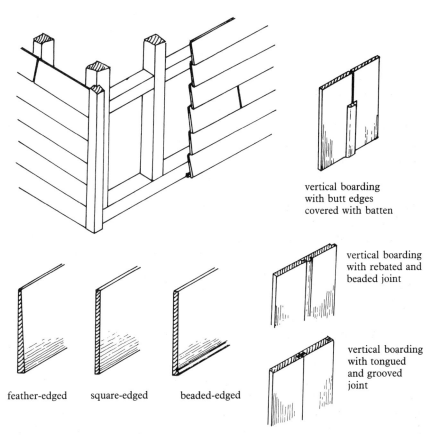

vertical boarding
with butt edges
covered with batten

vertical boarding
with rebated and
beaded joint

vertical boarding
with tongued
and grooved
joint

feather-edged   square-edged   beaded-edged

57. Weatherboarding

to tile-hanging or plastering as a cladding material was probably the need for economy, and it is, therefore, found principally on small houses, cottages, farm buildings and mills.

Weatherboarding comprises timber boards fixed either horizontally or vertically to the face of the building. Horizontal boarding is by far the most common and most attractive, with each board overlapping the one beneath, thus casting a shadow. The boards are generally feather-edged – boards tapered across their width – and chamfered along the bottom edge, but other types were used, such as square-edged and, in the eighteenth and early part of the nineteenth century, beaded. Vertical boarding is far less common but it can be found on timber-framed church towers and belfries in Essex (Blackmore, Margaretting, Stock, Marks Tey, Good Easter and Doddinghurst), in West Sussex (Itchingfield) and in Kent (High Halden). The use of vertical boarding was also common on agricultural buildings: it is known that many of the early farm buildings were clad with vertical boarding (the barns at Frindsbury, Kent, and Upminster, Greater London) and the style remained popular in Sussex and Hampshire

58. Paul's Farm, Leigh Kent

and may well have been used elsewhere in the South-East. In Cambridgeshire vertical weatherboarding was used as a cladding to smock mills (the derelict mills at Swaffham Prior and Sawtry), while in Yorkshire it was also a feature of many of the postmills. Little now survives; there are the barns at Frindsbury and Upminster, and a few timber-framed granaries in southern England (one formerly on the Goodwood Estate has been re-erected at the Weald and Downland Open Air Museum at Singleton) and a little can still be found in the West – for instance, the large barn at Malt House, Little Stretton, Shropshire. In these cases the boards may be tongued and grooved, rebated and beaded, or butted with the joints covered by narrow cover strips.

The cladding of horizontal barns and other farm buildings with horizontal weatherboarding commenced in about 1600 and has continued in eastern England and the South-East until this century. This technique, however, never became popular on domestic buildings until the eighteenth century, even then generally being restricted to the construction of the slight, timber-framed cottages built at this time or, like other cladding materials, (59) applied to the face of old

59. Weatherboarded Wealden house, Eynsford, Kent

timber-framed houses when they were modernized. The use of weatherboarding as a cladding material on cottages continued well into the nineteenth century, with some of the cottages at Tillingham, Essex, being erected as late as 1881. Houses are not necessarily weatherboarded all over; often it is confined to the front or rear, the upper storey or to a gable end, while along the Hertfordshire-Essex border the weatherboard, usually tarred, is used up to the ground-floor window sill (60) or, slightly less common, carried up to the top of the window or door with plaster above.

The early weatherboarding was of oak or, more commonly, elm, pegged to the frame and left untreated, but later, particularly in the eighteenth and nineteenth centuries, it was of softwood nailed to the face of the studs, treated with tar, in the case of barns and other farm buildings, or painted, when used on domestic buildings. In parts of Essex, however, especially along the coast, one can still find old tarred weatherboarding on cottages, giving greater protection against the salt air and the weather (61). At the corners a vertical rebated batten was provided, up to which the boarding could be fitted, while at the reveals to windows and doors a smaller rectangular batten was fixed for the boards to fit against.

60. Cottages, Cottered, Hertfordshire

61. Weatherboarded cottage, West Mersea, Essex

The use of horizontal weatherboarding in the cladding of timber-framed barns as well as other farm buildings can be seen throughout the South-East and the East of England. These large timber-framed, weatherboarded and tarred buildings under a well-mellowed red-tiled roof are certainly one of the features of Surrey, Kent, Sussex and Essex and to a lesser extent of Suffolk, Cambridgeshire and Hertfordshire. In the West and the west Midlands the use of weatherboarding on farm buildings is somewhat rare, although examples can be found, for instance at Manor Farm, More, Shropshire. Horizontal weatherboarding both tarred and white painted is a feature of windmills – post and smock – as it is with the majority of timber-framed watermills of eastern England and the South-East.

Like plaster and stucco, weatherboarding was used to simulate stone. Often it was used as a cladding to brick buildings but not infrequently it was also used on timber-framed buildings. The cheapest way was to face the house with boards which were scored vertically at regular intervals to give a 'stone-effect', a method used on a number of the buildings along the Pantiles at Tunbridge Wells. The vertical scoring of these timbers was by necessity shallow, and in better-class work individual blocks were used either with butt-joints, the fine division between the blocks resembling mortar joints or the blocks chamfered to suggest rustication. This type of cladding can be seen on a number of buildings in Kent, particularly in Tenterden and Rolvenden.

Brick and Stone Cladding

During the seventeenth and eighteenth centuries, with the increasing production of bricks, new brick buildings began to be built in most parts of the country, formerly the domain of timber. In all these areas there was a desire for the owners of old timber-framed buildings to modernize their properties by either entirely encasing them in brick-work or more commonly providing a new brick façade retaining the old building behind. These brick façades are a feature so common that west Midland towns such as Alcester, Warwickshire, and Pershore, Hereford & Worcester, look brick-built whereas they are to a large extent only brick-fronted. In the South-East and eastern England too this was fashionable, and many streets which in appearance are Georgian are often only brick-fronted, with the old timber-framed building hidden behind. New brick façades were not restricted to towns and villages, and there are a number of isolated farmhouses which have been similarly modernized. Similarly, other detached buildings were encased or largely encased in brickwork, notable examples being a number of timber-framed churches in Cheshire – Baddiley, Cholmondeley Chapel and Swettenham.

In addition, from the late sixteenth century onwards it became a common practice to underbuild the jetties, and many which today appear on first evidence to be plain brick or tile-hung are on closer examination former jettied houses. The advantage of this undertaking was two-fold: it provided extra space to the ground-floor rooms – usually some eighteen inches, and at the same time the front of the house could be modernized. Generally a brick wall was built up under the projecting jetty, and in the case of the Wealden house this brickwork was carried up to eaves level between the projecting end bays, to support the floors or wall-plates. When all the timbers were securely fixed, the front wall beneath the jetties or wall-plate could be removed without fear of structural damage. The whole of the upper storey would then be clad with tiles or sometimes weatherboarded, and with the insertion of contemporary windows and doorways the modernization would be complete. There are numerous examples of this type of construction to be found in the South-East, particularly in some of the towns of the Weald – for instance, Burwash, East Sussex, in which the original character of the building has been completely lost. Not all jetties were underbuilt; one can cite such examples as Detillens, Limpsfield, Surrey, in which the original jetty was cut off and replaced by a Georgian brick façade.

Brick was not the only material used in the cladding of old timber-framed buildings; where there was a plentiful supply of stone, this too was widely used. Of all areas, this was particularly true in Yorkshire, where there are numerous buildings, both houses and barns, which externally give few clues that they originated as timber-framed buildings, the oak frame and roof timbers not being dispensed with but retained to provide strength and stability. Guiseley Rectory, West Yorkshire, rebuilt in 1601 in stone, is one example which from the outside appears to be entirely of this date, with a symmetrical façade, yet the porch leads to a medieval cross-passage and an aisled hall which still retains its arcade posts. There are a number of other aisled houses in West Yorkshire, particularly around Halifax, which were partly rebuilt and clad in stone in the seventeenth century. This practice of rebuilding or cladding the external walls of timber-framed buildings continued into the eighteenth century – as for example at Green Farm, Stocksbridge.

Architectural Features and Details

So far the structural elements of timber-framed buildings have been discussed but there are many other details and features, both functional and decorative, that form an important and often integral part of these buildings, adding considerably to their character.

Roof-Coverings

The traditional roof-coverings for a timber-framed building are thatch, tiles, pantiles, slates, stone-slates or flags and occasionally shingles. Concrete tiles and asbestos slates sometimes to be found are twentieth-century innovations and are aesthetically objectionable.

Today thatch (62) is essentially a rural material, but this was not always so. In medieval times most buildings, except those of some importance, would have been thatched, including most of those in towns. There are many instances of fires in towns for which thatch was to blame, and in many towns a coat of whitewash was applied to the thatch to give it some protection against sparks. In London, in 1212, a coat of lime plaster was made compulsory on existing thatch to reduce the risk of fire, and at the same time a restriction was made on the use of the material on any new roof. Other towns followed suit, but outside the town thatch remained popular in most parts of the country well into the sixteenth century, when in some parts it began to be replaced with more permanent materials (63).

Reed, straw (wheat, rye, oats and barley), heather and other vegetable products such as flax, sedge and even broom were at one time all used for thatching, but today only reed and wheat straw, with sedge still in demand for ridges. Reed is the best and, although initially more expensive, if well laid will last at least sixty years and in a few cases as long as a hundred. It is laid so that only the sharp, butt-ends of the stalks are exposed, the water being shed from tip to tip on its way down the roof. Wheat straw, also known as 'long-straw', often needs to be remade after fifteen years or so: being rather short, it is liable to be attacked by both birds and the weather. For these reasons long-straw thatch is often protected with wire netting. Roofs constructed of wheat straw have their own distinctive appearance, for the straw is applied lengthwise, giving a more gentle, moulded appearance than that obtained with reed. A speciality of the South-West is what is known as

110

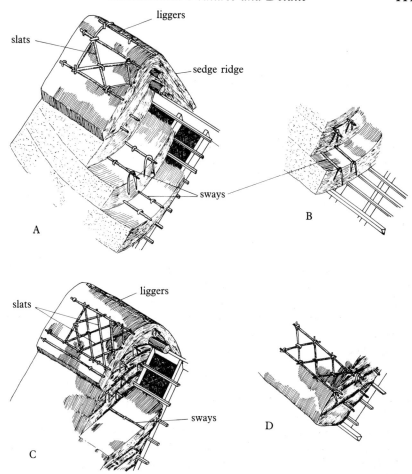

A. detail of ridge in Norfolk reed; B. detail at eaves in Norfolk reed; C. detail of ridge in straw; D. detail at eaves in straw.

62. Roof-coverings – Thatch

'wheat-reed'. Botanically it has no connection with true reed but owes its name to the method of laying, which is similar to true reed, in that only the ends of the straw are exposed, producing a longer-lasting and neater roof.

Basically four methods were used in securing the thatch to the roof structure: sewing the thatch to the rafters, pinning it down with hazel 'sways' secured by timber hooks, working the thatch into layers of turf or a foundation of brushwood or wattle, or securing it by means of a series of weighted ropes passing over the surface. All four methods were used, either individually or in a combination of two or more

63. Cottage, Steyning, West Sussex

methods. Today the second method is most commonly employed, sometimes combined with the first.

(64) Although there are exceptions to the rule that thatch is a rural material, it is to be found mostly on country cottages and small houses. Suffolk has more thatched buildings than any other county, and thatch is a feature of many timber-framed and plastered cottages as well as the occasional farmhouse and barn. It is also to be found in many of the other counties of eastern England, particularly Hertfordshire, Cambridgeshire and the northern part of Essex. In Kent, Surrey and East Sussex, because of a plentiful supply of excellent plain tiles from quite an early time, thatch is comparatively rare even on small houses. In West Sussex and Hampshire, there is much more, and it is a feature of many timber-framed cottages, farmhouses and occasional farm buildings. Again, in the West thatch was once the traditional roofing material and is still to be found on some of the timber-framed cottages in the area, particularly in Hereford & Worcester.

Plain clay tiles (65) have been used in the South-East and eastern England for many centuries, and the large expanse of undulating red clay tiles on many of the old timber-framed houses and barns is one of the features of these areas. These clay tiles followed the same

64. Cottages, Wherwell, Hampshire

development as brick-making, for they were usually made at the brickworks, often being fired with bricks within the same kiln. The size of the tiles varied greatly, despite an attempt to standardize size and manufacture in 1477, when a statute declared, for the first time, that the size should be 10½ by 6¼ by ⅝ inches, but whether it had much influence is doubtful, for in Kent they continued to measure

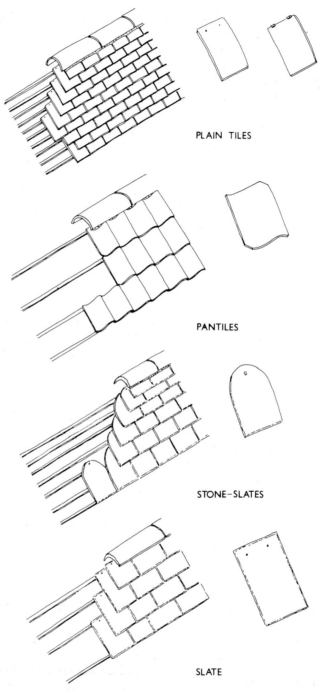

PLAIN TILES

PANTILES

STONE-SLATES

SLATE

65. Roof-coverings – tiles, pantiles, slates

nine by six inches, and in Sussex the width was often 6¾ inches, while in Leicestershire plain tiles have always measured eleven by seven inches.

The earliest surviving tiles have large central 'nibs' on which to hang them, but by the fifteenth century these were replaced by peg-tiles, fixed to riven oak laths by means of small timber pegs – usually oak – driven through holes in the tiles and hooked over the laths. It was not until the nineteenth century that peg-tiles began to be replaced by tiles with nibs cast onto the back to hook over the batten. Tiles are usually laid to a pitch of forty-five degrees or more, with some of the memorable tiled roofs in the Weald being between fifty and sixty degrees. Tiles were laid to a double-lap – that is to say, there is a double thickness of tile over the entire roof, with each tile overlapping two others, leaving only about four inches exposed. The tiles were originally laid on a bed of hay, straw or moss, a process which continued in some parts, such as Surrey, until the beginning of this century and can still on occasion be found on old roofs. To weatherproof the roof completely, the tiles were usually 'torched' – pointed in lime hair mortar on the underside.

As previously stated, the best and earliest of the plain clay-tiled roofs are to be found in the South-East and eastern England. Being hand-made, each of the old peg-tiles varied slightly in size, shape and texture, each with a slight camber in various shades of red, the colour of those from the Weald being particularly fine, producing a roof of unusual character and charm. Not all tiles were red; in Cambridgeshire, for instance, the Gault yields a dull yellow tile, and a feature around Elsworth, Eltisley and the neighbouring part of Suffolk, around Mildenhall, are roofs of variegated colours – yellows, browns, pinks, greys and some reds, all arranged in a haphazard fashion. In Shropshire and Hereford & Worcester they are often brown, whereas in Staffordshire they are of an unusual dark purply colour with a slightly shiny surface.

The S-shaped clay pantiles (65) were first imported from Holland during the seventeenth century and were at the beginning of the following century supplemented with pantiles manufactured in England. The size 13½ by 9½ by ½ inches was first laid down in the reign of George I, and these dimensions have been maintained ever since. Pantiles are single-lap tiles, each tile lapping the one beneath, but in addition the S shape made it possible for such tiles to form a sideways lap with the adjacent tile. Because of this a pantiled roof was light and often a suitable replacement for thatch on many timber-framed buildings. In addition the pantiles could be laid at a far lower pitch than plain tiles, as long as the roof was adequately torched to prevent rain and snow penetration. Pantiles are to be found generally on the eastern side of England (the only place elsewhere is around Bridgwater, Somerset), from London northwards and as far inland as the eastern part of Leicestershire and Nottinghamshire, and they are a feature of many timber-framed buildings particularly in Suffolk and parts of Norfolk, and in York. Generally, pantiles are various shades of red and orange but in Suffolk and Norfolk they were sometimes black glazed, reflecting the light of the vast East Anglian skies.

Slate (65) is to be found in parts of Cornwall, Devon, Leicestershire and the Lake District, but unfortunately the majority of tiles seen in this country are of the blue-grey slate from Wales, the least attractive of all Britain's slates. It was not until the nineteenth century, with the improvement in transportation, that the use of Welsh slate became widespread. Able to be split into thin layers of uniform thickness, they produced a light roof and were frequently used not only on new buildings but to replace thatch. This was particularly true in the Welsh Marches, where Welsh slates became the universal roofing material. In eastern England and the South-East too they were used to replace thatch as well, often to roof the softwood cottages that were erected in these areas during the nineteenth century. English slate was rarely used for the roofing of timber-framed buildings, mainly because where slate was found timber-framed buildings were rare. It can, however, be seen in Totnes and elsewhere in Devon, in Launceston, Cornwall, and on an occasional timber-framed house in Leicestershire. Unlike Welsh slate, which was laid in regular courses, English slate is laid in diminishing courses. Originally all slates were bedded on straw, hay or moss and fixed with oak pegs fitted into holes in the slates and hooked over battens.

Sandstone flags were also used where available in the roofing of timber-framed buildings and, in all areas where readily available, were preferred to clay tiles. These flags are thick and heavy and can be as much as four feet wide and three inches thick, fixed with oak pegs hooked over the battens and laid in diminishing courses – the widest at the eaves and the narrowest at the ridge – and bedded in some form of vegetable material such as straw, hay or moss. Today they are often bedded in mortar. In the South-East, in a triangle formed roughly by Crawley, Horsham and Steyning, most buildings built to last were, it appears, roofed with Horsham slates, including small farm buildings such as granaries, of which a great many are timber-framed. In the Welsh border counties, although many have been replaced with tiles and Welsh slate, many sandstone roofs still exist. In Hereford & Worcester they come from the Old Red Sandstone and can still be seen in, for example, Pembridge and Eardisland.

In the Welsh border counties too, sandstone roofs can be found but here the sandstone comes from the Ordovician and Silurian rocks and further north from the Coal Measures and Millstone Grit. Although many have been replaced with tiles and Welsh slates, roofs covered with these sandstone flags are to be seen on timber-framed buildings in the area including the timber-framed churches at Lower Peover and Marton and in many of the major houses, such as Little Morton Hall, Rufford Old Hall and Ordsall Hall, Salford.

Less significant in their application to timber-framed buildings are the limestone slates which, because of the nature of the stone, could be split into relatively thin slabs, producing a much lighter roof than that obtainable with sandstone flags. They can on occasion be found on timber-framed buildings in those marginal areas between the predominantly stone regions of the limestone belt and the predominantly timber ones to the west and east.

Shingles – small pieces of wood, between four and ten inches wide and about a foot long – were also widely employed in England as a roofing material from Roman times until about the twelfth century, when they began to be replaced by clay tiles, which were more durable and becoming competitive in price. For centuries these shingles were of cleft oak so riven as to produce a shingle which was slightly thicker at the lower end, which was often rounded. Nowadays few of these old shingles survive, being replaced with Canadian cedar which, fortunately, like oak, mellows to a silvery-grey. These are substantially larger than the traditional oak ones and are cheaper to produce and lay. The traditional way of fixing shingles was by means of oak pegs to timber battens but this has now given way to copper nails.

Although shingle continued to be used in some parts for the roofing of cottages up to the eighteenth century, today they are to be seen principally on church spires, particularly in the South-East but also in Essex, especially on the timber-framed belfries and towers in that county, as well as in parts of Hampshire, Berkshire and Hertfordshire. They can also be found in parts of Shropshire, Hereford & Worcester and Gloucestershire, in the Forest of Dean.

It was these coverings, more than any other item, which determined the roof shape, for each material had its appropriate pitch, and whereas thatch, plain tiles and limestone stone-slates could all incorporate hips, valleys and dormers, the slates, sandstone flags and pantiles were more appropriate to a simple roof without valleys or dormers. These considerations have led to the use of two basic roof shapes, the hipped, in which all four sides slope, and the gabled, in which only the two opposite sides slope, with the other two finishing up to the gable walls which project above the eaves. Within these two main groups there are several variations.

Another, but unrelated, roof type is the gambrel, commonly called the mansard, which occurred in the eastern counties towards the end of the eighteenth century and enjoyed popularity at the lower end of the social scale, providing a cheap and effective way of creating a room in the roof space with sufficient headroom to be used as a normal first-floor room. The roof has two pitches on each side of the ridge, the lower one much steeper than the upper, with the lower sometimes incorporating a dormer.

In addition there were local traditions which also affected the roof shape. In the eastern counties gabled roofs were predominant, with hipped, although not rare, being far less common, whereas in the South-East and in particular in Kent, Surrey and East Sussex, the situation was reversed. A feature widely used in the South-East is the half-hipped roof, which gives a part-gable at the end of the house, which often incorporated a window to light the roof space or attic. Another feature of the area is the small gablet incorporated in these half-hipped roofs. Again, unlike in the East, dormers were not widely used, and most of those that exist today are almost certainly later insertions.

Sometimes gables were used to break up the roof slope either to provide attic accommodation, in which case they often incorporated a window, or as an architectural feature. In some instances these secondary gables, as they are known, were added to an older house when the floor was inserted into the open hall, adding to the existing gables of the cross-wing.

Bargeboards

Bargeboards (wide boards fixed to the end of gable roofs immediately below the tile, forming the overhang) were a feature of many fifteenth- and sixteenth-century timber-framed buildings and followed the slope of the roof (66). Introduced to provide protection to the exposed ends of the roof timbers as well as affording some protection for the walls, these boards were also selected for decorative detail, often elaborately carved, shaped and pierced, and were an important part of the decorative treatment of the building. The earliest surviving examples belong to the fifteenth century; those foiled, possibly with carved spandrels

Bargeboards – a few examples of the numerous types and shapes used during the 15th and 16th centuries.

66. Bargeboards

and often cusped in the Gothic tradition are generally of pre-Reformation date, after which they generally became more straight-sided and simply moulded or moulded and carved. Towards the end of the sixteenth century, running designs based on the vine were largely replaced by scroll-work, strap-work, dentils, the guilloche pattern and other Renaissance forms of decoration. The pendant, both carved and moulded and occasionally pierced, was frequently used in the Elizabethan and Jacobean period, usually at the apex but sometimes at the eaves as well. Decorative bargeboards ceased to be used in the seventeenth century, when timber-framed houses began to be clad in plaster, tile or weatherboarding and the distance between wall and bargeboard diminished until the bargeboard was fixed flush to the wall, the generous overhang at the gable being no longer required to protect the walls.

Pargeting

The external face of a plastered wall was often decorated by ornamental enrichments. Today this is known as pargeting, a term originally meaning any type of external plaster sheathing (67). The derivation of the word can be traced to the French word *pargeter* – to throw or cast over a surface. The art of pargeting, a craft little known outside Britain, developed in the sixteenth century, reaching its zenith in the latter part of the following century.

Pargeting can be found in many parts of the country, and examples can be cited at York, Maidstone, Newark, Banbury and Hereford & Worcester, but it is in Suffolk and Essex and the surrounding parts of Hertfordshire, Norfolk and Cambridgeshire that most can be seen. Originally pargeting was far more common than it is today but, due to the deterioration of old plaster over the years and the restoration and repair of many old plastered buildings, much has been lost. Yet despite this there is still much to be seen, some original, other replacements of the seventeenth and eighteenth centuries, in and around the villages of south-west Suffolk, north-west Essex and the eastern part of Hertfordshire.

There are two forms of pargeting to be found: incised work, also known as stick, scratch or combed work, and relief or raised work. Of these two, incised work appeared first and is by far the most common. At first it was restricted to larger houses but it remained in favour much longer than relief work, continuing in use well into the eighteenth century, when it was often employed in the construction of cottages. The process was simple, and tools were home-made – a pointed stick, a number of sticks tied together to form a fan, a rectangular piece of wood, a wooden comb or even a large nail. The process was either to impress a pattern into the wet plaster or to

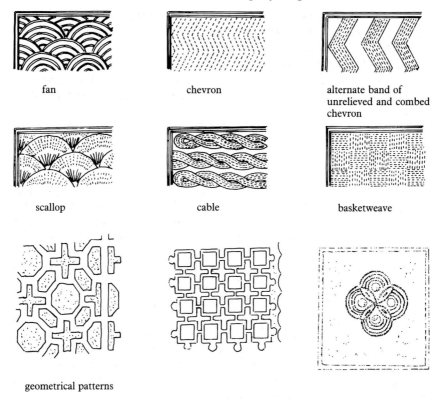

fan

chevron

alternate band of unrelieved and combed chevron

scallop

cable

basketweave

geometrical patterns

67. Pargeting

inscribe one with the use of the fan or comb. The chevron, herringbone and basket weave were all produced by the use of a rectangular piece of wood pressed into the plaster to form a soft V-shaped impression. Sometimes the whole face of the wall would be covered with an 'overall' design but more frequently the walls would be divided into rectangular panels, often varying in size. Generally each panel had a scratched border, with the remainder filled in with one of a variety of patterns.

Perhaps the most common of the older patterns is the chevron, of which there are various designs, repeated over the entire panel. Basket weave is another common pattern; the older form, which comprised rectangular patterns of broken lines of D-shaped indentations formed by a comb, is now rare and has generally been replaced by a simplified modern version, formed by the use of a series of square blocks stamped on the face of the plaster. The fan pattern is perhaps the most popular type now in use. Originally it was a combed pattern, very irregular and often placed diagonally, but today the pattern is generally produced with the aid of stamps pressed into the plaster.

Another – and the simplest – form of decoration, one frequently used on cottages, was 'sparrow-picking'. This consisted simply of holes formed by a tool comprising a triangular piece of wood with teeth on one side and a handle on the other which was stabbed over the face of the plaster. One difficulty with incised pargeting was that it soon lost its sharpness over the years with each successive coat of lime or colour wash.

Much more ornate is the pargeting in relief. The work was carried out in a soft lime plaster, reinforced with hair and a variety of other ingredients including chopped straw, wood scrapings, manure and even cheese. Geometrical patterns of interlacing squares and circles were popular in the seventeenth century. These 'stamped' patterns can still be seen – for instance, at the Sun Inn, Saffron Walden, Essex, and on a house in the High Street, Lavenham, Suffolk. These overall geometrical patterns were formed by placing templates of wood onto the undercoat of the plaster, with the finishing coat brought up to it and often roughened or sparrow-picked, so forming a contrast between the main wall surface and the smooth face of the pattern once the template has been removed. Repetitive work in relief, such as string courses or friezes in a vine or other floral designs, were often formed by means of moulds, and it is not uncommon to find patterns obviously from the same mould on houses fairly close together. N. Pevsner observed two similar patterns at Yoxford and Sibton in Suffolk. The best work was undoubtedly that undertaken free hand, thus avoiding repetition. Decorative oval frames comprising a raised band or garland were another common pattern. These sometimes enclosed floral motifs, as at Yew Tree Farm, Finningham, Suffolk, but more often enclosed initials or a date or sometimes both. This form of decoration was popular during the seventeenth century and continued into the first quarter of the eighteenth.

There are many examples of relief pargeting to be found in eastern England. In Essex there is Colneford House, Earls Colne, with a richly pargeted front with a date of 1685; the group of houses in Church Street, Saffron Walden, decorated in geometrical pattern foliage, birds and also figures (one, the former Sun Inn, has the date 1676 and the figures of Thomas Hickathrift and the Wisbech giant); Garrison House, Wivenhoe, with a gorgeous display of mid seventeenth-century pargeting: large foliated scrolls and strapwork above a weatherboarded ground floor; and Crown House, Newport, late sixteenth or early seventeenth century, with the front arranged in moulded panels, those on the ground floor left blank but filled in with garlands, swags and leafy branches.

Notable examples in Suffolk are the Ancient House, Clare, of 1473, overlooking the churchyard, and the Ancient House (also known as

Sparrow's House), Ipswich, which depicts among other things a large coat of arms of Charles II, Neptune, a shepherd and shepherdess, a man on horseback, a tree heavy with fruit, figures in a chariot and two horses, and a series depicting the continents of Europe, Asia, Africa and America, with Atlas. There are some good examples still to be found in Lavenham: in Church Street are depicted emblems of the wool trade – mitre, spur-rowel and fleur-de-lys, and 68 Water Street also has the remains of some bold pargeting.

Good pargeting can also be found in parts of Hertfordshire, particularly near the Essex border, at, for instance, Fore Street, Hertford, and in the High Street, Ashwell; the cottage next to St John's Guildhall has some excellent fancy pargeting of 1681. Kent too has a few good examples: the best and earliest is on a house in Bank Street, Maidstone, dated 1611; another, not dated, is the Queen Elizabeth guest chamber, Canterbury, while work of a considerably later date can be seen at Week Street, Maidstone, dated 1680 and at 121 West Street, Faversham, dated 1697.

External Decoration

Limewash was the traditional external finish to timber-framed buildings, giving additional waterproofing and decorative finish to the external plastering. It has now been largely replaced by a wide range of commercially produced paints, usually with a cement base. The latter form a hard, impervious layer which, although restricting the penetration of moisture, also restricts the old plaster wall breathing and drying out, resulting in the cracking and peeling off of the paint. Limewash on the other hand is absorbed into the plaster, allowing it to breathe and dry out, an important feature if, as is often the case, no damp-proof course is provided. In addition, with the inevitable movement of the timber frame, it does not crack like modern paints.

Traditionally limewash comprised two ingredients, quicklime and a water-repellent, usually tallow, originally obtained from Russia, or linseed oil. Other ingredients were added, such as cow-dung, size, animal glue and even egg yolks, milk and beer to help to bind the material together. Alum and salt were added to prevent scaling. Colour was obtained by adding various pigments, the most popular of the medieval ones being the dull reds, browns and yellows mainly from oxides in clay; these had to suffice for many cottages well into the seventeenth century. At the beginning of that century, however, other pigments began to appear made by the application of heat on clay stained with the oxides of both iron and manganese to produce stronger tones, such as burnt umber and sienna. Later, greens, vermillion and blue were produced from copper, sulphur and cobalt, but these were expensive and generally restricted to decorative features such as pargeting.

Limewash was a cheap form of protection and, although its application was a traditional craft, required little skill in either its manufacture or application. The quicklime was at first broken down into small lumps and 'slaked' by the addition of hot water, after which it was mixed gradually with water and stirred until a smooth consistency was achieved. The tallow was then melted until it became a transparent liquid and added and stirred into the lime until a smooth texture was obtained. Colour was then added, care being taken to ensure an even distribution of the pigments. The mixture was then left for upwards of two weeks before being finally diluted with water to the right consistency. The limewash was then applied to the wall by means of a brush tied onto a long pole or by a special liming brush.

External timbers were also treated, for medieval manuscripts and paintings frequently show a contrast between the timbers and infill panels. It is known that in eastern counties and the South-East the oak face of the framing was limewashed over with the panels; or left in their natural state to weather into a silvery hue. Whether this was general practice throughout the country is uncertain; today much of the exposed framing in the West, the west Midlands, Cheshire and Lancashire is blackened and known as 'magpie' or 'black-and-white' construction, but this seems to be a later rather than an early form of decoration (although there is reference to the blacking of timber as early as 1574), for a permanent black was not widely available until pitch and tar were manufactured from coal in the nineteenth century; it seems therefore that most were treated in Victorian times or later. Such is the passion for the black-and-white buildings in these areas that it is not uncommon to find brick buildings treated to simulate timber-framing. However, there is evidence that timbers were treated prior to this to darken the frame, for bullocks' blood, mixed with soot, rudd or red ochre, was used to produce a rich matt surface. Also more buildings must have been brightly painted in reds, greens, yellows and golds than the single remaining example of the White Hart, Newark, Nottinghamshire.

Open Hearths, Smoke Bays, Firehoods, Chimneys and Fireplaces

Few medieval houses possess chimneys (68) as such, although a few examples are known in the stone-built Norman hall houses. In the typical timber-framed dwellings of the medieval period the central hearth in the open hall was the only means of heating. It comprised little more than a slab of stone and billet bars used to support the logs, the smoke escaping as best it could through a smoke hole at or near the apex of the roof or through a smoke louvre in the gablet. Evidence

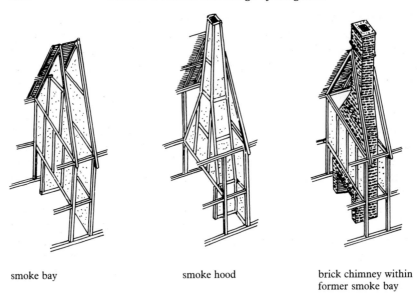

smoke bay   smoke hood   brick chimney within
                                                          former smoke bay

68. Chimney development

of the smoke holes or louvres is rare, for later alterations have generally
obliterated all traces of these original features.

As the upper floors of most end bays projected into the roof space,
it was necessary to prevent smoke from the adjoining hall drifting in.
In most cases the partitions between the hall and storeyed end bays were
timber-framed, infilled with wattle-and-daub, and in most medieval
houses the smoke was allowed to drift from the hall through the
triangular space between the partition rafters and collars, with the
smoke then escaping through the gablet. To prevent smoke entering
the rooms below, a plaster lining was laid over the collars and, as at
Fadben, Thundridge, Hertfordshire, the plaster was carried up to
meet the gablet collar, thus completely sealing the room below. This
arrangement to extract the smoke was usually provided at both ends
of the hall. Another common feature appears to have been the provision
of a projecting hood to the gablets, presumably to keep the weather
out, and one survives at Stanton's Farm, Black Notley, Essex, now
covered by a later roof.

With the discomfort caused by the open hearth, it became desirable
to provide some method of channelling the smoke from the ground
floor to the roof. From the evidence so far available, it seems that the
method generally adopted in a timber-framed house was to introduce
a smoke bay – a bay four or five feet in length which ran the full height
of the house. The hearth was located in the centre of this bay and was
plastered from first floor to ridge level. In many cases these bays were

introduced into the former open hall when the floors were inserted, the floor extending over one bay only, with the second bay being turned into a smoke bay. Most of these conversions seem to be from about 1500, and it was not long before this improvement was adopted for new houses built with two storeys throughout. Smoke bays continued to be in general use for at least another hundred years, and it seems that, despite the increased production of cheap bricks that accelerated the introduction of brick chimneys, some at least continued in use until about 1700. There is now much evidence of the widespread use of smoke bays in timber-framed buildings not only in South-East and eastern England, where many are to be seen, but also in the west Midlands.

An alternative to the smoke bay was the smoke hood, a chimney made of timber with a wattle-and-daub infilling and usually plastered internally to protect the timbers. The structure itself, which tapered to an outlet in the roof, was built against a timber-framed partition, usually with two return walls, and was supported at the front by the mantel beam above the fireplace. Such were the fire-resistant properties of these structures that several still survive and in a few cases have remained in use until recent years. The smoke hood was probably first introduced at the end of the fifteenth century, when it was often inserted into the open hall, usually prior to the insertion of the first floor, and probably continued to be built in many of the smaller houses until the beginning of the eighteenth century, for instance at Gravel Pit Hall, Wareside, Hertfordshire.

A variation of the smoke hood was the firehood, a feature widely used in the North. The open hearth was rarely employed even in the earliest timber-framed open halls to be found in the North; instead, built against a stone reredos at the lower end of the hall, there was a timber and plastered firehood. As in the smoke hood in the South, the front of the firehood was supported by a bressummer beam at mid-wall height, the full width of the building, with the upper portion of the stack supported by a pair of collars attached to the purlins. In some cases with a through-passage behind the reredos, the side of the hearth was screened off from the entry into the hall by means of a short screen running between the end of the reredos and the bressummer, which was frequently supported by a timber post. This short wall was known as the 'heck'. In later houses in the North the adoption of the firehood became universal, and it was the equivalent of the brick chimney in the South. Today few survive, nearly all being replaced by stone-built chimneys in the seventeenth century.

With these timber and plastered structures, the fire risk was considerable, especially in towns. As early as 1419 the City of London introduced regulations that in future chimneys were to be constructed of stone, tile or brick 'and not of plaster or wood under pain of being pulled down'. In the following centuries many other towns and villages brought out regulations governing the construction of chimneys, but it is evident that timber and plaster continued to be used. At Clare, Suffolk, in 1621, a decision was made by the headboroughs that every chimney should in future be built of brick and stand 4½ feet above the roof; but nearly a century later, in 1719, people were still being fined for the use of timber and clay chimneys.

Brick chimneys and fireplaces began generally to appear in the second half of the sixteenth century not only in new timber-framed houses but also in many of the medieval former open-hall houses. The modernization of the open halls was spread over a considerable period, most being undertaken in the sixteenth century, but it was not until the following century that the process was complete. Obviously in most of these later examples the new brick stacks replaced earlier smoke bays or smoke hoods, and there is much evidence that these stacks were often built within a former smoke bay. In a timber-framed house which had a brick or stone chimney from the start, the frame was usually designed by means of a short bay, perhaps some four or five feet in length, to accommodate it. Where a chimney had been inserted, the timbers were often cut resting on or built into the stack. Chimneys of brick were undoubtedly the most common in much of the lowland zone but in the stone-bearing areas of the country stone was generally used, the stone gable end stack being a feature of many of the houses of Hereford & Worcester and Shropshire. The decorative brick chimneys of Tudor times often towering over quite modest timber-framed houses are a feature of eastern England. In the sixteenth century octagonal shafts were popular, giving way to the later diagonally set, square shafts, frequently joined together in concertina fashion in the seventeenth century. This is true of the South-East, where they are squarer, decorated perhaps with recessed vertical bands and oversailing courses at the top. Later brick stacks, not only in eastern England and the South-East but elsewhere, became much smaller, decorated only with oversailing courses.

Brick stacks were built without foundations and were of massive size which not only gave the large fireplaces required but also helped to distribute the load. Gradually during the seventeenth century the chimneys which had previously had a separate shaft for each flue were superseded by large brick chimneys containing all the flues, decorated with vertical projecting or recessed bands with oversailing courses. The width of early fireplaces provided in the average house was often from eight to twelve feet, while in the chambers above they were probably only three feet wide. They also varied in appearance, depending on their position and use. Those in the kitchen were generally spanned by a larger oak beam, probably decorated only with a stop chamfer, although there are examples, especially the earlier ones, which have a flat four-centred arch with a carved pattern in the spandrels. Elsewhere in the house they were often constructed of either brick or stone with a four-centred arch over. Within the hearth the log fire was supported on iron 'dogs' to improve the draught, and at the rear a cast-iron fireback was provided to reflect the heat and also to protect the rear from excessive heat.

To one side or to the back of the hearth in the kitchen, an oven for bread-making was often constructed. This was a domed structure two feet or so in diameter internally, provided with an opening but no flue. The interior of the oven was heated by burning wood, furze or bracken, and when hot the ash was raked out, the bread inserted and the opening sealed. In the flue itself above the fire, irons were often built in to enable bacon and hams to be cured in the smoke from the log fire. A separate smoking chamber was sometimes provided to cure the bacon and ham. This comprised a chamber to the side of the flue with an opening at low level and a corbelled flue at the top leading back to the main flue.

Towards the end of the eighteenth century and the beginning of the nineteenth century, many of the large, open-hearth fireplaces of the preceding centuries were reduced in size to accommodate the new type of coal-burning grates. In the kitchen too, changes appeared from the end of the eighteenth century: the new cast-iron cooking range began to replace the pot crane, pot hangers and other cooking-aids which had for almost four hundred years been in common use in the kitchen.

Doorways and Doors

The typical doorway of the fourteenth and early fifteenth centuries was constructed of a simple two-centred equilateral arch formed by two solid pieces shaped to form the arch and door jambs all in one and specially selected from a tree with a pronounced curved growth. Another early but less common doorway profile is the three-centred arch.

Towards the end of the fifteenth century – from about 1480 to 1500 – the four-centred arch cut from a solid lintel appeared, from which developed the depressed pointed arch, a feature popular in many late Tudor and Jacobean timber-framed buildings, where a false timber arch usually with sunk spandrels was tenoned and rebated to the jambs and let into the horizontal lintel at the head.

Occasionally the three-centred arch, now depressed, which dates from the fourteenth century until the sixteenth century, the ogee-arch, which dates from about the same period, or the shouldered-arch, which is typical of the late fifteenth and early sixteenth centuries, was preferred. By the seventeenth century the plain square frame was widely used, occasionally on better-class work with some sort of moulding.

The doorway to the main entrance usually received some form of decorative treatment. In the average building the posts and lintels were given shallow mouldings, those on the post being stopped before reaching the bottom, with the spandrel often sunk and carved. In larger timber-framed houses – those belonging to rich merchants and the like – the posts were often richly carved and, in pre-Reformation times, enriched with sculptured figures. According to the status of the house, internal doorways were similarly treated depending on their position. In the average house the doorway to the parlour would be arched and moulded, whereas the stair doorway would have a plain, straight head.

During the eighteenth century the doorway became the focal point of the front elevation, and during this period, when many old timber-framed buildings were being modernized, the opportunity was often taken to provide a new doorway. Frequently it was flanked by pilasters supporting a frieze or cornice above. In some instances this cornice projected to form a hood which could be either curved or flat supported by large carved brackets, known as 'consoles'. Indicative of the late seventeenth and early eighteenth centuries is the use of the pilaster on pedestals and the shell hood. Also of early eighteenth-century date is the use of the pediment both triangular and segmental. In the second half of the century broken pediments, often with a fanlight over the door, gained popularity, the fanlight later becoming a highly ornamental feature. Also a feature of the late eighteenth and early nineteenth centuries was the fluted pilaster with the entablature over resting directly on the abaci of the caps of the pilasters. Many of these Renaissance features can be found on old timber-framed houses, especially those in towns and villages.

The earliest entrance doors (69) were ledged ones, the simplest consisting of vertical boards often of varying widths secured at the back by horizontal battens or ledges and, when the door was wide, with additional diagonal braces to prevent the door from sagging. A stronger and more elaborate form was one in which the inner face was constructed of a continuous series of horizontal battens, the two layers joined by nails driven from the outer face and cleated over on the inside. The boards were either butt jointed, half lapped or occasionally tongued and grooved at each joint and fixed to the batten by either wooden pegs or nail studs with the gap between the boards covered with a moulded cover strip. Alternatively the joint could be moulded either with a simple beaded mould or a somewhat more elaborate

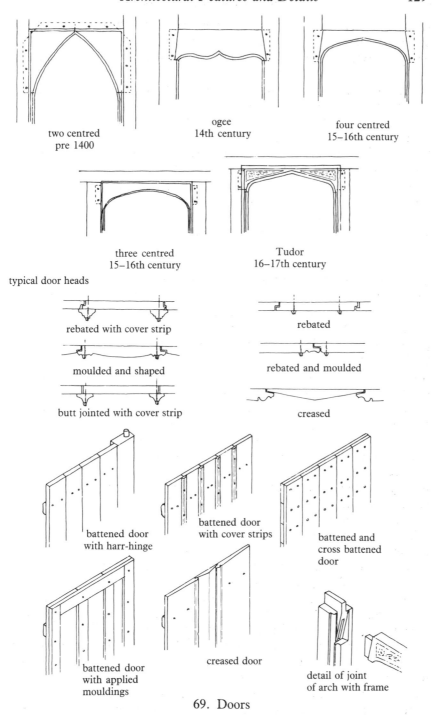

two centred
pre 1400

ogee
14th century

four centred
15–16th century

three centred
15–16th century

Tudor
16–17th century

typical door heads

rebated with cover strip

rebated

moulded and shaped

rebated and moulded

butt jointed with cover strip

creased

battened door
with harr-hinge

battened door
with cover strips

battened and
cross battened
door

battened door
with applied
mouldings

creased door

detail of joint
of arch with frame

69. Doors

moulding. Although the door was sometimes shaped to conform with the shape of the arch, often the top of the doorway carried on up behind the arched head.

Towards the end of the sixteenth century there appeared another type of battened door, the so-called 'creased' door which had vertical mouldings so designed as to give a stronger vertical emphasis by the creation of a shadow. The door comprised three vertical boards, the two outer ones wider than the central one, with the outer ones splayed, moulded and rebated to fit over the twice-splayed central one. The creased door remained a feature of many buildings during the seventeenth century, but towards the end, and particularly in the following century with the improved techniques in joinery, the battened door, in whichever form, had generally been replaced, particularly for the front entrance door, by the panelled door. A transitional form, sometimes to be found, is a battened door formed in the normal way but which has on its outer face applied mitred mouldings to simulate a panelled door. These doors, although rare, can still be found and are of late seventeenth- or early eighteenth-century date. Later panelled doors had raised and fielded panels and bolection moulds. In many houses, however, the old battened door was still used on the rear or kitchen entrance and other entries of little significance.

Internal doors followed much the same development as external doors. They were generally of lighter construction, those of battened construction seldom having the moulded cover strip found on external doors, while the panelled doors were often plain with no moulding around the panel. In late Tudor and Jacobean times internal doors were often panelled to match the wall panelling which was then becoming popular. The early linen-fold is somewhat rare, but the later simple rectangular Jacobean style was common in many of the larger timber-framed houses. Like the external battened door, by the eighteenth century the internal battened door was used only in doorways of little significance, although the use of panelled doors was in many smaller houses restricted to the parlour.

As previously mentioned, medieval doors had no frame and were hung directly to the opening either on 'harr-hinges' or on wrought-iron 'strap-and-hook hinges'. Harr-hinges were a simple arrangement in which the vertical board on the hanging side of the door was increased in thickness – the harr-tree, the ends extending beyond the door at top and bottom and shaped to form dowels which fitted and rotated in holes in the lintel and sill. Strap-and-hook hinges were largely restricted to important buildings during the medieval period but because of the width and weight of many battened doors they continued to be used throughout the Tudor and Stuart period. In many cases the strap fitted around both sides of the door, and the end of the external face of the strap was frequently shaped, usually in the fleur-de-lis, and the hook, also known as the 'ride', was fixed directly to the timber jamb. It would not have been until the sixteenth century that in the South-East iron strap hinges began to be used in smaller houses, the harr-hinge probably continuing, especially in remote areas, until cheaper iron became more readily available in the eighteenth century. Towards the end of the seventeenth century, when the lighter panelled doors became fashionable, doors were hung on H-hinges or HL-hinges fixed to the face of the frame and door. The familiar 'cockshead' hinge used on internal doors and furniture is a variant of these hinges.

Like hinges, metal door furniture (70) was usually restricted to larger buildings. Handles normally comprised a ring with a spindle passing through the centre of a decorative iron cover plate and operating a latch on the inner face of the door. Heavy iron bolts were also provided to external doors, together with the 'stock-lock' – a lock within a wooden case. The escutcheons were also a feature, usually square but sometimes circular and always delicately worked, often with Gothic tracery or cusped decoration. In most of the smaller

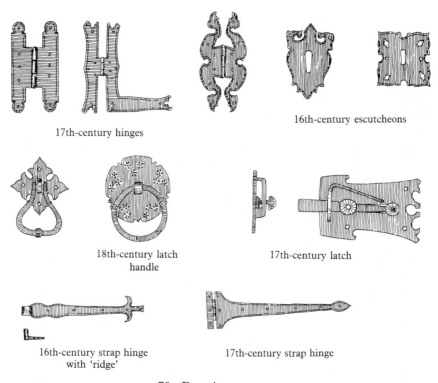

17th-century hinges

16th-century escutcheons

18th-century latch
handle

17th-century latch

16th-century strap hinge
with 'ridge'

17th-century strap hinge

70. Door ironmongery

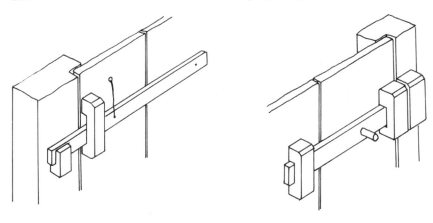

71. Wooden latches and bolts

timber-framed buildings, however, all door fittings, with the exception of hinges, were made of wood until the eighteenth century, and even then the iron fitments would be restricted to doors of important rooms.

Wooden latches (71), precursors of the later iron thumb latch, were a common feature. They could be worked from the outside by a string tied to the latch and passing through a hole in the door or by a wooden peg attached to the latch and passing through a slot to the outside. These latches were made secure by the insertion of a peg or the like into the staple, thus preventing the latch being raised. Wooden bars placed across the inside of the door, and wooden bolts, were also common features to enable the door to be secured from the inside.

Windows
Early windows were unglazed even in superior houses, and they remained so in all but the largest houses until the end of the sixteenth century, when for the first time the manufacture of glass became more widespread, but it was probably the following century before it was used universally. In place of glass, oiled paper or the horn of cattle, obtained by peeling or shaving thin slices from the horn, as well as lattices of wood, wickerwork and even reeds were all employed, but oiled cloth, preferably linen stiffened by a wooden lattice arranged in a diamond pattern and fitted to each opening, was the most common. Consequently, prior to the use of glass, windows, being a source of draught, were usually kept to a minimum and were generally situated away from the prevailing winds.

In most cases these early unglazed windows were fitted with some form of battened wooden shutters (72) to afford some protection from the elements and to provide some security. Hinged shutters, fitted

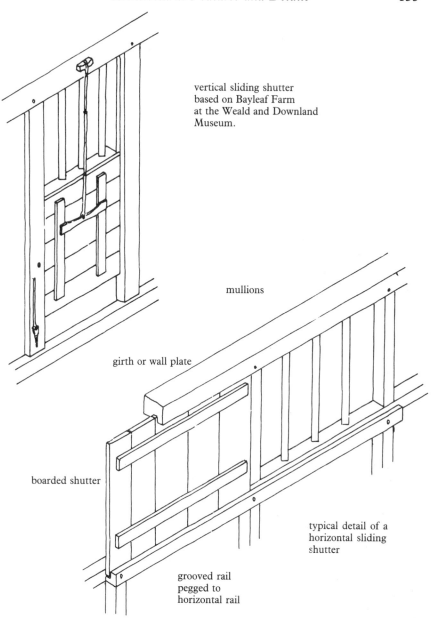

vertical sliding shutter
based on Bayleaf Farm
at the Weald and Downland
Museum.

mullions

girth or wall plate

boarded shutter

typical detail of a
horizontal sliding
shutter

grooved rail
pegged to
horizontal rail

72. Window shutters

either externally or internally, were frequently used on larger houses, especially on the large windows to the open hall, but it seems that horizontally sliding shutters, fitted internally, were most commonly provided in smaller houses, obviating the necessity of expensive iron hinges. However, in most cases, as the whole complex was easily removed, little evidence remains apart from the peg holes by which the grooved runners were fixed to the framing. Vertical sliding shutters were less common and were perhaps of a slightly later date. In the reconstructed Bayleaf Farmhouse at the Weald and Downland Open Air Museum, three differing forms of shutters were used including an unusual form in which the shutter slides up and down in vertical grooves. These vertical sliding shutters occur in the solar wing of the house, which seems to have been added at a later date.

In the fifteenth century, windows in the important rooms of a timber-framed house of any significance had some form of tracery, often of Gothic design, in their heads. Although in some of the important houses these may have been glazed, the majority were not, there being no evidence of a glazing rebate or fillet, with the tracery carved on the inside as well as the outside. Later, with the increased use of glass, the pierced tracery was replaced by a small depressed arch which was usually plain except for a hollow chamfer with small sunk or pierced spandrels. Occasionally the arch retained the last vestige of Gothic tracery and was cusped. In all these cases, the moulding was only on the outside, the inner face being flat with any glazing carried up behind it.

In most timber-framed houses, however, the window would have been square-headed and was usually situated at high level either beneath the first-floor bressummer or at eaves level. Unglazed windows were divided by plain square mullions (73), set diagonally, about six inches or slightly wider apart, with each light usually sub-divided vertically by a slender intermediate bar. These early unglazed windows can still be found in many timber-framed houses, although in nearly all cases they have been blocked in. However, as early glass lattices required no structural preparation, other than the provision of vertical bars to which they could be tied, it is often difficult to decide if such a window was originally glazed or not. Where the window was covered with oiled cloth, a slightly different arrangement occurred. The window was fully framed as for an unglazed window but the square mullions were not set diagonally. Externally, around each light, was a rebate to which the cloth, probably stiffened with a diamond-patterned lattice, was fitted. The cloth was supported internally by a smaller intermediate vertical member similar to that used for unglazed windows.

A similar arrangement was also provided when glass was introduced.

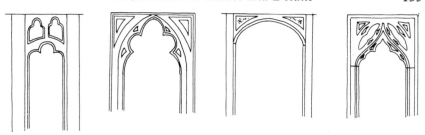

examples of Gothic tracery and shaped heads to 15th and early 16th-century windows

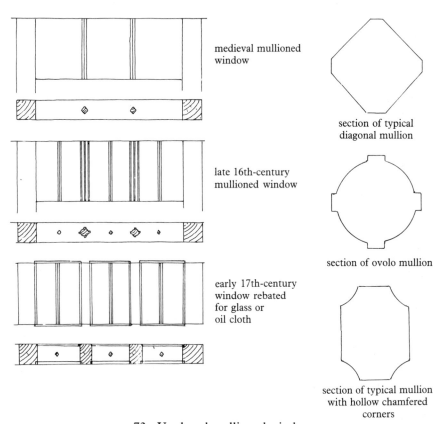

medieval mullioned window

section of typical diagonal mullion

late 16th-century mullioned window

section of ovolo mullion

early 17th-century window rebated for glass or oil cloth

section of typical mullion with hollow chamfered corners

73. Unglazed mullioned windows

The mullions, being no longer placed diagonally, were generally set wider apart than before. Although on occasion they remained square in section, they were often moulded. At first the mullions and jambs were splayed; later they were hollow-chamfered, although this method had been widely used in many of the unglazed traceried windows of the fifteenth century. Early in the seventeenth century the hollow-chamfered mullion was replaced almost universally by the simple ovolo-moulded one, which, because of the side fillets, enabled easier fixing of the glazing. These mullioned windows were seldom of any great height, the characteristic feature being long, horizontal runs of narrow-mullioned lights ranging from two and eight.

The best of the medieval glass in Europe was manufactured in Normandy, but although glass from here and other places on the Continent was imported into England, the amount was small. The Norman process produced glass blown into a disc, or 'crown', by the use of a glass-blower's pontil, the molten material at the end of the pontil being spun round and round in the palms of the hand, with the bubble on the end flattened out by a wooden bat to produce a disc which averaged about three feet in diameter. The disc was always thicker towards the centre, culminating in the 'bull's eye' where the glass was attached to the pontil. The glass so produced was much favoured for its brilliant 'fire finish', whereas early English glass (which was blown in cylinders or 'muffs' which when split along its length gradually opened up and flattened as it cooled) was frequently rough, speckled with a greenish tint. In 1567 the Privy Council issued a patent to introduce the foreign glass industry into England, where crown glass began to be manufactured for the first time; by 1589 there were fifteen factories manufacturing glass in England. As competition increased, so the price fell.

Because of the manufacturing process of early glass – both cylinder and crown – the panes were by necessity small, rarely exceeding six inches by four. In order to make a window of reasonable size, these panes were set in lead cames, which in turn were joined together to form a lattice known as a 'leaded light' (74). Because of the expense of glass, the quarries were diamond-shaped, although not the symmetrical diamond pattern we are today accustomed to; more often than not the leading was made up irregularly, thus allowing even the smallest pieces to be used at the edges. At the beginning of the seventeenth century a new process using coal as a fuel instead of wood was introduced and later in the century, when glass manufacture became more widespread, more dependable and a little cheaper, diamond quarries were replaced with square ones. In many of the larger houses leaded lights of a variety of patterns were used. In 1615 a work entitled *A Booke of Sundry Draughtes Principally Serving for Glasiers* was published containing over one hundred designs. One notable example is Little Morton Hall, Cheshire, where it is said that no two lights amongst those in the long gallery have the same design of leadwork. Stained glass windows were also fashionable in many of the larger Tudor houses – sometimes pictorial but generally of heraldic design. The most notable and earliest surviving example of this can be seen at Ockwells Manor, near Bray,

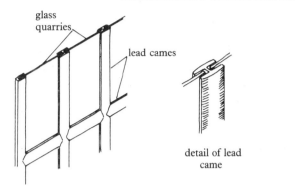

glass
quarries

lead cames

detail of lead
came

pierced lead ventilator
from a window at Dedham,
Essex

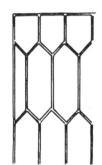

various 'leaded lights' patterns

74. Leaded lights

Berkshire, where there are eighteen shields, showing the arms of the
founder of the house, his sovereign and friends. The windows are
contemporary with the house, which was built in about 1466.

When fixed, leaded lights were stiffened by horizontal saddle bars
set inside the glazing and housed into the mullions and jambs, the
leaded lights being secured to them with lead tape or later with wire.
When installed in an existing building, these lights were often secured
by nailing directly to the mullions of the previously unglazed windows.
The lights were therefore narrow, usually around six to eight inches
wide but in new buildings the windows were designed to take slightly
wider panels, often between eight and ten inches, fitted to the mullions
and supported by an intermediate vertical bar set diagonally.

Opening lights, even in larger houses, were kept to a minimum,

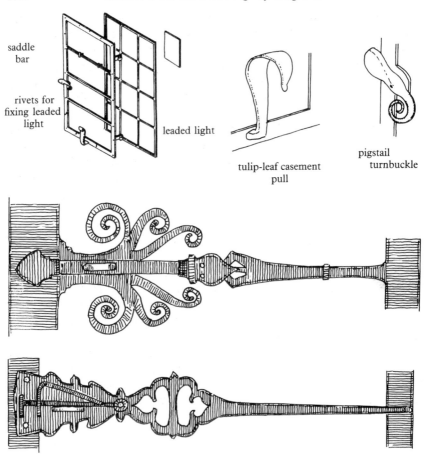

saddle
bar

rivets for
fixing leaded
light

leaded light

tulip-leaf casement
pull

pigstail
turnbuckle

Two examples of the elaborately decorated latch plates used in the 17th century.

75. Wrought iron windows

and in smaller dwellings, or where the number of open lights were inadequate, ventilation was provided by omitting a quarry and replacing it with a pierced lead plate. Opening lights were made from wrought iron (75). Those of late sixteenth- and early seventeenth-century date comprised an inner frame often one inch or more wide and in some cases only one-eighth of an inch thick, mounted on hinges in an outer frame usually of a similar section. The saddle bars were welded outside the plane of the frame for diamond-shaped panes but later, in the seventeenth century, when square panes became popular, these were butt-welded in the plane of the frame and so arranged to correspond with the horizontal line of the lead cames. The latch-plates were elaborately decorated but towards the end of the seventeenth century became more compact. Stays were not provided to early wrought-iron casements, for, being narrow and generally less than two feet high, it was not necessary, but later, when the height of windows increased, a stay comprising a twisted square rod was generally provided, engaging with a ring in the base of the tulip-leaf handle. The tulip-leaf handle, a feature throughout most of the seventeenth century, was replaced by a round rod ending in a spiral or boss. At first the leaded lights were secured to the casement with lead tape or wire in the usual way but later they were often riveted to the wrought-iron frame.

Windows over one light high were rare in the fifteenth and sixteenth centuries. Only, for instance, in the open hall would there be windows of any height, and here they would be sub-divided by a transom. These windows would have at first been unglazed, with separate shutters to the upper and lower lights. The shutters would be either of the hinged type, which could be fixed externally or internally, or of the sliding variety, fixed internally. It was also normal to place these large windows on opposite sides of the hall so those on the windward side could be closed. Later these windows would have been glazed but few now survive for they would have had to be removed or altered when the floor was later inserted into the open hall.

Full-height bay windows were also used in the open halls of the larger houses built off a brick base occasionally dominating the front of a timber-framed house. Oriel windows too were a common feature in the medieval period and had the advantage that they could be placed anywhere on a timber-framed building – under the projecting overhang of a gable, beneath the eaves, over an entrance or at ground-floor level.

An early feature of these windows was the corbelled timber base wrought out of the solid which could be either moulded or carved. Later, towards the end of the sixteenth century, it became customary to support the sill on shaped brackets. Oriel windows are a particular feature of many Wealden-type houses in Kent and Sussex as well as many of the timber-framed houses in towns and villages. They seem to have been a vulnerable feature, but their former presence can often be identified from joints in the surviving timbers. Bay and oriel windows are a feature of many jettied buildings, often situated beneath the jetty, the underside of the oversailing forming the top of the window. The many bay windows with sash windows, especially those in towns and villages, added to earlier timber-framed houses, are of course, from the Georgian period or even later. In the latter half of the seventeenth century the long, horizontal ranges of mullioned windows began to give way in the larger houses to taller windows. They were divided horizontally by a transom and could be up to six lights wide, although they were often only two lights divided by a single mullion and were generally divided horizontally by a transom so placed that the light above it was smaller than that below, so forming a 'cross'. Leaded lights, but by now with square panes replacing those of a diamond shape, with the open lights formed with wrought-iron casements as previously described, were still used.

Towards the end of the seventeenth century the vertical sliding sash window made of softwood was first introduced, each sash divided into small panes by glazing bars which were often rectangular in section and heavy in appearance. At first the upper sashes were fixed, only the lower ones sliding in grooves and held open by means of a wedge or hook. It was not, in fact, until the end of the eighteenth century that the now familiar double-hung counterbalanced sash replaced this older system. Later, with the general improvement in glass and joinery techniques, the glazing bars began to be reduced in size and moulded.

The introduction of the sash window coincided with the decline of timber-framed buildings, in most areas, except for the construction of cottages and the like, but in many timber-framed houses built before the end of the seventeenth century sash windows replaced the earlier mullioned ones, and in many cases they would probably have been the first glazed windows these houses received. It was a comparatively easy process to cut a new opening in the studwork and to block in the existing windows, and it is not uncommon to see these earlier blocked windows alongside later sash ones.

In many houses the installation of sash windows was confined to the front and other important elevations, with wrought-iron casements continuing to be used in less conspicuous positions.

Sash windows were not, however, universally adopted. Throughout the country timber casements or wrought-iron casements within timber frames continued to be used in many of the smaller houses where the low ceilings made the tall vertical sliding sash impracticable. A cheap alternative to the vertical sliding sash was the horizontal sliding sash, the so-called 'Yorkshire' sliding sash, in which one light was fixed and the other sliding. It was first introduced at the beginning of the eighteenth century and became extremely popular in many small timber-framed houses and cottages throughout the country, for it was particularly suited to houses with low ceilings. There are also local variations, in Suffolk for instance, where windows are often divided into small panes with only the central and lower panes formed into a casement.

To overcome this difficulty of low ceilings, some houses have vertical sliding sashes with the sashes of unequal height, the upper one smaller than the lower one. This alters the overall proportion of the window from vertical to horizontal. Sometimes this horizontal window shape, which is perhaps more suited to many of the long, low houses, is obtained by the use of narrow fixed sashes to either side of the main sliding sash.

Mouldings and Carvings

We have seen previously that doors and window frames, as well as bargeboard boards, were all moulded and sometimes carved, but other elements of the timber-framed building – the open truss of the hall, wall-plates, ceiling beams and joists, bressummers, fascias and corner posts – were frequently decorated. At the vernacular level this might be limited to a simple chamfer or other form of moulding to the ceiling beams but in buildings at a higher social level mouldings and carvings often abound.

The mouldings of the thirteenth and fourteenth centuries were often deeply undercut, with the frequent use of three-quarter hollows, the heavy bowtells – with fillets – and even scroll mouldings. Yet we see that the carpenters of the period, particularly those in Essex, Kent, Sussex and Hereford & Worcester, were capable of producing such mouldings from mature oak. In the fifteenth century and later, the mouldings, somewhat simpler, with their hollows less deep, are all well represented in timber-framed buildings.

Inside most houses it was in the hall that mouldings were most commonly used. The beam at the upper end of the hall was often, but not always, moulded, for it was the focal part of the hall with panelling below, attached to which ran a low bench and a coved canopy above and the high table in front of it. The open truss of the hall, the great arch-braces and the spere-truss are all usually moulded with the heavy rolled mouldings preceding the double ovolo moulds in the fourteenth century and the plain chamfers – both plain and hollow – in the fifteenth century. These mouldings were often taken down the supporting wall posts.

Arcade-post and other columns also received decoration with moulded caps and bases; the crown-post was also similarly treated when exposed to view. The wide, shallow mouldings of the fifteenth and sixteenth centuries had an effect on such timbers as bressummers, fascias and ceiling beams for these allowed the use of repetitive carvings such as the vine pattern, and later such motifs as strapwork, running foliage, grotesque animals and human forms and many others.

Floors

The ground floor in most medieval buildings, except possibly for the homes of the nobility, prior to the end of the sixteenth century, would have been little more than compacted earth strewn with rushes or straw and perhaps treated with ox-blood and ashes which hardened sufficiently to prevent dusting and wear and which could also be polished. In most cases the earth for these floors was dug and raked to a fine tilth, and water was added until it was the consistency of mortar. It was then spread in position, and when the surplus water dried and the earth began to harden, it was compacted by treading and ramming with a heavy wooden rammer until a hard, true surface was achieved.

Other materials were added to help the earth bind together: the *Dictionanum Rusticum*, first published in 1709, states that floors should be made from loamy clay with one-third new soft horse-dung mixed with a small quantity of coal ashes. Before being laid, the mixture was tempered, resting for ten days, tempered again and rested for a further three days. J. Lawrence in *The Modern Land Steward*, published in 1806, states that the floors should be made from one third lime, one third coal ashes and one third loamy clay and horse-dung, all tempered to a 'tough and glewy' consistency.

In Sussex the ground floors often consisted of rammed chalk which comprised lumps of chalk sealed with sour milk and lightly tempered, producing a durable and smooth floor. This durability can be seen at The Clergy House, Alfriston, Sussex, when during the renovation of the building in 1977 a new rammed chalk floor was laid, four inches of chalk lumps sealed with thirty gallons of sour milk, which is standing up well to the thousands of feet that have since walked over it. Lime and gypsum were all added, where available, being regarded as an invaluable material.

The use of these floors continued in some areas into the nineteenth century but generally they began to be replaced by floors of a more substantial nature by the seventeenth century. In those areas where brick production was gaining popularity, bricks of a size similar to those in wall construction began to be used, laid either directly onto the earth or onto a bed of sand. In eastern England, and in particular in Suffolk, clay tiles, known as 'pammetts', again laid directly onto the earth, were commonly employed. Where stone was readily available, stone flags were used. However, in districts where there was little brick manufacture or where the stones were unsuitable for use as paving, earth floors and floors made with lime and gypsum remained in constant use.

These solid floors, no matter of what material, were cold and damp for they relied almost solely on the impervious nature of the floor, and rarely was any form of damp-proof membrane introduced. It was not until the beginning of the eighteenth century that the boarded ground floor on joists began to be introduced into houses, and even then it was almost entirely restricted to the parlour, the hall-cum-kitchen and service rooms still retaining the old solid floors. Even so, these boarded floors too were often constructed with the joists resting directly on the

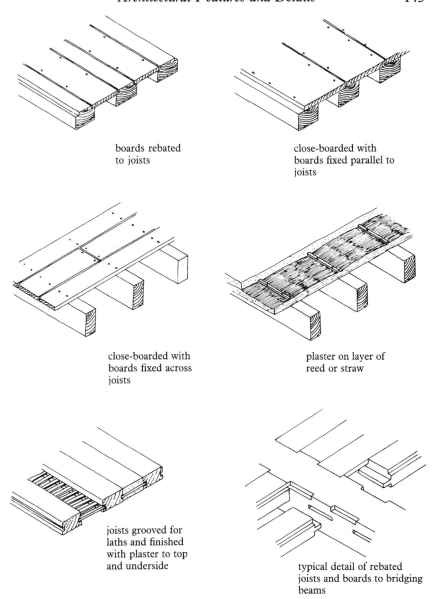

boards rebated
to joists

close-boarded with
boards fixed parallel to
joists

close-boarded with
boards fixed across
joists

plaster on layer of
reed or straw

joists grooved for
laths and finished
with plaster to top
and underside

typical detail of rebated
joists and boards to bridging
beams

76. Upper floor construction

ground, and this together with inadequate ventilation caused many to
rot.

The upper floors in early buildings (76) were in nearly all cases of
boarded construction, being regarded as superior to other types of
flooring. There is clear evidence that floor-boards were not always

fixed, often being inserted by the tenant and, like the glass of windows, not infrequently included in an inventory along with furniture, often described as 'loose and moveable'.

A few old oak floors still survive, the characteristic feature being the uneven wear – the softer parts being worn away, with the rays standing proud. However, most have worn, shrunk and split over the years and have generally been replaced with boards constructed of softwood. Although sawmills, driven by wind, water and animals, first appeared in the sixteenth century, until the seventeenth century most floor-boards in Britain were cleft or pit-sawn, as previously stated. The length of boards obtained by cleaving depended greatly on the quality of the timber and so generally were shorter than pit-sawn ones, sometimes only a few feet long, and rarely of any great width. Pit-sawn boards could be obtained by three methods: the log could be quartered and then cut obliquely across the medullary rays at a very acute angle, finally being adzed to produce boards of a similar thickness, or it could be squared to the right width and cut up, producing boards of the same width, usually about twelve inches wide; more commonly the log was not quartered or squared but slabbed, producing boards of varying widths, a common feature of many old floors, as at Little Chesterford Manor, Essex, where the boards vary between one and three feet. The first two methods were wasteful, so the third was more commonly used, there being very little waste, though boards often twisted and buckled if not securely fixed.

In the days of closely placed joists, the boards ran parallel to them, either fitted into rebates, with the joists forming part of the floor, or more commonly laid over them. Later, when the joists were set wider apart, the floor-boards were fixed at right angles and not parallel to them, in order to distribute the weight. This was even true in a house jettied on two adjacent faces with the joists meeting the dragon-beam at the angle, the floor-boards being mitred above the beam. This type of flooring enabled, for the first time, boards of varying widths to be used. Few, if any, boards would span the whole room, and the carpenter's main aim was to fill in the area and produce a sound floor with the boards available. Boards varied not only in width but also in thickness. To overcome this, if the board was too thick, the underside was hewn away with an adze; if the board was too thin, it would be packed at each joist. Oak was, as always, the carpenter's first choice for flooring, but in the sixteenth century elm competed with it, and in the eighteenth century softwood replaced it.

Not all upper floors were boarded: in some timber-framed buildings lime and ash floors and gypsum floors were also popular. From the sixteenth century onwards this became a feature of many timber-framed houses, the most famous being Little Morton Hall, Cheshire.

Generally a layer of reed or straw was placed over the floor joists and secured by a batten but sometimes either sawn timber laths or wattle were fixed across or between the joists. In those instances it was not uncommon for the top of the joists to form part of the floor. Onto this base was spread a layer of plaster two or three inches thick, trowelled smooth and allowed to dry slowly to prevent cracking.

Ceilings

The joists and beams of the upper floors were left exposed, and the floor upon them, whether of timber or plaster, constituted the ceiling of the room below. In the medieval houses with the open hall, the only upper floor would be over the parlour and perhaps over the service room. In these rooms the beams would be rarely moulded. In fact, the rude square joists of the parlour ceiling in particular are a common feature of many medieval houses. It was not until the late fifteenth and early sixteenth centuries that in some of the more pretentious houses the exposed joists and beams became richly moulded and in some cases carved. A feature of many of the houses of eastern England is the rich carving of the beam soffit, as at Paycocke's House, Coggeshall, Essex. In the main, however, from the sixteenth century onwards the decoration was generally restricted in the average house to a chamfer or ovolo mould to the edge of the timber. These decorations were usually stopped near the end of the timber with a variety of designs, a feature which can help in dating a building. Even so, in many small houses only the principal timbers would receive any form of decoration, the joists between remaining plain.

As previously stated, the flooring upon the joists and beams formed the ceiling of the room below. When boards were used, these were at first left exposed, with the boards and sometimes the joists as well often decorated with painted designs. This feature is today rare in England, due no doubt to the replacement of old floor-boards, but adjoining Cwmmau Farm, Brilley, Hereford & Worcester, in what appears to have been an earlier house, the beams and joists have been painted with a chevron pattern. Alternatively, the ceiling would be completed by the whitewashing of the underside of the boards.

The fashion of plastering between the joists first occurred in the sixteenth century. In some districts a layer of reed or straw was placed over the joists and secured in position by the floor-boards to provide a base for the plaster. In other areas straw or reed was secured to the underside of the boards by short strips of timber lath fixed between the joists, and the plaster was applied to this. Later the reed and straw were replaced with timber laths fixed directly to the underside of the boards as a key for the plaster.

In the fifteenth century boarded ceilings were used; some still exist in East Anglia – as at Garrads House, Water Street, Lavenham, Suffolk. The boards were thin, between about a quarter and three-eighths of an inch, either running parallel to the joists and lying between them or, in better work, with the joists covered with narrow boards, sometimes V-jointed, running at right angles to the joists and parallel to the bridging joist which remained exposed. At Garrads House, narrow ribs with bosses at their intersections were planted on the face of the boards. These ceilings were, it seems, generally decorated with distemper.

The ceilings of exposed beams with plaster between remained and still remain in many houses but from the end of the seventeenth century onwards there came an increasing desire in both new and old houses for the ceiling to be 'underdrawn' in plaster. In many of the older houses the deeper main beams remained exposed, but early in the seventeenth century it became fashionable to plaster these as well, often finished with a continuous moulded cornice which ran around the beam and the adjoining wall. By the beginning of the eighteenth century beams projecting below the ceiling line were avoided, with sometimes separate ceiling joists framed into the main beams and independent of the floor joists above. Laths were generally but not universally used as a backing for the plaster, for in parts of South Yorkshire and the east Midlands they were replaced with thick-stemmed reed-grass fixed to the underside of the joists and secured to them with battens.

The plastered ceiling of most vernacular houses remained plain with little or no decoration but by the end of the seventeenth century in many of the more pretentious houses ornamental moulded plasterwork became fashionable. Moulded ceilings first appeared in the principal rooms of the great houses during the sixteenth century, and those of the Elizabethan period are usually characterized by small moulded ribs applied in geometric patterns. At the intersection of the ribs are often ornamental bosses, and between the ribs a somewhat restrained use of decorative motifs which are usually restricted to heraldic bosses, shields, sprigs of foliage, the Tudor rose and the fleur-de-lis. In the larger houses many of the ceilings were of the pendant type where the moulded ribs descended into pendants with bosses or other forms of decoration at the junction. Moulded ceilings of the Jacobean period are far more ornate, divided into panels by moulded trabeations – wide ribs in high relief – providing greater space on the soffit for running ornamentation, usually comprising flowers and foliage. The panels are more freely filled with motifs than earlier ceilings; pendants of fruits, heraldic devices, wreaths of leaves and berries and cherubs are all typical. Later moulded ceilings became more dignified and restrained, with simpler patterns employed. A centre-piece became a common feature. First, in the second half of the seventeenth century, it was in high relief and richly decorated but later, towards the end of the century, although the centre-piece was retained, the mouldings were often plain and in low relief. The centre-piece remained a feature in the eighteenth century, again in low relief and often connected to the moulded cornice by a delicate moulding.

Staircases

Early stairs (77) were either a simple ladder or at its best the more elaborate companion-way – a straight flight with the steps formed of triangular oak blocks with the first five or six set vertically one above the other. Evidence of these steep companion-ways are sometimes to be found in the layout of the ceiling joists where an almost square but small stair trap or opening has been infilled with later timbers.

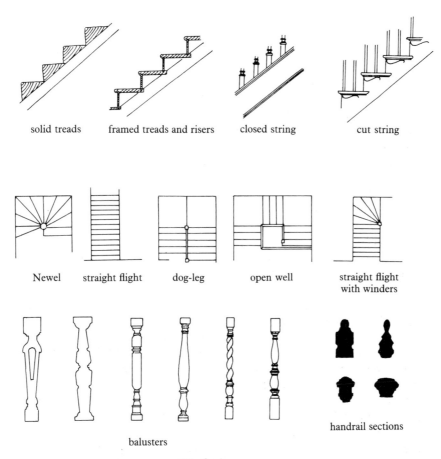

solid treads   framed treads and risers   closed string   cut string

Newel   straight flight   dog-leg   open well   straight flight with winders

balusters   handrail sections

77. Staircases

However, the most common medieval type of stair, a type which continued to be built through much of the sixteenth century in ordinary houses, consisted of steps formed of baulks of solid timber triangular in section. Straight flights, dog-legs, winders and newel stairs were constructed with these steps. Straight flights, in which the steps were pegged to two inclined bearers, usually set at an angle of forty-five degrees, were the most usual. Newel stairs (tapered treads rising around a centrical post) were preferred in many buildings, particularly small houses, for they occupied less room and could be conveniently placed beside the axial stack, which in many cases were constructed at the same time. The solid steps were housed at one end to the newel post – a circular or octagonal post – which went from floor to ceiling and on occasion for the full height of the building and at the other end to the studs and wall posts. Straight flights often incorporated winders at the top or bottom, constructed in the same way as newel stairs.

Examples of straight flights, sometimes with winders, still exist today in many old timber-framed houses of the fifteenth and sixteenth centuries, though not always in their original positions, and sometimes hidden beneath later softwood treads and risers which have been nailed to the original solid treads. Some of these treads can be seen at the Guildhall, Lavenham, Suffolk, and there is a modern reconstruction of a stair at Bayleaf Farm, at the Weald and Downland Open Air Museum, Singleton, Sussex. Surviving examples of newel stairs with solid timber steps are rare but evidence of their former existence can sometimes be seen in the irregular mortices in studs and wall posts which represent the outer fixing of the treads.

A variation of the newel stairs in which solid treads, four inches or so thick, are housed into the newel is also to be found. One such example is at Read Hall, Mickfield, Suffolk, which dates from about the middle of the fifteenth century and has the risers built of brick and plaster.

Newel stairs remained the most popular in nearly all small houses until the eighteenth century, although, where space permitted, straight flights were preferred. By the end of the sixteenth century, however, the solid steps began to be replaced by the framed stairs with separate strings, treads and risers. The dog-legged staircase was particularly common in smaller houses in the seventeenth century, as was the open-well staircase, from the middle of the seventeenth century. The late Elizabethan and Jacobean staircases were of heavier construction than the more delicate ones of the following century. Generally they had heavy square newels which projected above the handrail, finished with a carved or moulded cap and below the strings the end finished with a similar-fashioned pendant. Wide moulded handrails and closed strings with the balusters housed into the string and handrail were also characteristic features of the period. The early splat balusters – flat balusters shaped, tapered or occasionally pierced – are fairly common. These were superseded by the more elaborate turned baluster. The twisted baluster was also a feature of many staircases constructed after the Restoration. Towards the end of the eighteenth century, with improved joinery techniques, the more delicate cut-string stair constructed of softwood developed.

With the introduction of the two-storeyed hall block and with the chambering-over of many open halls, only one staircase was necessary to serve the upper floor, and although in many houses the stairs were situated alongside the newly built chimneystack, in some cases, especially with the dog-legged type, it required more space. Often the stairs were situated in the hall itself, but occasionally the staircase was accommodated in a projecting annexe at the rear of the building, usually with access from the hall.

Internal Partitions
In most houses, from the fifteenth century onwards, the private rooms were separated from the main living-rooms by partitions (78). These were usually non-structural and built in timber. The use of edge-to-edge horizontal plank partitions is today rare (one example can be seen at the Court House, Milton Regis, Kent) but vertical boarding in one form or another is much more common. An early type has the vertical boards overlapping one another – in medieval times known as clap-boarding, a term still used in the United States for horizontal boarding. In some instances the boards were not merely overlapped but carefully tongued and grooved, producing two faces, one of overlapping boards and the other flush. The flush face was always the best side, and the

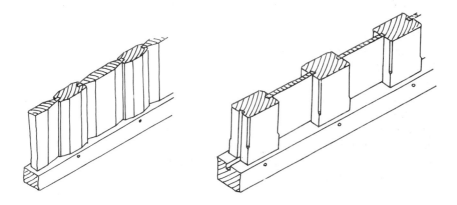

78. Internal partitions

smooth face presented an ideal surface on which to apply some form of painted decoration.

Another medieval and most common type of partition was the so-called 'plank-and-muntin' partition, which consisted of alternate vertical boards or planks housed into the edges of the muntins, which in turn were framed into the sill and ceiling beam. The muntins were often only chamfered, but on better-class work they were sometimes moulded on the living-room side, while the planks might be given a simplified type of linenfold pattern. The partition generally incorporated a doorway, a shaped door-head being housed to the jambs and head and sometimes a built-in bench with pew-like shaped ends. When the chamfer or moulding stops some way from the floor it implies the former presence of such a bench. There are many surviving examples of this type of partition from the end of the fifteenth century until the end of the seventeenth century.

From about the middle of the seventeenth century the framed partition began to appear in vernacular buildings. Here horizontal rails were framed into the muntins to form square panels which were filled in with thin timber housed on all edges to the muntins and rails. Both the muntins and the rails were moulded.

Wall Panelling

Wall panelling was first introduced into timber-framed houses in the late fifteenth century, when it was referred to as 'sealing'. The earliest form of panelling was similar to that used in partitions and comprised little more than vertical oak boards, with the edges either simply overlapping or tongued and grooved into each other – a form, according to N. Lloyd in his *A History of the English House*, frequently found in fifteenth- and sixteenth-century houses in Kent. In some instances of sixteenth-century work the 'clapboarding' was ribbed. Another form of sealing, or wainscoting, as it was later known, comprised thin boards set into grooves in heavy muntins with these uprights framed into a sill and head. In some instances a horizontal middle rail was introduced. This type of panelling too was obviously a development of the plank-and-muntin screens and partitions previously described.

These early forms of wall panelling soon established panelling as a method of adding comfort to rooms. Because panelling had no structural importance, the heavy sections previously used were progressively reduced in thickness until by about 1550 the panelling was often only one inch thick. At the same time the muntins were set closer together, with horizontal rails being introduced in the Elizabethan period to form small, nearly square panels.

In Tudor and Jacobean panelling the horizontal rails were usually one continuous length framed at the end into styles, with the panels formed by muntins pegged and morticed-and-tenoned between them. At first only the muntins were moulded, with the rails left square with a scratched bead above and below each panel; later the top edge of the rails was chamfered either continuous with the muntin scribed over the chamfer or with the chamfer stopped on either side of the muntin. As the mouldings were wrought out of the solid, when the edges of the rails were moulded, as well as the muntins and styles, this caused a problem at the junction. It was overcome either by the introduction of a mason's mitre, in which the muntins were butted square with the rails, and the mouldings of the rails returned to meet those on the muntins, or occasionally by having the muntins scribed over the mouldings or the rails. The true joiner's mitre, in which the mouldings were cut at forty-five degrees, did not come into common use until the beginning of the seventeenth century. It was not until well into that century that applied mouldings cut and mitred at the corners were adopted. This method proved to be a great advance, being both quicker and cheaper, and it had the added advantage of being less wasteful.

The panels too were often decorated, and in the early Tudor period the linenfold pattern was the characteristic embellishment, in which the panels were carved with vertical grooves to resemble folded linen. The term 'linenfold', so widely used today, is a comparatively modern word, first used in the nineteenth century. There were other motifs, with the most ornate treatment attained in the reign of Henry VIII, when the subjects included carved animals, shields and bunches of grapes twined between ribbed patterns. Another popular design was the use of Renaissance-type heads in profile carved in round medallions. A feature of some Jacobean panelling is its division into bays with pilasters supporting a rudimentary frieze, the whole connected with strapwork and arabesques. In some cases the panels are large, overlaid with moulded strips of wood to form diamond or other shapes. In the second quarter of the seventeenth century the size of the panels increased, and bolection mouldings were freely adopted.

The use of panelling declined in the second half of the seventeenth century, and it was not until the beginning of the following century that it regained popularity. Whereas in the preceding centuries the panelling had been of oak, the timber was now invariably pine. A feature of early Georgian panelling was the raised and fielded panels framed in bolection mouldings with large panels above a dado rail and squat ones of the same width below. Later in the eighteenth century in many unpretentious houses the panels became plain, with the bolection mouldings replaced by a simple moulding run out of the solid. Georgian panelling is fairly common in timber-framed houses and was provided in many older buildings when modernization took place in the eighteenth century. Often later wall panelling was taken up to dado height only.

Interior Wall Decorations

Wall panelling was expensive and rarely reached down to ordinary houses, where other forms of decoration were employed. As early as the fourteenth century the wattle-and-daub infilling was decorated with simple combed designs similar to those associated with pargeting in the seventeenth century, while in larger houses the use of mural decorations and tapestry remained the vogue. During the fifteenth century, however, the desire for a similar form of wall decoration penetrated down the social scale. It took the form of a painted hanging of cloth or canvas, a cheap substitute for tapestry. That such hangings became extremely common during the sixteenth century is evident from the domestic inventories of the period, which abound in references to 'painted cloths' and 'painted hangings' for walls.

It was about the middle of the sixteenth century that wall paintings – that is to say, decorative designs painted directly onto the face of the plaster – first emerged in the domestic house. These early paintings were generally executed in colours in which the pigments were diluted with glue or mixed with white of egg to form a distemper. The earliest form of these paintings was pictorial, often of a religious nature. More common and perhaps later in date are ones of a floral or geometrical pattern, sometimes in an all-over design but more frequently of a repetitive nature in panels or bands often contained within a decorative border. Strapwork was another popular design in Tudor times. Although many of these patterns were repetitive, most repeats appear to have been undertaken free-hand, and it was not until the Reformation that stencilling became widely accepted. Decorative paintings were used not only on plasterwork but often on timber partitions, and doors were similarly treated. In stud walls too, where the timbers were exposed, it was common for the studs to be whitened and the wall painting continued across. Individual timbers such as roof timbers too, it seems, were also painted, generally with vines and simple floral patterns.

Of the numerous wall paintings which must have once existed, relatively few now survive; most have been destroyed with old plaster or obliterated by successive coats of whitewash. In recent years the stripping of old wallpaper and the removal of old whitewash have revealed many remnants of these paintings. Few are fit for preservation but many good examples of all types still remain.

Wall-painting continued throughout the eighteenth century, and surviving examples are all of a repetitive nature, almost certainly undertaken with the aid of stencils. In design, they followed much the same pattern as the early wallpapers. Although wallpaper in England had been known since Tudor times, it was not until the early part of the eighteenth century that it began to gain popularity. The designs were usually block printed on sheets of rectangular paper which, though small in size, were the largest capable of being produced by the hand methods then employed. Colour was added to the design either by hand painting or more commonly with the aid of a stencil.

Churches and Other Ecclesiastical Buildings

The use of timber in the construction of church buildings must, at one time, have been widespread in all those areas where there was a plentiful supply of wood, and the further one could go back in time, the more common they would undoubtedly have been.

There are numerous examples of surviving Saxon churches built of stone but there seems little doubt that many were built of timber. The stave-built nave at Greensted-juxta-Ongar, Essex (79), is the sole survivor. Traditionally, it is where St Edmund's body rested on its journey from London to Bury St Edmunds in 1013, but it appears to date from before this: dendro-magnetic tests carried out in 1960 suggested a date of about 835 for most of the staves of the present church, although there were some timbers which were dated to building of the mid-seventh century. This makes it the oldest wooden church not only in England but probably the world. Excavations have also revealed traces of two earlier chancels with timber walls. The nave is built of split oak logs (staves) set vertically and jointed together by oak tongues let into grooves. Originally the timbers would undoubtedly have been set in the ground but the ends of these would have decayed considerably before the introduction of a timber sill in the sixteenth century. The present brick plinth and oak sill date from the restoration in 1852, when more decay to the ends of the staves resulted in the further reduction in the height of the wall. Stave construction may have been a common form, yet it has no influence on later timber-framed work, for it was built without the aid of framed joints, which, as we have seen, is an essential element in true timber-framed construction.

Timber-framed churches were much more common than is evident today; many have been destroyed, due no doubt in part to decay and neglect but also to the desire to rebuild in a more fashionable material, such as brick. F. H. Crosseley lists twenty-seven timber-framed churches that once existed in Cheshire; today only two survive – at Lower Peover and Marton – while in only some six others does timber-frame work survive. Other counties have fared even worse: only two remain in Shropshire, one in Hereford & Worcester, one in Hampshire; in Essex there is Black Chapel, North End, which has a priest's house attached; there are the remains of two in Staffordshire

79. Greensted-juxta-Ongar church, Essex

and a chancel in Suffolk. Those that do exist have been in the main sadly mutilated.

Perhaps more interesting and certainly more numerous are the timber-framed towers and belfries, some detached, some built outside the west wall of the nave and some within the west end of the church, that survive in all timber-framed areas. Unlike timber churches, which were far more numerous in the Welsh border counties of England, timber-framed towers and belfries are to be found in the South-East. Essex, for instance has some sixty-five examples, some of thirteenth-century date. Unlike timber churches, these timber-framed structures have in the main not been restored or altered and so are of great interest, particularly in the use of notched lap-joints in those of thirteenth-century date.

Churches
Of the few timber-framed churches that have survived, the earliest are those in Cheshire. Professor Walter Horn of Berkeley University (California) considers the church at Lower Peover may be of thirteenth-century date (a chapel was founded here in 1269) but that it is more likely to be fourteenth century, and he claims this, together with the one at Marton (80), to be the earliest of their kind in Europe.

80. Marton church, Cheshire

The building was smaller and simpler than it is today, though the arcades and much of the internal timbers have remained substantially unaltered. Originally it had a single-pitch roof with only narrow aisles, with low side walls about six feet high. The church was enlarged to its present width between 1450 and 1500 but it still retained its single-pitch roof, which was a common feature of the timber-framed churches of Cheshire. Sadly, during the restoration of 1852 the external walls were largely rebuilt – the position and size of the windows were altered, as was the studwork, which was originally upright studs and horizontal cross members; and the roof, which originally covered the nave and low aisles under a continuous roof, was altered to provide three separate gable roofs, thus considerably altering its original appearance.

As previously stated, the church at Marton is fourteenth-century, the earliest part being the nave, the chancel a later addition. The tower is built separately from the nave, the timber uprights and cross-piers reminiscent of those built in Essex. Like other churches, Marton was altered during the nineteenth century: in 1804 the church roof was lowered, the dormer windows were removed and the minstrel gallery was discarded, while in extensive restoration work in 1871 the tower was reconstructed and the entrance to the church revised.

In a few other churches in Cheshire and the neighbouring part of Greater Manchester there are remains of timber work: Charkirk Chapel, Romiley, still retains its timber-framed chancel, though largely rebuilt in brick in 1716; at Warburton the north side is timber-framed; at Baddiley, of the old timber-framed church only the small chancel remains visible, the remainder being encased in brickwork in 1811; at Holmes Chapel the church was encased in 1719 but much of the original timber core remains; at Whitegate, although largely rebuilt in brick in 1728, the timber arcade posts still survive; at Cholmondeley Castle the timber-framed chancel was encased in 1716, and a similar fate overtook the church at Swettenham in 1711; at Siddington, though at first sight the church has a considerable amount of exposed timber, most of the black-and-white effect is obtained by the use of black paint on white painted brickwork.

In Shropshire the two remaining timber-framed churches are at Melverley and Halston. They are both of fifteenth- and sixteenth-century date. As with other timber-framed churches, both have been rebuilt and repaired in part. At Melverley this work is far more extensive than at Halston, with both the belfry and the porch renewed. Despite the restoration work, the church, situated in meadows above the River Vyrnwy, has great charm, a humble building with the interior largely unspoilt and with its timbering more like a barn than a church. The church is some forty-four feet long, divided into six bays, and twenty-two feet in width, built in the traditional western school of carpentry with most of the bays divided by a horizontal member forming two panels with each panel divided by close studwork. The church at Halston is situated behind Halston Hall and is of similar size to that at Melverley, being forty feet long and some twenty-three feet in width. Here the walls are divided into large open panels, the main studs being divided horizontally by a single horizontal member to divide the bays into two unequal panels.

Hereford & Worcester has one completely timber-framed church, that at Besford, which Mr F. W. B. Charles attributes to the late fourteenth century. The framing is in large panels – almost five feet square – with some bold diagonal braces and at the west end curved wall braces. Two early features of note are the ogee north doorway and a west window with a quatrefoil in a roundel in the spandrel between two ogee-headed lights. The church was extensively restored in 1881, when the walls were taken down and re-erected; the bell-turret also dates from this time. Within the church there survives a rood screen, also of late fourteenth-century date, with a loft above. A similar timber-framed church once stood at Newland.

Outside the West, only the church at Mattingley, Hampshire, and the Black Chapel, North End, Essex, survives. Mattingley is timber-framed throughout and late medieval, although the aisles were added in 1867 when the church was restored. The timbers are closely spaced; those to the chancel are seven inches apart and filled with brick-nogging. Inside the church the arcade posts clearly show that they were originally the wall posts of an aisleless church. The church at Rotherwick, in the same county, is timber-framed, the nave being faced in brick as early as the sixteenth century. Some early exposed timber work can be seen at Hartley Wespall, also in Hampshire; here the timbers to the west wall, dating from the early fourteenth century, form one enormous boldly cusped lozenge cut by a cusped middle post with smaller cusped timbers in the gable. No other church has anything to compare with it. The church also had a timber-framed tower, similar to that at Yateley, but this was greatly altered in the restoration of 1868–9 when most of the church was rebuilt. The chapel at North End, near Great Waltham, is both charming and rare; the charm is not evident from the outside for the timber frame is roughcast and painted, but the inside, with its mixture of Georgian pew boxes and fifteenth-century benches and screen, is very pleasing. It is rare because attached and built at right angles to this medieval chapel is a timber-framed priest's house.

Elsewhere in the country little now survives of timber-framed churches. In Staffordshire there is the church at Rushton Spencer, which one would not recognize as a timber-framed building until one enters it, for only here does it reveal the remains of its timber frame, the posts which form the narrow west aisle, being the remains of the original external wall framing. Greater Manchester has a church at Denton built about 1530 but of that period only the timber posts of the nave and some of the roof timbers with cusped arch-braces survive; the rest is Victorian, and the gay black-and-white exterior is obtained by the use of paint. The church at Crowfield, Suffolk, has a timber-framed chancel with exposed timbers both externally and internally and is the only one in the county in which a major part is of timber, a strange fact considering the wealth of timber-framed domestic buildings within the county.

Occasionally timber-framed churches had aisles from the outset (Holmes Chapel and Marton) but the majority, including those at Lower Peover and Mattingley, were later additions – Lower Peover in the fifteenth century and Mattingley in 1867. Of the fourteen or so timber-framed churches with aisles that once existed in Cheshire and the neighbouring part of Greater Manchester, only a handful now survive; besides those at Marton and Lower Peover, they are to be found at Warburton and Whitegate, where despite at least two rebuildings, the eight columns of the earlier arcade survive, and of course at Holmes Chapel, which has the finest. In some instances the timber piers have been encased in brickwork while, when the former timber church at Castle Bromwich, West Midlands, was rebuilt in brick in 1726–31, the timber arcades there were retained and encased in plaster.

Arcades of timber are also to be found within churches built of stone. The earliest is probably the one on the south side at Navestock, Essex, which dates from about 1250. The arcade, excluding the contemporary south chapel, is of four bays constructed of rough work but later cleverly and very effectively disguised by plaster to imitate stone. The arches too are also of plaster faced as stone. Two more important timber arcades in Essex are at Shenfield and Theydon Garnon; the one at Shenfield has been drastically restored. The arcade at Theydon Garnon dates from 1644, when the brick north aisle was built; it is of five bays with octagonal piers and semi-circular arches with a pendant drop for a keystone in each.

A very impressive fifteenth-century timber arcade exists at Ribbesford, Hereford & Worcester, while at Betley, Staffordshire, there is one of early seventeenth-century date above which is a timber-framed clerestory. In Hampshire, at Crawley, there survive rough wooden posts with longitudinal arched braces instead of arcades. A timber arcade of unmoulded posts can be seen at Wingham, Kent; these were, according to early nineteenth-century illustrations, at one time plastered to look like Doric columns but the plaster was removed during the restoration of 1874–5. The church at Selmeston, east Sussex, has a south arcade of oak piers in fourteenth-century style, but apparently they are replacements of the original in the rebuilding of 1867. At Nymet Rowland, Devon, there is a three-bay arcade all moulded as if it were stone. Why it was constructed of oak in an area where stone was plentiful is curious. At Winkfield, Berkshire, the nave is divided by two rows of octagonal wooden piers carrying arched braces instead of arches.

Towers and Belfries

Much more numerous and far more interesting than the timber-framed churches that survive are the timber-framed towers and belfries attached to stone churches. Towers are structures built outside the west wall of the nave, whereas a belfry is a turret which seems to stand on or near the west end of the church but which in actual fact stands on posts visible from within the church. These are quite distinct from the bell-turrets or cots which survive in many parts of the country which, being only of slight construction, are supported either by the tie-beams of the roof structure or on beams from the tops of walls. Timber-framed towers and belfries are found mainly in two areas, the eastern and the western parts of England.

There are two distinct types of timber-framed towers – those which are simple square towers and those which have additional bracing and posts producing an aisled effect on two, three and sometimes four sides. Of the two the square, unbuttressed tower is the least common, there being only a half-a-dozen or so examples still surviving. Four – the churches at Perivale, Greater London (81), Upleadon, Gloucestershire, Michelmersh, Hampshire, and Cotheridge, Hereford & Worcester – still retain their early pyramidal shaped roof. Those at Warndon and Dormston, both in Hereford & Worcester, have gabled roofs, and the church at Greensted-juxta-Ongar carries a shingled broach spire.

The oldest of these towers is probably the one at Cotheridge, whose lower part may be of about 1300, formed of solid timbering consisting of wide oak planks some four inches thick, tongued and grooved to each other and reminiscent of the nave walls at Greensted-juxta-Ongar. The upper part of this tower is weatherboarded and modern. The towers to both Warndon and Dormston (82) are ascribed to the fifteenth century, and both have a singularly domestic appearance; the one at Warndon has very closely spaced studs on the three flank walls as well as the ground floor of the west wall, while the remarkable feature at Dormston is the heavy internal bracing. The tower at Upleadon (83) is most attractive, probably built about 1500. It has close-set studs, broken only by three horizontal cross members with no bracing visible externally, so enhancing the impression of height,

81. Perivale church tower, Greater London

82. Dormston church tower, Hereford & Worcester

83. Upleadon church tower, Gloucestershire

but inside there are large cross-braces crossing each other, the ceiling level continuing up beyond the belfry. The infilling to the studs is stone on the east side, otherwise it is mostly of eighteenth-century brick. Of the other three, Perivale and Michelmersh are of fifteenth- or sixteenth-century date, while that at Greensted is probably eighteenth century. All three are clad externally with weatherboarding.

The tower at Dormston stands on a stone plinth several feet high, and there are some other churches in western England in which the towers are formed part stone and part in timber. At Kington (84), in the same county, the ground floor forming the porch is of stone and was constructed to take a timber-framed tower. The close-studding

84. Kington church tower, Hereford & Worcester

dates the tower to the fifteenth or even sixteenth century, but Mr
F. W. B. Charles has suggested that, since the upper stage has curved
braces, it may well be contemporary with the stone base, which
contains fourteenth-century windows. At Brimfield, Hereford & Worcester, and Milson, Shropshire, the division is more or less equal, but

far more numerous are the examples in which the stone tower is capped with a timber-framed belfry, as at Hampton Bishop, Defford and Winforton, all in Hereford & Worcester, and Bitterley, Shropshire. Also in Shropshire, along the Welsh border, there are a few examples of the two-stepped timber-framed belfries with pyramid-shaped roofs. These are to be found at Clun, Hopesay and More, all giving a degree of charm to the otherwise grim-looking squat stone towers. A similar form of construction can be seen at Rumburgh, Suffolk, where a timber-framed bell-chamber with a tiled roof caps a large square stone tower with some traces of thirteenth-century work. Whether this stone tower was ever complete and why it is now capped with timber is unknown.

At Marks Tey, Essex, the upper part of the brick tower was rebuilt in the seventeenth century in timber after it had been damaged in the siege of Colchester in 1648. The upper part of the tower and even the battlements are covered with vertical weatherboarding. In the same county the tower at Little Totham, commenced early in the sixteenth century of knapped flints was, for some reason, abandoned and later completed in timber, covered with weatherboarding and capped with a pyramid roof.

Far more numerous than the square towers are those in which, around the free-standing tower, additional posts and braces are introduced to form aisles. This type of construction is to be found mainly in the South-East and in Essex, which has more than any other county and is justly famous for these and the timber-framed belfries. Each tower was individually designed, no two being alike, often of rough work with few, if any refinements or mouldings, yet so massive are these structures that they cannot but be impressive. The basic arrangement is four posts either upright or inclined connected from north to south and sometimes from east to west by tie-beams which are supported by arch-braces. In addition, diagonal but slightly straighter cross-braces were introduced, usually from east to west rather than from north to south. Additional posts, arch-braces and diagonal cross-braces are all used outside the main tower to form aisles with lean-to roofs. So varied are these structures that it is impossible to generalize, for though some have these aisles on two or four sides, they are more usually to three sides, while the tower at West Hanningfield, Essex (85), is unique in that it is built on a cruciform plan.

As already mentioned, Essex has more timber-framed towers than any other county. One of the earliest is the magnificent tower at Navestock (86) which has recently been radio-carbon tested and a date of 1193 put on its timbers. It is oblong and carried on four stout cant posts with octagonal shafts attached and with the arch-braces meeting in a foliage boss, with aisles to the north and south and in addition a

85. West Hanningfield church tower, Essex

86. Navestock church tower, Essex

west aisle to form a semi-octagonal arrangement. Also of thirteenth-
or possibly fourteenth-century date is the tower at West Hanningfield.
As mentioned above, the ground-floor plan is cruciform with a square
upper part provided with a curious-looking oriel on the west side. The
construction internally is of special interest and well worth a visit.

Another and one of equal interest is to be found at Stock, which
C. A. Hewett considers to be late thirteenth-century. The ground floor
is set around four posts with braces and trellis-strutting. Externally
the tower is very elegant; the bottom stage is clad with dark vertical
weatherboarding with a doorway and three wooden tracery panels over
to the west wall, and there is one three-light traceried window to each
of the north and south walls. Above the pent-roof is a very tall white
horizontal weatherboarded bell-stage and a tall thin broach spire.

An octagonal arrangement similar to that at Navestock can be found
at Mundon, a church now, sadly, abandoned but fortunately in the
care of the Friends of Friendless Churches and remarkable in that the
tower is only a little higher than the nave roof. The tower at Magdalen
Laver is probably of sixteenth-century date and is unusual in that the
four central posts carry beams with queen-posts and have diagonal
cross-braces. The tower has the customary aisles to the north, south
and west, each with a pent-roof and above the bell-stage a pyramidal
roof. The church at Margaretting (87) is another well worth the visit,
for its tower is supported on ten posts connected from north to
south by arch-braces. Outside, the ground floor is clad with vertical
weatherboarding, and the roofs are hipped on three sides but straight
on the east side, as at Navestock. The bell-stage is vertical and clad
with shingles, as is the broach spire above.

The finest of all the towers in Essex, and perhaps of England, is to
be found at Blackmore, built, it has been suggested by C. A. Hewett,
in about 1480. Externally it has on the ground floor three lean-to roofs.
Above these rises a square section clad with vertical weatherboarding,
then four lean-to roofs, then the square bell-stage clad in horizontal
weatherboarding and finally the shingled broach spire. Internally the
tower is even more impressive, for it possesses ten free-standing posts,
making a nave and two side aisles. The posts are connected with a
number of elaborate tie-beams, arch-braces and diagonal cross-braces.
Others of interest are at Bulphan (unusual in that it is tile-hung with
ornamental tiles), Ramsden Bellhouse, Great Easton and Bobbing-
worth.

Towers of a nature similar to these in Essex can be found in
the South-East. Surrey has three notable examples: the churches at
Burstow, Newdigate and Great Bookham. Burstow (88) is perhaps the
finest, the tower constructed around the usual four posts with diagonal
bracing and aisled on the north, south and west sides, the aisles covered

87. Margaretting church tower, Essex

88. Burstow church tower, Surrey

by lean-to roofs. The lower stage is weatherboarded, the slightly battered upper bell-stage shingled, rising to a delicate shingled broach spire with four corner pinnacles. The date is probably sixteenth century and later than the one at Newdigate. This tower is of a type similar to that at Burstow but is shorter, with the spire both smaller and bolder. The ground-floor section is of black weatherboarding, the upper section above the pent-roofs white weatherboarding and the spire shingled. The tower at Great Bookham is similar except that the bottom stage is of flint. Inside, the framing also differs in that the four posts are supported with diamond and cross-bracing instead of the simpler diagonal bracing found at Burstow and Newdigate.

Kent has a notable example at High Halden, which has been dated by Mr Rigold as thirteenth century. It has a large, semi-octagonal ground floor similar to those at Navestock and Mundon, then a square bell-stage and finally a short broach spire. The ground-floor stage is clad with vertical weatherboarding, the bell-stage shingled, as is the spire. There are six posts which carry the upper stage, which, unlike most, is constructed independently. Kent had a similar tower at Monks Horton prior to the restoration of the church in 1847. The tower at Yateley, Hampshire, is fifteenth-century and, like those in Essex, has aisles to the north, south and west, originally separated from the central one by arch-braces, but these have been replaced by straight scissor-bracing. Sussex also has a timber-framed tower at Itchingfield. It differs from most in that it has aisles only to the north and south but not to the west. It has, however, the usual four posts with the customary diagonal bracing between them. Like most towers it is weatherboarded, this time with large vertical boards below and with shingles above. The tower is attributable to the fifteenth century, when it was butted up against an old west front. A tower similar to that at Itchingfield, with aisles only to the north and south, can be found at Greenford, Greater London. It has four main posts, is clad externally with dark oak weatherboarding and has a shingled broach spire.

Outside the home counties this form of timber-framed tower with aisles is rare. The tower at the timber-framed church at Marton has three aisles, but the structure has, sadly, been drastically altered, and too much reliance cannot be put on it. Much more important is the north tower at Pirton, Hereford & Worcester (89), which probably dates from the fifteenth century or may be even earlier, although the pyramidal roof is modern. It has narrow-spaced studs with two aisles formed with large cruck-like braces and, internally, between the nave and aisles, double scissor-braces of considerable size.

Timber belfries built within the western end of the nave walls are more plentiful. These independent structures, supported on timber posts resting upon the nave of the church, varying in number from

89. Pirton church tower, Hereford & Worcester

two to eight, carry an impressive belfry above the roof. These must not be confused with the bell-turrets or cots, which are supported either from the roof structure or, more commonly, by beams held from the tops of walls, sometimes using a mixture of timber beams and uprights built into the walls.

Once again, most are to be found in Essex, fairly closely grouped in the southern half of the county. The number of posts varies greatly: at Netteswell, Ovington and Willingale there are only two, at Doddinghurst, Hutton, Little Burstead and Mountnessing six, at Black Notley, Chigwell and Sutton eight, but the majority, such as those at Broxted, Hadleigh, Horndon-on-the-Hill, Shopland, South Hanningfield, Stanford Rivers, Stapleford Tawney, Stondon Massay and White Notley, have four posts. The belfry at Wakes Colne also has four posts but these are arranged in a row from north to south. They are constructed in much the same way as the towers in the county, with the posts connected with cross-beams and arch-braces, although only at Sutton are the posts so arranged as to form a kind of nave with side aisles, which is a feature of most of the external towers. Trellis-strutting, some of considerable size, is also a feature of many of the belfries (Horndon-on-the-Hill, Black Notley, Doddinghurst, Hutton, Mountnessing, Sutton). Most of these Essex belfries are of fifteenth-century date, but the one at Doddinghurst has been dated by C. A. Hewett as from the first half of the thirteenth century.

Belfries constructed similarly to those of Essex can be found in the South-East, particularly Surrey. At Byfleet there are two posts supporting beams built into the outer wall on three sides, while at Capel the bell-stage and spire are supported off beams on two posts and the west wall. The ones at Crowhurst, Dunsfold, Elstead, Horley, Alford, Bisley and Tandridge all have the usual four posts, but those at Elstead and Bisley, though having independent frames within the nave, are not structurally clear of it, being bonded to the outer walls. The belfry at Alford is unusual in the absence of cross and diagonal bracing usually associated with timber-framed belfries, the corner posts with small curved braces carrying horizontal beams.

The most unusual of the belfries is at Thursley, where an enormous timber structure was built to carry a very modest bell-chamber. Unlike other belfries, which are placed to the west end of the nave, this one was built half-way down the nave and so designed that the view towards the altar was not obscured. It was placed within the existing nave, the four corner posts (each thirty inches square) built against but just clear of the north and south walls. These support tie-beams on arch-braces and, from east to west, are joined by four-centred arches which carry beams on which stand two more posts, one each side, supporting two more tie-beams on arch-braces. This elaborate and sophisticated structure supports only a vast platform, yet it looks as if it was intended to support a complete belfry.

Similar in some ways to that at Thursley is the belfry at Rogate, Sussex, for here, between the four large corner posts (on the north and south sides only), are a series of arches and not the customary cross-braces. Another example in Sussex is at Tangmere, which has four posts but this time with diagonal cross-bracing. At Cowden, Kent, the tapered belfry stage is carried on six massive posts with arch-braces in both directions. It is an attractive belfry which carries a pyramid roof out of which is a very slim spire. Unlike the belfries of Essex, which are generally weatherboarded, the belfries of the South-East are clad with shingles, as are the spires.

Similar belfries can be found on the outskirts of London, namely at Northolt, Cowley, Ickenham and Kingsbury, all of which have small timber belfries surmounted by small spires supported in each case by substantial timbers which spring from the ground floor. A similar structure can be found at Didcot, Oxfordshire, where the belfry, topped with a broach spire at the west end of the south tower, is supported on a remarkable arrangement of stout timber posts, struts and braces.

Belfries can also be found, but far fewer in number, in the West. In Hereford & Worcester the church at White Ladies Aston has a belfry with a spire which is supported on heavy timbers inside the nave. More common is the use of a timber-framed cross wall at the west end of the nave to support the belfry and separating the nave from the belfry, as at Knighton-on-Teme, which has square panels, Broadwas, Bransford, which is of seventeenth-century date, Mamble, which has, behind a timber wall to the nave, a system of scissor-braces on which the belfry sits, and Bayton, which has a similar wall reconstructed in 1905. Another excellent example in the county is at Vowchurch, built about 1522 and unusual in that the exposed section above the main roof has exposed timbers whereas elsewhere most are clad. Internally the posts, which incidentally are not braced with scissor-bracing, are original even if they have received some Jacobean decoration. Another one with exposed timbers externally is at Tredington, Gloucestershire, although this is a rebuild of 1883.

Detached Belfries and Bell-Cages

Detached church towers are to be found in many parts of the country, and a few of them were built of timber. One at Holmer, Hereford & Worcester, is a detached square tower, the lower part of stone and the upper part timber, capped with a pyramid roof, while there are others at Brookland, Kent, and Pembridge and Yarpole, both in Hereford & Worcester, which are formed of timber and could more correctly be called detached belfries.

90. Brookland church belfry, Kent

The one at Brookland (90) is an interesting structure, octagonal in shape, some sixty feet high and thirty-six feet across, formed of three overlapping and diminishing stages all supported on four massive vertical posts. The posts are braced by scissor-bracing to the north and south and with four pairs of arch-braces from east to west. The lower stage is thirteenth-century; the upper stages are fifteenth-century. The whole structure is covered with shingles. A detached belfry similar to that at Brookland once stood at Benenden; it was much larger, some 134 feet high (almost twice the size of the one at Brookland), octagonal in shape with three stages and stood on nine posts (as opposed to the four at Brookland). This belfry was destroyed in 1672, when the church was struck by lightning.

The fourteenth-century detached belfry at Pembridge (91) is also octagonal in shape and, despite the low stone wall and pent-roof around the base, is a completely free-standing timber structure supported on eight timbers built in three diminishing stages, the upper stages square and clad in weatherboarding and the structure capped with a pyramid roof. The belfry at Yarpole is much smaller, though probably of more interest for it is more complete, with some of its cross-bracing still intact; it is built in two stages, again free-standing, with the lower stage encased in stone and the upper stage weatherboarded.

At East Bergholt, Suffolk, the bells are housed not in a belfry but in a single-storey open timber-framed bell-cage (92). This unique cage was built about 1500 after construction of the church tower had been abandoned. Externally the walls above the cross rail are formed into a grille with horizontal timbers woven through the vertical ones; the steeply pitched pyramid roof has a louvred top. Internally the five bells are supported on heavy oak timbers. Another curious structure houses the bells at Wrabness, Essex, the detached single-storeyed weatherboarded building of seventeenth- or perhaps eighteenth-century date being little more than a 'little shed like a village lock-up'.

Porches

By the end of the Middle Ages most churches had a porch on the south side – or on the north side if the manor house was to the north, and a few even had porches on both sides. Although there are references to porches being built in the thirteenth century, it was not until the beginning of the fourteenth that they were regarded as a necessary part of the village church. From this time they played an important part in ceremony: it was here that women knelt to be 'churched' after the birth of a child, that part of the baptismal and marriage service was held, that penitents received absolution, that penance was done and where legal business was conducted. In addition it had the practical use of protecting the door from the elements.

91. Pembridge church belfry, Hereford & Worcester

92. Bell cage, East Bergholt, Suffolk

Porches built of timber are to be found in all those areas where timber was the predominant building material and are usually attached to earlier stone churches. In general these porches were single-storey, one or two bays in length, with the sides divided horizontally by a middle rail either panelled or filled in solid below and with an open tracery above or, in the sixteenth and seventeenth centuries, with open balusters above. In many instances the lower part below the middle rails is of stone, flint or brick but these are probably not original. Not all porch sides were open; some, such as those at Defford, Hereford & Worcester, were filled in solid with the timbers exposed. At Bradwell-juxta-Mare, Essex, a porch of two bays, the entrance bay is open and traceried, with the bay nearest the church filled in.

The roofs of many early porches are steep but in the fifteenth century they became less so. They are constructed in a variety of ways, often being miniatures of those to be found within the church. Crown-posts, king-posts and arch-braced collar-beams were all used, the most unusual being that at South Benfleet, Essex, which has a hammer-beam roof. At Boxford, Suffolk, there is wooden groining springing from clustered shafts with undercut mouldings to the cap, while, at Metfield, in the same county, there is elaborate vaulting with lierne ribs and carved bosses. Bargeboards too were frequently provided, often boldly cusped, as at White Notley, Essex, Little Eversden, Cambridgeshire, and Huddington, Hereford & Worcester, sometimes moulded, as at Cardington, Shropshire, or traceried, as at Eye, Hereford & Worcester. Two-centred arches are provided to many of the early examples, the door jamb and arch formed of two slabs of oak following the grain of the wood, as at Warndon, Hereford & Worcester, Munslow, Shropshire, Somersham, Suffolk, and High Halden, Kent, while later examples are generally provided with a four-centred arch. Less common are those provided with a ogee-arch – for instance, at Bradwell-juxta-Mare, Essex, and Huddington, Hereford & Worcester.

Upper chambers built over porches are a common enough feature of churches, and there are a few instances in which this was carried out in timber.

At Berkswell, West Midlands (93), the jettied upper floor with closely set studs was a priest's room reached by an external staircase, while the upper storey of the porch at Little Hampden, Buckinghamshire, is a belfry. Perhaps the finest of these two-storey porches is the one at Radwinter, Essex (94), which is jettied on three sides. The lower part, with the dragon-beamed and jettied first floor, is probably early fourteenth-century, while the attractive upper storey is of 1870, although it obviously replaced a similar structure.

As previously stated, porches first appeared in the fourteenth century, and there are some built of timber that still exist from that date. Most are to be found in Essex, which has no fewer than fourteen which have been ascribed to this period. The ones at Aldham and Frating, perhaps the best, have curious S-shaped braces above the collar to the roof to form an ogee bracing. Essex also possesses some exceptionally good timber porches of a slightly later date, chiefly of the latter part of the fifteenth century. The best examples are those at Margaretting, Doddinghurst, Laindon, Runwell and South Benfleet. As we have seen, timber was freely used in Surrey for church towers and belfries and was also widely used in the construction of porches. Next to Essex it probably has more than any county, many dating from the fourteenth and fifteenth centuries, often with well-cusped bargeboards. Among the most notable are those at Bisley, of late fourteenth-century date; of the fifteenth or sixteenth century are those at Elstead, Ewhurst, Merrow, Pyrford, Seale and Wisley. Timber porches were also popular in Sussex, though in many cases they are a mixture of timber and stone. Some of the earliest are probably those at Barnham, West

93. Berkswell church porch, West Midlands

Chiltington and Rustington. Hampshire too has some notable examples, for instance at Warblington and South Hayling, while Kent has a good variety, including those at Brookland, of fourteenth-century date, Horsmonden and Shoreham. Suffolk too has many of note; the earliest is undoubtedly at Somersham, which is certainly early

94. Radwinter church porch, Essex

fourteenth-century, while the most notable porch in the county is the
early fourteenth-century one at Boxford. In Hertfordshire the oldest
is probably that at Hunsdon; another of interest in the county is
the one at Stanstead Abbotts, of fifteenth-century date. In contrast
timber-framed porches are rare in Cambridge; in fact, there are only
two – at Bassingbourn and Little Eversden, reputed to be built about
1400. Another of note, in Bedfordshire, is at Salford, which has one

beam with dogtooth carving and some work dating from the thirteenth
century.

Timber porches, sometimes of great age, can be found in the West
of England. The earliest perhaps is the one at Warndon, Hereford &
Worcester, which F. W. B. Charles considers possibly contemporary
with the church, which is twelfth century. Others of note in the county
are at Eye, Dormston and Crowle, all probably built in the fourteenth
century, and the late Perpendicular one at Huddington from the
fifteenth. Shropshire too has some fine porches – for instance, at
Milson, probably fourteenth-century, Munslow and Lydbury North.
In the West, timber porches continued to be constructed well after
they had generally stopped in the South and East – the only one in
Essex, for instance, of seventeenth-century date appears to be that at
Mundon, whereas in the West one can cite such examples as Cardington, dated 1639, Loppington, dated 1658, and Atcham, all in Shropshire, and Orleton, of 1680, in Hereford & Worcester.

Lych-Gates

Many churches have a lych-gate built over the main entrance to
the enclosed area around the church, the name deriving from the
Anglo-Saxon *lich*, meaning corpse. The gate marks the division
between consecrated and unconsecrated ground, where the bearers
sheltered with the coffin, resting the coffin on a lych or coffin-stone
while the priest said part of the burial service.

Lych-gates, like porches, were built of stone or timber or a mixture
of both, as at Rustington and Pulborough, Sussex, with stone below
and timber above, or on occasion combined with a house. In medieval
times few churchyards were without one of some kind, and they
continued in use until the end of the eighteenth century, after which
many, especially those constructed of timber, became decayed and
have subsequently been demolished. In Cheshire, for instance, in the
eighteenth century the lych-gates were frequently replaced by iron
gates, as at Bunbury, Malpas and Tilston.

A timber lych-gate was constructed in one of two ways: straddling
the path or running along the path. In both cases it was essential to
provide a roof large enough to give adequate protection from the
weather, for the structure was generally open. The roof might be held
up by two, four or (in the case of those at Boughton Monchelsea, Kent,
Garsington, Oxfordshire, and Whitbourne, Hereford & Worcester) six
posts, the whole strengthened by braces and struts. In the main the
roofs are either hipped, sometimes on all four sides, especially when
the ridge runs transversely to the path, or gabled – some, such as those
at Monnington-on-Wye, Hereford & Worcester, and Clun, Shropshire,
gabled on all four sides. The majority of lych-gates are single structures,

95. Ashwell lych-gate, Hertfordshire

but at Ashwell, Hertfordshire (95), there is a rare example of a double lych-gate of fifteenth-century date.

Although the majority of these timber-framed lych-gates have now disappeared, many destroyed or damaged after the Reformation and since rebuilt (particularly during the Gothic revival of Victorian times), there are some which are of considerable age and interest. One of the oldest surviving is at St George's Church, Beckenham, Greater London, a thirteenth-century gate restored early this century. There still survive some from the fourteenth and fifteenth centuries, such as those at Isleham, Cambridgeshire, and Boughton Monchelsea, Kent.

As previously mentioned, lych-gates are sometimes built in conjunction with houses, often a church house. In these cases access to the

96. Smarden lych-gate, Kent

churchyard was gained through a passage within the building. There are several good examples of this: at Hartfield, Sussex, the cottage, thought to be of 1520, has the upper jettied floor extending over the lych-gate; at Penshurst and Smarden (96), both in Kent, the lych-gates are formed between two half-timbered cottages bridged by a third; at Bray, Berkshire, there is a fifteenth-century timber-framed gatehouse. At Finchingfield and Felsted, both in Essex, the lych-gates are formed within former guildhalls.

Priests' Houses
The idea that every parish should have a house and land with its church originated at the Lateran Council of 1215, when the Pope ordered that a reasonable living, with secure tenure, should be provided by those who had appropriated churches. Most of these medieval priests' houses would at first have differed little from the simple

dwellings of their more humble parishioners, but the few that have survived are mainly those of more prosperous benefices. In size and structure these resemble those of the laity of the same period and social standing, yet often they differ from the typical medieval hall-house in that separate quarters were provided for the servant or housekeeper, generally with no direct access to the rest of the house. In addition these medieval priests' houses had to serve for other needs – for instance, to provide hospitality for travellers and passing wayfarers, so guest rooms were also required.

Examples of churches with attached timber-framed priests' houses are extremely rare. One has already been mentioned, that at the Black Chapel, North End, Essex, and the other surviving example is also in Essex, at Laindon. Here the church itself is built of stone, the priest's house being a two-storeyed, timber-framed narthex at the west end. The ground floor is a living-room, the upper floor a bedroom separated from the nave of the church by a rood-loft type parapet. Unfortunately the upper floor has been turned into an organ loft. Another attached

97. Clergy house, Alfriston, East Sussex

98. St William College, York

timber-framed priest's house was at Flaunden, Hertfordshire, where the house was combined with a large timber-framed tower.

More commonly, however, priests' houses were separate buildings either within or overlooking the churchyard. The most famous of these early timber-framed priests' houses is the one at Alfriston, East Sussex (97), built for a small community of parish priests around 1350. (It has the added distinction of being the first building and the second property to come into the care of the National Trust.) After the Reformation, the house became the vicarage of St Andrew's Church until about 1790, when it was converted into two farm labourers' cottages. The building became derelict in the 1880s and was acquired by the Trust in 1896 at a cost of £10. It is a standard Wealden house with a central open hall, with service rooms to the west end and a solar above, but it differs in one important respect, in that separate servants' quarters, comprising a living-room and bedroom, were provided at the east end of the building, with a rear door but with no direct access to the remainder of the house.

Before the Reformation priests often lived in small communities where they might share a common life under discipline. These were often chantry priests, and special buildings were set aside for their

99. Ashleworth vicarage, Gloucestershire

use, a feature being the large upper floor open to the roof. Perhaps the most famous is St William College, York (98), founded in 1461 in the house of the prior of Hexham. Following the Reformation the college was dissolved, and the building became Crown property. After a succession of private owners, the building is today administered by the college trustees.

Another building of interest is the Chantry House, Henley, Oxfordshire, built in about 1400 as a dwelling for chantry priests. This rare, unspoilt, timber-framed building, formerly known as Chapel House, is situated overlooking the churchyard of St Mary's and is connected to the church by a porch. Like the house at Alfriston, after the Reformation it was put to several uses: in 1664 it was a school, the grammar school using the upper floor and Lady Periam's Bluecoat School the lower floor; later it formed part of the adjoining Red Lion Hotel before being restored to the church as a memorial to a rector who died in 1915.

After the Reformation the clergy were allowed to marry, and it is

100. Gawsworth old rectory, Cheshire

from this period that most priests' houses or vicarages and rectories belong. Those constructed of timber are to be found in all those areas where timber was once plentiful. They differed little from ordinary houses of the period, although they vary considerably in size depending on the stipend, from quite small houses, such as the one overlooking the churchyard at Clare, Suffolk, to such striking houses as Ashleworth vicarage, Gloucestershire (99), and Gawsworth old rectory near Macclesfield, Cheshire (100), built in 1470.

Public and Communal Buildings

Timber-framed buildings used by the public can be classified into three groups.

The first comprises civic buildings, used in the administration of the community, such as guildhalls, market halls and crosses, town halls, moot halls and court houses, and the closely related church and town houses. Although many of these buildings have distinct and separate origins and initially might have served different purposes, over the years the functions have become intermingled, with their use changing through a period of time, often being used for more than one purpose at the same time. For instance, Elstow moot hall originally used as a market house in connection with the fairs held on the adjacent green, later became a meeting-place for Elstow manor court, and later still the upper floor was used for Nonconformist worship on Sundays and a school during the week.

The second group are those buildings which depended upon a charitable trust, such as a guild or a wealthy benefactor, or perhaps the local administration. To this group belong almshouses, hospitals and schools. In the third group are those buildings which are privately owned but used by the public, such as shops, inns and public houses.

Guildhalls

A guildhall originally denoted the building used by a medieval guild for its meetings, but over the centuries the word has come to apply to various buildings serving as a municipal hall which are a common feature of many towns and villages in England.

The majority of guildhalls were built for guilds – that is, fraternities of a religious and social nature, and so were frequently sited near the church, perhaps at the edge of the churchyard, as at Hadleigh (101), Eye and Fressingfield, all in Suffolk, Ashdon, Felsted, Clavering (102) and Finchingfield (103), all in Essex, Knowle, West Midlands (104), Rickmansworth, Hertfordshire, and Linton, Cambridgeshire, while the guildhall at Henley-in-Arden is attached to the church. Although many of these religious guilds are of great antiquity, guildhalls are rarely so. The majority, for some reason, are late fifteenth or early sixteenth century, probably indicating the increasing wealth of the

101. Hadleigh guildhall, Suffolk

102. Clavering guildhall, Essex

103. Finchingfield guildhall, Essex

nation during this period. There are some earlier examples: the former guildhall in Church Street, Stratford-upon-Avon (105) (now known as the Grammar School), for instance, was built in 1417 for the Guild of the Holy Cross following the amalgamation of the Guilds of Our Lady and St John the Baptist in 1403.

The most common form of guildhall built for these religious guilds is one which is long, relatively narrow and of two storeys, although Church House, Hawstead, Suffolk, when built as a parish guildhall had a three-bay open hall at one end and at the other end a large service area including a kitchen on the ground floor with three rooms above. However, most appear to be continuously jettied along one side and in a single range. Generally they were five, six or seven bays long, though some are smaller – Barley, Hertfordshire, for instance, is only four bays. The upper storey was usually divided into two, one large room which could accommodate all the members at once and a smaller ante-chamber or a combined ante-chamber, service room and perhaps

104. Knowle guildhall, West Midlands

RJBROWN '85

105. Stratford-upon-Avon guildhall and almshouses, Warwickshire

kitchen. Access to the upper floor was usually gained by an internal
staircase, but on occasion an external staircase was provided, as was
the case at Ashdon and Rickmansworth, both of which have a first-floor
door visible, Ashdon at the rear, Rickmansworth at the end. The
ground floor was used for a variety of purposes, now not clear.
Sometimes, as at Trinity guildhall (later the grammar school), Felsted,
lock-up shops were provided, perhaps to provide the guild with extra

money. More often it seems it provided accommodation, perhaps for the poor or other needy sections of society. At Clavering the ground-floor end room overlooking the churchyard had an external doorway but no direct communication with the remainder of the ground floor. The room, which has an oriel window, probably constituted the living-quarters of a priest, but the purpose of the remainder of the ground-floor rooms is unknown.

Timber-framed guildhalls of this type are a common feature in many of the villages in the eastern counties, and apart from those already

106. Ashwell guildhall, Hertfordshire

mentioned one can cite such examples as Whittlesford and Dul-
lingham, both in Cambridgeshire, Ashwell, Hertfordshire (106),
and in Suffolk, Kelsale, Fressingfield, Laxfield and Stoke-by-
Nayland.

Guildhalls similar to those found in eastern England can be seen
elsewhere. That at Stratford-upon-Avon has already been mentioned;
it is like many other guildhalls, a long, relatively narrow building
jettied the entire length but unlike most, in which the guildhall proper
was on the first floor, at Stratford it was on the ground floor. The
upper room, open to the roof, was known as the 'Over Hall'. In Church
Lane, Ledbury, Hereford & Worcester, there is a similar building
almost certainly a former guildhall – possibly for the Guild of Holy
Trinity – which was, like the one at Stratford, later used as the
grammar school. At Aston Cantlow, Warwickshire (107), there is a
small guildhall formerly connected with the Fraternity of the Blessed
Virgin.

In contrast to these religious guildhalls are those belonging to

107. Former guildhall, Aston Cantlow, Warwickshire

merchant guilds and craft guilds whose interests were more specialized. Merchant guilds began to appear in the eleventh century, were well established by the twelfth and by the end of the thirteenth existed in more than a hundred towns. They were an alliance of merchants and traders of a town who were involved in the control of markets, buying and selling, the checking of weights and measures and the collection of tolls. These guilds also had a charitable side: they appointed chaplains and helped both sick and poor, particularly their own members and their families who had fallen on hard times. During the thirteenth and fourteenth centuries these merchant guilds began to be

108. Lavenham guildhall, Suffolk

replaced by a number of smaller craft guilds, concerned with a single trade or group of allied trades; by so doing they hoped to maintain standards much as the merchant guilds had earlier.

Although these were primarily trade guilds, religion often played a considerable part in their affairs. The famous half-timbered guildhall at Lavenham, Suffolk (108), was built in about 1528 by the Guild of Corpus Christi and was one of three guilds in the town founded to regulate the wool trade but religious festivals were celebrated with

109. Thaxted guildhall, Essex

processions from the guildhall to the church, and religious feasts, particularly that of Corpus Christi, were held in the hall. The Wool Hall, built for another guild, that of Our Lady, also survives at Lavenham, if only just, for in 1911 it was completely dismantled, its timbers numbered and plans made for its re-erection near Ascot but strong protests resulted in its return and the restoration of the building. It now forms part of the Swan Hotel.

The halls of the craft guilds varied greatly in size and design: the early ones – for instance, the guildhall at Thaxted, Essex (109), built for the Guild of Cutlers early in the fifteenth century, and the one at Much Wenlock, Shropshire (110) whose lower part is said to be medieval but whose timber parts date from 1577, have open ground floors, the upper floor being supported on columns. These open ground floors were undoubtedly used for trading, combining the guild requirements with those of the market hall.

Merchant guilds were not only concerned with local trade: some were formed to give protection to their members abroad. The first of such companies which became prominent was the Merchants of the Staple, a group who obtained a monopoly of the overseas trade of raw wool, the largest of all English exports at that time. By the beginning of the sixteenth century the wool trade had begun to decline and with it the company. The one company of real significance was then the Merchant Adventurers, who held a monopoly of the trade with the Netherlands and western Germany. Its seat of government was in Antwerp, although subordinate courts were held in London and provincial ports. The most famous of their buildings was the Merchant Adventurers' Hall at York (111), built between 1357 and 1361 for the Guild of Our Lord Jesus Christ and the Blessed Virgin, which was early in the fifteenth century absorbed by the Guild of Mercers and Merchants who in about 1580 became the Merchant Adventurers. The great hall is entirely timber-framed, divided into two aisles by a central row of posts and has an open timber roof. Below this hall is an undercroft also divided into two aisles by a row of massive oak posts with four-way braces. Externally there is much exposed studding, particularly impressive to the south and west.

Guilds of religious nature were suppressed following the Charities Act of 1547, their property confiscated by the Crown and later sold by the Court of Augmentations for secular use. Some became private houses while many others became parish property. Sometimes they were used as the town hall; others were divided up into a series of tenements, or into shops or workshops for local traders and craftsmen. Some, as we have already seen, were used as schools. Many more finally became the parish workhouse and almshouse. The guildhall at Lavenham is typical. It is known for instance that after 1547 the

110. Much Wenlock guildhall, Shropshire

guildhall was used for secular purposes only, regulating a much-reduced wool trade; it became parish property in 1596 and was used as the town hall for nearly eighty years, after which it became a prison and later a workhouse, then, with the adjoining cottages, an almshouse, and finally a wool store. Fortunately, in 1887 it was purchased by Sir Cuthbert Quilter, who undertook the repair of the building, which is now in the ownership of the National Trust and is open to the public. Another is St Anthony's Hall, York, now part of the university but originally the hall of the guild of St Anthony. After the Dissolution,

111. Merchant Adventurers' Hall, York

the hall became a poorhouse, a house of correction and a school. The building dates from 1446–53 and was, later in the century, doubled in size. It is a stone below and timber above. Craft guilds were not so drastically affected by the Act: the guildhall of the butchers' guild, Hereford, was built in 1621 – another building attributed to John Abel, the King's carpenter. Now isolated, it was once part of a row of twelve belonging to the fraternity.

In 1835 the legal powers of the guilds were ended, but long before this they had been declining, due in part to state control, in part to the rise of new industries and to the movement of some industries from town to countryside.

Many former guildhalls are now museums, such as those at Lavenham and Ledbury, already mentioned, and the one at Carlisle, a fifteenth-century former town house which became the meeting-place of eight trade guilds.

Market Crosses and Halls

Crosses and halls were important features of the medieval market, being the centre for the commercial activities of the town and the central feature of the market square. Most towns had a market cross and often a market hall as well, although the two terms are often confused and many market crosses appear to have been quite substantial buildings with many of the features of a market hall. Most of these buildings date from the new wave of market charters in the sixteenth and seventeenth centuries. Although many of the best known are built of stone, there were at one time many of timber, which lent itself equally as well as stone to the functional demands of these buildings, the chief need being an open ground-floor plan, which was easily achieved in timber.

Sadly many have been swept aside, often – as at Petworth and Horsham, both in West Sussex, and Saffron Walden, Essex – to be rebuilt in stone as town halls. Others were demolished during the nineteenth century, when they no longer served the purpose for which they were built. This was due to the radical change in the trading conditions when private shops and other commercial outlets took trade away from the traditional trading areas. Despite this there are some timber-framed market crosses and halls which still survive.

Market crosses are generally single-storey open arcades built for the use of 'poore people to sell their chafer there . . .'. They are often constructed of stone, as at Chichester, West Sussex, and Malmesbury, Wiltshire, but there still survive a few constructed of timber. Perhaps the largest of these single-storey structures is the one at Dunster, Somerset, an octagonal market cross built in about 1589 by George Luttrell and repaired in 1647. It is built around a stone core and has a pitched roof with dormers. Another, this time of seventeenth-century date, is to be seen in the market square at Pembridge, Hereford & Worcester. It has been suggested that the notches in the posts were for supporting counters on which wares for sale could be displayed. Others of interest are the sixteenth-century hexagonal one at Mildenhall, Suffolk; that at North Walsham, Norfolk, an octagonal timber structure rebuilt after the fire of 1602 and altered in the late nineteenth century to mark the Diamond Jubilee of Queen Victoria; one at Oakham, Leicestershire, built around a stone pillar, and the one at Abbots Bromley, Staffordshire. Much less common is the market cross with an upper floor; one can be found at Wymondham, Norfolk (112), an octagonal building built around the market cross, the upper floor supported on eight timber posts. The building dates from 1617.

This structure differs little in design from those market halls which began to appear in the sixteenth and seventeenth centuries with an upper chamber over an open arcade where goods could be sold or stalls set up by licensed traders. The upper storeys were used either as a general meeting room or by some particular trade – the one at Ledbury, Hereford & Worcester, for instance, was built as a corn market and

112. Wymondham market cross, Norfolk

the one at Horndon on the Hill, Essex, as a wool hall. In this respect they were similar to the early guildhalls. The upper floor of these structures is usually reached by an external staircase.

Hereford & Worcester was at one time rich with these timber-framed market halls. The one at Ledbury, which has already been mentioned, was begun about 1617 and was not completed until after 1655. It was attributed to John Abel but as with others – that at Weobley (destroyed about 1860), the magnificent one at Hereford (destroyed in 1862) – there is no documentary evidence of this. The finest surviving market hall known to be the work of Abel is at Leominster (113). It was built in 1633 and stood at the top of Broad Street until in 1853 it was offered for sale, bought by John Arkwright and re-erected on its present site. Known as The Grange, it was at first a private house but is now the offices of the district council. Like other market halls, it was originally open on the ground floor and used as a butter market. Features of this hall are the ogee-shaped braces and the profusion of Renaissance decoration. Besides the hall at Leominster, Abel is also known to have been responsible for the erection of those at Brecon (1624) and Kington (1654).

Close by, at Newent, Gloucestershire, is another late sixteenth- early seventeenth-century timber-framed market hall, containing a large room on the first floor reached by an external staircase. As in so many of these buildings, the ground floor is open, the upper floor being supported on twelve timber posts.

In the South-East and eastern England these halls were at one time a common feature in most market towns. Sadly, few remain, nearly all having been destroyed in the eighteenth and nineteenth centuries, although a few, for instance, one at Harwich, Essex, survived until recent times. Of the few that remain, the one at Horndon (114) is perhaps the best. Built early in the sixteenth century in connection with the wool trade, it was restored in 1969 with finance provided by the John Poley Trust. At Sawbridgeworth, Hertfordshire, there is the former market house, a two-storey plastered jettied building with a gable wing with another long, partially weatherboarded wing. Another is to be found in the square near the church at Midhurst, West Sussex; built in 1552, it has been much altered and now forms part of the nearby Spread Eagle inn. The market hall from Titchfield, Hampshire, has been re-erected at the Weald and Downland Open Air Museum, Singleton, and is typical of what probably happened to many of these buildings. Built at the beginning of the seventeenth century, it finally became redundant and was moved from the old High Street in about 1850, after which it was used for a number of purposes before becoming derelict in spite of spasmodic attempts to raise money for its repair. Eventually a 'dangerous building' notice was served by the local

113. The Grange, Leominster, Hereford & Worcester

114. Horndon-on-the-Hill woolmarket, Essex

council, insisting upon its immediate demolition. Fortunately it was saved by the museum and re-erected at its site in 1972.

Town and Moot Halls

Closely associated with market halls and guildhalls are town and moot halls, which can include such buildings as court halls and church and town houses. It is often difficult to distinguish between them all, for all represent a centre for control and supervision. Certainly in the case of market halls the upper floor was often used as a council chamber, and the one at Leominster was often referred to as the town hall. Many guildhalls, following the suppression of the guilds in the mid-sixteenth century, became parish property and were used as town halls, such as the one at Lavenham, Suffolk. The guildhall at Faversham, Kent, was built in the market place in 1574 as a market hall, was converted into a guildhall in 1604 and later became the council chamber. The Guildhall, Leicester (115), was originally built for the Guildhall of Corpus Christi, founded in 1347, from about which time the east part of the north range of the hall probably dates. However, by 1495 at the latest it served as the town hall, and it remained in use until 1875, when the new town hall was built. It is a fine timber-framed L-shaped building on a stone base; the north range, which is the oldest, is of base-cruck construction and is long and low with narrowly spaced studs, while the east range is taller with very large timbers. In 1556 Thaxted was granted a royal charter and assumed full borough status, and the old guildhall served as the town hall until James II withdrew the charter.

In construction and layout too there is a close similarity between market halls and many town halls and indeed some guildhalls, in that

115. Leicester guildhall, Leicestershire

the ground floor was open with the upper floor supported on timber columns. This was not always so, for the west part of the moot hall, Elstow, Bedfordshire, was divided into six shops, each with its own doorway and broad single-light windows. Similarly at Great Dunmow, Essex, the fine timber-framed town house, built shortly after the town became a borough in 1556, had shops on the ground floor with the upper floor used for town meetings.

These town or moot halls were, like the market halls and some guildhalls, situated in the centre of the towns commercial activities. The one at Bridgnorth, Shropshire, built in 1648–52 after much of the town was burnt down in 1646, is in the centre of the high street, the one at Fordwich, Kent (116), on the quay, and that at Aldeburgh, Suffolk, in what was the town centre before the sea pushed its position back. The town hall at Fordwich was built, it is believed, shortly before 1544 with a court room and jury room on the first floor, with the ground floor, which was apparently open, later formed into a

116. Fordwich town hall, Kent

storeroom and prison. Today it is used as a parish room and museum and is open to the public. The building is most attractive, being jettied on all four sides, the upper storey infilled with herringbone brick nogging, beneath a large hipped roof. The moot hall at Aldeburgh dates from between 1520 and 1540, with the brick nogging to the upper floor inserted in 1654. Like the one at Fordwich, it was originally open on the ground floor, as is evident from the original timber arches which still survive. The ground floor at Bridgnorth had an open arcade of stone but is now faced with brick, with timber above, and has clock turrets to the north and south.

The moot hall at Elstow, which is situated in a field – a former fair-green – to the north of the church, was built about 1500. The upper floor is jettied and contains the main room with its original roof. As previously stated, the three bays at the west end of the ground floor

117. Town hall, Wootton Bassett, Wiltshire

were used as shops while the fourth bay at the east end contained the staircase to the chamber above. The fifth bay was added to the east end about a hundred years later, and the massive brick chimney may indicate that this end was used as a cottage.

One of the last-built of these timber-framed town halls can be seen at Wootton Bassett (117), Wiltshire. It was built in 1700 and like earlier town halls has an open ground floor with the timber-framed upper floor carried on fifteen stone columns, the whole structure being 'very conservative for 1700'. Close by, at Faringdon, Oxfordshire, is a similar building: again the upper storey is supported on stone columns but the upper part here is plastered and is probably of a later date than the columns.

The free-standing court hall at Milton Regis, Kent, stands in a 'embryonic' square. Restored in the 1960s, it has been dated by Mr Rigold to the early part of the fifteenth century. The building is two-storeyed with closely spaced studs and with a continuous overhang on the east side only. On the ground floor are two lock-ups. The court house, Berkhamsted, also dates from the Tudor period, and although the ground floor has been rebuilt, the upper floor retains its closely spaced studding. The building has also been known, according to documentary evidence, as 'town house' and 'church house' and was where the corporation of Berkhamsted met and where the ancient manorial courts were held until the late 1880s.

The use of the term 'town house' is fairly common, particularly in the eastern counties, to describe 'general-purpose' halls. They occurred in those places which did not rate as a market town or borough yet needed some building to serve the juridical, administrative, mercantile, educational and merely social needs of the parish. Many, such as the town house at Barley, Hertfordshire, were former guildhalls.

Church houses, built near or adjoining the church, or churchyard, are a feature of some villages, particularly in the South-West and in eastern England. Those in the South-West are of stone – those in Devon at Chagford, Drewsteignton, South Tawton and Widecombe-in-the-Moor are all excellent examples – while those in the East are of course built of timber. These houses were maintained by the churchwardens and were in effect forerunners of the village hall used for parish festivals and holidays, especially after an Act of 1571 forbade the use of the church itself for feasting. At these festivities church ales, brewed from gifts of malt, were sold to increase the church's income, as well as for the benefit of the poor of the village. After the Reformation the brewing of church ales was frowned upon by both the Puritans and the magistracy, and so church houses began gradually to disappear and with them the ales. Some former guildhalls and church houses, such as the Fox and Goose Inn, Fressingfield, Suffolk, became ale-houses.

118. Court house, Long Crendon, Buckinghamshire

Others were destroyed, while some were converted to other uses, perhaps as the village hall before in most cases becoming almshouses or even workhouses. Among the most notable timber-framed examples are those at Cockfield, a handsome fifteenth-century building with one original doorway, and Yoxford, both in Suffolk.

Lock-ups

There are examples of a timber lock-up forming part of the ground floor of a guildhall or market hall, as for instance at Thaxted, Essex, and Milton Regis, Kent, but of free-standing timber-framed parish lock-ups, although one time common enough, only a few still survive – for instance at Tollesbury, Essex, which is little more than a timber-framed, weather-boarded shed with an iron grille in the door. It stands in the churchyard and has recently been reconstructed. Another, also in Essex, stands near the churchyard at Canewdon. This too is little more than a shed and, although built in 1775, was moved to its present position in 1938, being given additional protection in 1967 when the cage was restored.

Perhaps the best example stands at Barley, Hertfordshire (119), well away from the village at Crosshill. Built in the seventeenth century, it is formed of studs approximately 4½ inches apart, with the spaces filled in with boards fitted into grooves in the studs. It appears that the spaces between the studs to the front, as well as those to the door, were open, for the boards to the front are secured by beading instead of being set in grooves, and the door has horizontal boards nailed to the back. Originally, within the cage, it is believed there was an iron post with chains. The cage, which was apparently last used in about 1890, was restored by the parish council in 1969.

Almshouses and Hospitals

Guilds were also associated with almshouses and hospitals, perhaps the most famous being the one associated with the Merchant Adventurers in York, which had attached to the fraternity a hospital for 'poor and feeble people'. In some guildhalls, as already mentioned, the ground floors were on occasion used for almsfolk. The ground floor of the guildhall at Finchingfield seems always to have been almshouses, and these together with the guildhall were given to the poor of the parish. The almshouses here remained in occupation until about 1930 and have now been converted into accommodation for elderly people. Similarly, at Hadleigh, Suffolk, a deed of 1438 refers to the 'market house' with almshouses beneath as being recently built. In other situations the almshouses were built alongside the guildhall, as at Stratford-upon-Avon. This long and continuous jettied range was built in about 1427, some ten years after the adjoining guildhall, but has since been enlarged and altered. After the suppression of the guilds in the sixteenth century, many guildhalls were converted to house the poor, particularly in the eighteenth and nineteenth centuries.

Not all almshouses and hospitals were connected with guilds or guildhalls. At Worcester, the 'Commandery' was originally the hospital of St Wulstan, founded in 1085 just outside the town walls. The

119. Lock-up, Barley, Hertfordshire

present timber-framed building dates from the late fifteenth century and derives its name from the masters of the hospital who from the late thirteenth century called themselves preceptors or commanders. The most interesting features are the great hall, which is impressive in both size and detail, and the wall and ceiling paintings depicting religious subjects in one of the first-floor rooms.

Many other hospitals were dependent on wealthy benefactors. After the Reformation large sums of money were still provided for charitable purposes, and a considerable proportion went towards the building and endowment of establishments to care for the poor and elderly. The majority are of course built of brick or stone but there are some interesting examples constructed of timber. One of the earliest is at Ewelme, Oxfordshire, founded in 1437 by the Earl and Countess of Suffolk to house thirteen poor men under the care of two chaplains. It is one of the earliest examples of an almshouse built on a collegiate plan with a timber-framed cloister around a courtyard, an arrangement unusual until the sixteenth century. The almshouses themselves are a good example of fifteenth-century timber-framed construction, based on three-foot-wide bays, being timber-framed with brick nogging to the courtyard and brick and stone externally. The group was originally thatched but is now tiled.

Another interesting group is to be found in St Mary's churchyard, Walthamstow, in the London borough of Waltham Forest. In 1527 George Monous, one-time Master of the Drapers' Company and former Lord Mayor of London, founded almshouses for thirteen poor people, a school for poor boys, a feast hall and a home for the schoolmaster

120. Almshouses, Pembridge, Hereford & Worcester

and parish clerk. The layout would appear to have been a central two-storey building, which housed the schoolmaster and clerk, flanked on either side by almshouses on the ground floor, with on the first floor the schoolroom on one side and the feast room the other. The latter was approached by an outside stair at the rear which was removed in about 1580, while the schoolroom had its own covered staircase, removed in about 1800, at the front. The west range was destroyed by bombs in 1940 and rebuilt in 1955 in red brick; the jettied centre section and east range were underbuilt and cased in brick. The school was closed in 1880 and is now, like the east range, flats for elderly people.

There are many interesting examples from the sixteenth and seventeenth centuries. At Thame, Oxfordshire, is a timber-framed group with brick nogging built in the 1550s as six dwellings. At Pembridge, Hereford & Worcester (120), there is another group of six built by

121. Stafford's almshouses, Old Harlow, Essex

Bryan Duppa in 1661, with jettied ends under a stone-slate roof. Also in the county – a most picturesque group – are Aubrey's almshouses, Berrington Street, Hereford, built in 1630, with all the characteristic features of that period. Old timber-framed almshouses can also be found in eastern England: at Old Harlow, next to the church, is Stafford's almshouse (121) built in 1630 by Julian Stafford, while at Thaxted, close by the church, is a row of almshouses also of seventeenth-century date.

More interesting are the few surviving examples of timber-framed hospitals. The medieval hospitals tried to cure both body and soul in one building, either by placing the wards within sight of the chapel or, more commonly, by forming a church-like building in which the chancel was the chapel and the nave the hospital ward. This is the arrangement at St Mary's Hospital, Chichester, West Sussex, in which the former ward space was divided not into cubicles but into seven (originally eight) self-contained flats, each with a bedroom and sitting-room, a unique arrangement which is still in use today. The building itself is of a great age, being probably built at the end of the thirteenth century, although the low range facing the street was rebuilt in 1905. The main building is an aisled hall with flint walls and timber framing carrying an enormous tiled roof sweeping down from forty-two feet at the ridge to seven feet at the eaves.

As previously stated, in the sixteenth century the work formerly undertaken by the church began to be carried out by wealthy bene-factors. Perhaps the most famous of these is Leycester's Hospital, Warwick(122), a delightful group, the fall of the street and the nineteenth-century staircase to the West Gate Chapel adding greatly to the overall effect. The hospital itself was founded by the Earl of Leicester in 1571, when he took over the premises of the guilds of the Holy Trinity and St George to house twelve poor brethren; it is still serving today as almshouses for ex-servicemen and their wives. The guilds had been formed in the fourteenth century, but the buildings must have been largely rebuilt in the fifteenth century and later increased in size by the addition of the two sixteenth-century timber-framed houses to the east of the stone archway. Through this archway one enters a courtyard which has on the east side an elegant wooden gallery on the ground floor as well as the floor above. The original guildhall is in the street wing, and in the west wing is another hall whose purpose is not now known. The master's house – where the master still lives – has a mid-nineteenth-century exterior with over-elaborate detailing.

Another medieval timber-framed hospital to be found in the Mid-lands is Bond's Hospital in Hill Street, Coventry, which together with Bablake School forms three sides of a courtyard open to the south. The hospital, which forms the north range, was founded in 1506 by

122. Leycester's hospital, Warwickshire

Thomas Bond, a city draper and former mayor, as a home for twelve elderly men, each having a bed-sitting-room. This range, containing the hospital, is mainly of 1506 although much restored – the west end was largely rebuilt in 1832 and the street face refaced and extended in 1846. The west range of the courtyard is entirely of 1832–4. A smaller but equally delightful hospital is Coventry's Ford's Hospital (123) in Greyfriars Lane, founded in 1529 by William Forde for the maintenance of five poor men and one woman. The street front is symmetrical, with its three oriel windows and three gables, and houses the common room and chapel. The central doorway leads into a long, narrow courtyard, some twelve feet wide and thirty-nine feet long. The building is an excellent example of its type with, at the front, buttress-shafts on both floors, moulded and carved bressummers, fine tracied windows and barge-boards. The same care has been taken in the inner court; the doorways have foliage carving in the spandrel, buttress-shafts again on both floors, excellent boldly moulded bressummers, and the front and back gables overlooking the courtyard carved barge-boards complete with finials. Ford's Hospital was badly bombed and was restored with pieces salvaged from this and other buildings in the town.

123. Ford's hospital, Coventry, West Midlands

Schools

As we have seen, early grammar schools were closely related to guilds: for instance, the Guild of the Holy Trinity at Finchingfield provided teaching for thirty scholars. After the suppression of the guilds in 1547, it was necessary, where a guild endowed a grammar school, to submit a petition to retain the school. Whether this was always granted is not clear but at Finchingfield a school was formed for the poor children of the parish in 1630 and the former guildhall used to house them. Grammar schools, as the name suggests, concentrated in medieval times on the teaching of grammar, not that of the spoken language but of Latin.

Because the guildhalls generally became parish property after their dissolution and because of the former connection between parishes, guilds and grammar schools, many former guildhalls were converted into schools, the often spacious first floors being ideal. Examples of this arrangement have already been mentioned – those at Stratford-upon-Avon, Ledbury and Felsted – but there are many other examples. In some cases, for instance at Barley, Hertfordshire, and Finchingfield, the school building was used in conjunction with other local needs, such as the council chambers and the village hall – in fact, any affairs of a common interest. This arrangement can also be found in other public buildings, such as the court hall, Milton Regis, and also the court house, Berkhamsted, both at some time used as a school. Another is the small building at Steeple Bumpstead, Essex: its original purpose is obscure, for though it was formed into the village school in 1592, it was unlikely to have been built as a school exclusively. Like other public buildings of that date, it had an open ground floor but was extensively altered in the eighteenth century and much restored since then. The grammar school, Steyning, West Sussex, was founded in 1614 in premises converted from the fifteenth-century buildings of the Guild of the Holy Trinity. At Needham Market, Suffolk, the grammar school was built in 1632 by Sir Francis Theobald of Barking Hall with materials from the former guildhall.

Two further timber-framed schools are to be found on the outskirts of Birmingham. One at Yardley (124), next to the church, dates probably from the fifteenth century, although it was not until the following century that the Trust school was formed, and its original purpose is not known. A similar building, also fifteenth-century, occupies a comparable position adjoining the churchyard at King's Norton and was for centuries an inn known as the Saracen's Head. The school at King's Norton, however, is on the north side of the churchyard and was originally the priest's house. Built in the fifteenth century, only the upper storey is half-timbered with the ground floor apparently underbuilt, probably towards the end of the sixteenth century.

124. School, Yardley, West Midlands

There are of course purpose-built timber-framed schools to be found. The earliest probably is Bablake School, Coventry, which forms the east range of the courtyard with Bond's Hospital. Founded by Thomas Wheatley, a former mayor, for twenty-one boys and a nurse, it now houses the offices of the Coventry General Charities. The school is the oldest of the three ranges, being built, it seems, in 1500. The back faces the road and has a stone ground floor with closely spaced studs above but to the courtyard there are open galleries to both the ground and first floors.

Schools of a slightly later date were built, as most public halls of the sixteenth and seventeenth centuries were, with open and pillared ground floors. One such example is Queen Elizabeth's Grammar School, Faversham, Kent. Built in 1587, the ground floor was originally open on two rows of timber columns with braces forming arches, as at the nearby guildhall. The upper part is now weatherboarded, but the timbers were originally exposed, with deep plastered coved eaves and shallow windows beneath. The building continued to be used as a school until 1880 and after being converted into tenements was purchased in 1887 by local Freemasons and adapted for use as their masonic hall. A similar school can be found in the square at Market Harborough, Leicestershire (125), a timber-framed building of 1614 with the open ground floor which served as a market space. The upper floor is pargeted, and on top is a small turret; undoubtedly some of its present appearance must be ascribed to the restoration of 1868.

Few of these schools are still used for scholastic pursuits. The old grammar school, Ledbury, continued in use until 1837 and was later divided into five tenements before in 1977–8 being restored by the Malvern Hills District Council as part of its contribution to the European Architectural Heritage Year; it is now open to the public. The Old School, Cradley, Hereford & Worcester, a fifteenth-century jettied building, is now the parish hall. Others – for instance, at Weobley, Hereford & Worcester, built about 1658, the old grammar school, in Barn Street, Lavenham, the one at Needham Market, Suffolk, and Hitchams School, Debenham, also in Suffolk – have been adapted into houses.

Shops
There is little doubt that the early 'shops' in England were no more than stalls or booths set up in the market-places or at fairs. The weekly markets provided all the needs for the community beyond that which they produced for themselves, while the annual fairs, with their temporary booths, provided additional goods not produced locally. From these, market rows often developed, with the temporary stalls becoming semi-permanent, then permanent, eventually evolving into small shops with living-accommodation over. One such example has recently been discovered by John Bailey at Middle Row, Dunstable, and is one of a terrace of four pairs of shops originally built in the medieval square. His investigations show that it was originally two separate buildings of identical construction built back-to-back, both jettied onto the street on the first and second floors with each

125. Grammar school, Market Harborough, Leicestershire

floor of each shop served by stairs built against the dividing party wall.

The earliest buildings thought originally to be shops are of stone. They are small with an undercroft and with living accommodation over, mostly of thirteenth-century date; examples can be seen in many of the medieval towns such as Stamford, Exeter, Guildford, Sandwich, Winchelsea and Rye. There is much documentary evidence of timber-framed town houses with lock-up shops to the ground floor, and sometimes with the upper floors containing lodging-rooms to house apprentices.

No early medieval timber-framed shops survive today but from the fifteenth century onwards examples can be seen. At Abbot's House, in Butcher Row, Shrewsbury (wrongly said to be the town house of the abbots of Lilleshall), the ground floor retains its shop front, said to be original with two narrow doorways and shop windows all with four-centred heads. The building probably dates from before the Reformation. Many more hide behind later façades, and time and alterations have obscured their original plan. In 1968, when the Shrewsbury Civic society restored to their original condition a group of timber-framed buildings known as Bear Step, it was discovered that forming part of the group were three sixteenth-century single-cell shops, interesting in that they opened off an open arcade. These arcades or walks, which once had market stalls along the edge of the pavement, were at one time a feature of many towns and can still be found in Winchester, Chester and Ludlow as well as in the small Devon market towns of Totnes – which has two, the Poultry and Butterwalks – Dartmouth, which still preserves much Tudor detail and carries the dates 1635 and 1640, and Plympton St Maurice (a rather fragmented walk).

Generally the medieval plan consisted of the shop facing the street with a chamber above and the open hall and service bay at the rear. Access to the hall and shop was by a passage at the side or sometimes by a passage which served the shop and went into a courtyard at the back with access to the hall by means of a cross-passage. Another, and perhaps more common, arrangement was for a shop at the front with a chamber over with access directly into an open hall at the rear. In some cases the hall was windowless. This arrangement can be seen at the fascinating row of medieval shops in Church Street, Tewkesbury, Gloucestershire. Here the accommodation is limited to a shop, hall and chamber all contained under a single pitched roof and with a store in an outshut at the rear.

Other rows of identical small shops can be seen at, for instance, York and Coventry. In Coventry a number of shops which survived the bombing of the Second World War are being dismantled and re-erected as one street – Spon Street. Some date back to the fifteenth and sixteenth centuries but, since they are used by modern commercial firms, give little idea of what a typical fifteenth- or sixteenth-century shop was like.

Timber-framed shop fronts from the fifteenth and sixteenth centuries have survived here and there. Eastern England has a number – probably due to the fact that they have been protected beneath a

126. Shop front, Lavenham, Suffolk

later covering of plaster and have only recently been revealed, the best known being at Lavenham, Suffolk (126). Essex probably has more than most, and examples can be seen at Kings Street, Saffron Walden, at Aubyns, Church Lane, Writtle, at Coggeshall and at Felsted. Elsewhere they can be seen at West Wycombe, Buckinghamshire, Lingfield, Surrey (127), Charing, Kent, Weobley, Hereford & Worcester, Ashwell, Hertfordshire, and Cerne Abbas, Dorset (128).

From examination of these medieval structures it is evident that the shop front comprised two or three unglazed openings, generally with four centred arches set below a square head. They often have some form of rebate to take some kind of internal shutter, or else the unglazed windows were secured at night by a pair of timber shutters, the upper one hinged from above, the lower one hinged from below. Both shutters opened outwards, the lower one let down to serve as an external counter during the day, and the upper one raised, providing shelter for the counter. These shutters can still be seen on a surviving

127. Shop front, Lingfield, Surrey

medieval shop at Lavenham. If sliding shutters were used, there is evidence that in some instances a shelf was provided pegged to the external face of the building just below the opening. In some instances the unglazed openings were fitted with a timber lattice, as can be seen at the medieval shop front at Charing. Not all shop fronts comprised two or three small openings: there is evidence that some had a single larger opening without mullions and arched spandrel panels, and this type survived well into the seventeenth century. In Cheapside, London, a row of identical timber-framed, gable-fronted, three-storey buildings, with shops under, built in 1585, still retain the unglazed shop front which remained an integral part of the structural frame, with the sill becoming the stall-board. Few shop fronts of this period survive for they have usually been replaced by later glazed shop fronts.

128. Former shop, Cerne Abbas, Dorset

Often these can be found inserted under the jettied first floor of a medieval building. However, the unglazed shop front continued to be used and still is today for some trades – butchers and greengrocers; and examples can still be seen – for instance, the butcher's shop, Brenchley, Kent, a sixteenth-century timber-framed building.

Alehouses and Inns

Inns and alehouses form another class of building designed for public use, those constructed of timber being some of the oldest and certainly the most picturesque. Alehouses and taverns must have existed in all medieval towns and, although most were probably secular in origin, in many towns and villages they had to compete with 'church ale' brewed and sold by the church. As we have seen, a church house, situated close by the churchyard, was usually used for this purpose. After the Reformation, however, the brewing of church ale ceased, and in a few cases the church house actually became the alehouse – for instance, the Fox and Goose Inn, Fressingfield, Suffolk.

More often, however, alternative accommodation was provided, either purpose-built premises close to the existing church house (which perhaps explains the close proximity of many to the church) or more likely an existing house or shop was adapted. These ale- or beerhouses were a common feature of many towns and villages from the seven-

129. The Fleece, Bretforton, Hereford & Worcester

teenth to the nineteenth century, and it is known in many instances that farmhouses and cottages were used, providing the occupants with additional income. In most cases alehouses died out during the nineteenth century, but some developed into the public houses known today. One of these alehouses, the Fleece, Bretforton, Hereford & Worcester (129), a farmhouse until 1840, has survived despite recent 'improvements', and the original concept is still much in evidence and gives some idea of what the old alehouses were like. Originally there was no bar; instead a hatch served all three bars. Behind the hatch was the 'tap-room', which also served as a beer-cellar. The beer, which as in most of these houses was brewed on the premises, was stored in a shed at the rear, brought into the tap and served from the hatch. Recently the hatch has been enlarged, and hand pumps have been installed. The building is now owned by the National Trust.

Although alehouses and taverns often provided limited accommodation for the traveller, their primary function was to sell ale, and in medieval times accommodation for travellers was usually provided by religious orders. Monasteries had a rule of hospitality which laid down that no traveller calling at the gates could be refused food and shelter. Hospices were often provided away from the monasteries, either on busy routes leading to or in towns which were popular centres for pilgrims visiting shrines. Greyfriars, Worcester (130), is one example of a guesthouse built for the Franciscans in about 1480. It has a lower and an upper hall, the whole façade being sixty-nine feet long with an archway leading into an inner courtyard flanked by two original wings.

Following the dissolution of the monasteries in the 1530s, the hospices began to disappear, and they passed into secular hands, often being run by the lord of the manor. Fortunately a few of these old guesthouses still survive; notable examples include the Star Inn, Alfriston, East Sussex, founded in the thirteenth century, parts of which date from about 1450; the King's Head, Aylesbury, Buckinghamshire, a timber-framed building dating from about 1450 which almost certainly started as a hospice attached to the Greyfriars monastery founded in 1386; the Falstaff, Canterbury, Kent, built in 1403, and the Pilgrim's Rest, Battle, East Sussex.

The George Inn, Norton St Philip, Somerset (131), was a hospice built by the Carthusian priory of Hinton and also served as a storehouse for the local wool trade. The original stone building dates from 1397, but a fire destroyed the upper floors which were rebuilt at the end of the fifteenth century in timber. There are other inns which incorporate parts of old hospices or which have been rebuilt on the site of an old hospice: the Ostrich Inn, Colnbrook, Buckinghamshire, founded in 1106 as a hospice, was rebuilt early in the sixteenth century; Ye Olde Bell, Hurley, Berkshire, founded as a hospice in 1135, was rebuilt at

130. Greyfriars, Worcester, Hereford & Worcester

the end of the sixteenth century, and the Bell, Tewkesbury, Gloucester-shire (132), may well have started as a monastic hospice in the thir-teenth century, for wall paintings of that date have been found on interior walls, although the building is mainly sixteenth-century and carries the date 1697.

131. The George Inn, Norton St Philip, Somerset

The Church and religious houses were not alone in providing accommodation for travellers, and there are many old inns still surviving which met the needs of the traveller. One of the finest is the Mermaid, Rye, East Sussex (133), rebuilt in 1420 on the site of an earlier tavern destroyed in 1377. Another is the Saracen's Head, Southwell, Nottinghamshire (134), an inn used by kings and nobles since the twelfth century.

By the end of the sixteenth century, hospices run by religious orders had been replaced by inns run by private enterprise, while more and more alehouses and taverns began to provide accommodation for the traveller. Many private houses began to be turned into inns to satisfy

132. The Bell, Tewkesbury, Gloucestershire

the needs of the traveller. Some notable examples are the Red Lion, Colchester, built in 1470 as a private house of a wealthy burgess and converted into an inn early in the sixteenth century; the Bull, Long Melford, Suffolk, built in about 1450 for a wealthy cloth merchant when the town had a flourishing woollen trade and becoming an inn in about 1570, and the Falcon and the White Swan, Stratford-upon-Avon, originally built for wealthy merchants. At the same time inns were also run by the lord of the manor, perhaps converting a former residence or constructing a purpose-built building – for instance, the Spread Eagle, Midhurst, West Sussex.

At the same time many new inns were built, often incorporating a

133. The Mermaid, Rye, East Sussex

134. The Saracen's Head, Southwell, Nottinghamshire

135. The George, Dorchester, Oxfordshire

136. The Llandoger Trow, Bristol, Avon

three-sided courtyard with two projecting wings at the rear, one for accommodation, frequently with an open gallery approached by an external staircase, the other one providing stabling. Perhaps the earliest of these inns incorporating galleried accommodation is the George, Dorchester, Oxfordshire (135), which still retains its staircase. Other notable examples are the New Inn, Gloucester, built in 1445, the White Horse, Romsey, Hampshire, and the George, Huntingdon, Cambridgeshire, which still retains an open gallery overlooking the yard with late seventeenth-century turned balusters and panelled posts and outer staircase. Often, as at the Bell, Thetford, Norfolk, an inn founded in 1493, and the White Horse, Romsey, these open galleries have been enclosed.

As roads improved, following the first Turnpike Acts in 1663, there rose an urgent need to provide more and better accommodation for the traveller. Inns had to provide rooms not only for the passengers of the stage-coaches and mail-coaches but also for those of private post-chaises and for horse-riders. As horses could be used over only a limited distance, inns had to provide extensive stabling for the horses which had to be changed at each stage. Although many inns were constructed to cater for this new demand, many of the old timber-framed inns were adapted, refurbished and enlarged, often given a pretentious Georgian façade; examples include the Bear at Devizes, Wiltshire, the White Horse, Dorking, and the Royal George, Knutsford, Cheshire, which dates from the fourteenth century. The courtyard plan remained popular but the open galleries had by now been abandoned. Some of the larger inns had two courtyards, the second courtyard surrounded by kitchens and other service rooms and stables. Private houses continued to be converted to cater for the growing demands – as was the Llandoger Trow, Bristol (136).

Houses

Timber-framed houses survive in England by the thousand (the total number can only be guessed at), ranging in size from the small two-roomed cottage to the large courtyard and quadrangular country houses of the fifteenth and sixteenth centuries. The earliest of these timber-framed houses date from the thirteenth century and are of manorial status, with the number of surviving examples increasing in each succeeding century until the end of the sixteenth century, after which the use of timber framing began to decline.

After the middle of the seventeenth century few traditional timber-framed houses were built. Lightly framed buildings, ranging in social stature from small detached farmhouses through groups of semi-detached houses to humble terraces, with a softwood frame and clad externally, continued to be constructed in parts of eastern England and the South-East from the late seventeenth century onwards and well into the nineteenth century. Timber-framed houses were at one time far more numerous than today, for many have been destroyed, especially in towns, and a large proportion of those that do survive have been altered and adapted to include the latest fashions, often obscuring their original plan. Those timber-framed houses located in rural areas are generally less altered than those in towns, where many have lost their identity when converted into office accommodation. Even so, timber-framed houses survive in a bewildering variety of forms, with local and personal factors often affecting the traditional pattern.

Medieval Houses

Most houses were designed for ground-floor living, but there were some which for some reason, usually defensive, were built for first-floor living. Generally these upper-hall type houses are of stone, built from about 1150 until around 1300, but there are a number of houses similar to them and of contemporary date built of timber. A number have later open-hall ranges built alongside, and it is often suggested that these earlier buildings were solar cross-wings to former ground-floor hall ranges which for some reason have disappeared. This theory cannot, of course, be disproved and in some cases may well be true, but the general arrangement and the high architectural standard of

237

some of these upper rooms, often with provision of a first-floor fireplace built at the same time as the house, coupled with the fact that there is generally no evidence of the existence of a former ground-floor hall, perhaps indicates that this is unlikely. It is equally unlikely that, at a time when such stone-built first-floor hall houses were being built, none was built in timber.

There are a few timber-framed buildings surviving from the end of the thirteenth century which are in arrangement similar to those first-floor hall houses built of stone. J. M. Fletcher cites two examples in Harwell, Oxfordshire. The southern range at Middle Farm (137) which was built about 1280, is of three bays, the upper floor being divided into a two-bay room to the front with a single-bay room at the rear. The height of the ground-floor room is at present about eight feet, but Mr Fletcher indicates that the original floor was probably less than six feet from the ground. Of slightly later date is the cross-wing at Wellshead Farm, a former parsonage and, like the south range at

137. Middle Farm, Harwell, Oxfordshire

Middle Farm, originally three bays long, although now part of the end bay has been demolished. From the evidence of the mortices in the posts, it seems that the original height of the first floor above ground level was about 5½ feet. In both these cases the ceiling height of the ground floor would have made them unsuitable for habitation, and they were probably used only for storage or as service rooms. At Steventon, Oxfordshire, similar ranges have been discovered at the old vicarage and priory.

However, as previously stated, the vast majority of medieval houses in England were not designed for first-floor living but for ground-floor living. The common, and indeed the only essential, feature of these medieval houses in England was the open hall, the nucleus around which lesser buildings were grouped, and this remained so until the sixteenth century. It was always the largest room in the house, open from the ground to the apex of the roof, which besides being the focus of life for a large household was also intended as a place of assembly for the transactions of public business, such as the manorial court. The principal features of these medieval halls, despite certain differences between various regions, were basically the same.

In or near the centre of the open hall was the open hearth (138), the smoke escaping as best it could through the small gablets at the junction of the hips and ridge or else through some form of louvre in the roof. Beyond the hearth was the 'upper end' which was occupied by the family and contained the high table and bench, possibly on a raised dais. This bench was usually fixed, being no more than a long, narrow oak plank some eleven inches wide and two feet high; it still remains in several of the halls of Lancashire and Cheshire. At Rufford Old Hall, Lancashire, it is about fourteen feet long and twenty-two inches high. Above the high table was often a moulded beam or covered canopy. These beams, often crenellated, are a feature of many Kentish halls of the fifteenth and sixteenth centuries. When such a beam is found, it may mark the springing of a former curved canopy over the high table. Most canopies have been destroyed, such as that at West Bromwich Old Hall, but there are a number, particularly in the North-West, which still survive. One of the finest is at Rufford Old Hall, which comprises moulded ribs forming thirty-six panels rising to a battlemented and moulded beam with scalloped soffit; above this the gable has a lattice work of quatre-foil panels. Even more ornate is the canopy at Adlington Hall, Cheshire, which contains sixty panels, with the bressummer carved and crenellated and with a drop tester of fourteen pendants with arches between. Most of the light in the open hall came from tall, unglazed windows on either side of the high table. In some cases a bay window was provided; examples from before the fifteenth century are rare, except for the possible one at Stanton's

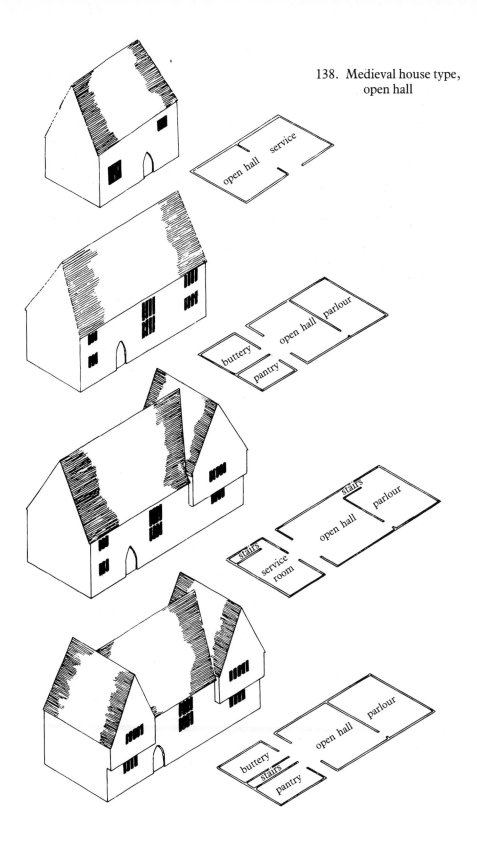

138. Medieval house type, open hall

open hall   service

buttery   open hall   parlour
pantry

stairs
stairs   open hall   parlour
service room

buttery   open hall   parlour
stairs
pantry

Farm, Black Notley, Essex, which may be original. In the halls of the North-West elaborate oriels of five to seven sides were provided, as at Ordsall Hall, Salford, and Rufford Old Hall.

At the other end, the 'lower end', the servants and retainers lived. In the open hall the social division between the family and the servants was marked by the central open truss. Even in the smallest house this division between the upper and lower ends is noticeable, with superior architectural details to all those parts not only in but also visible from the upper end.

The earliest surviving houses with an open hall are those of aisled construction (139) and are almost certainly of manorial status. These halls, which were larger than those in comparable later houses, had two large bays, approximately equal and each about sixteen feet in length. These aisled houses began as straight ranges of uniform construction under a lofty roof with low eaves. There is evidence, based on Fyfield Hall, Essex, and Old Court Cottage, Limpsfield,

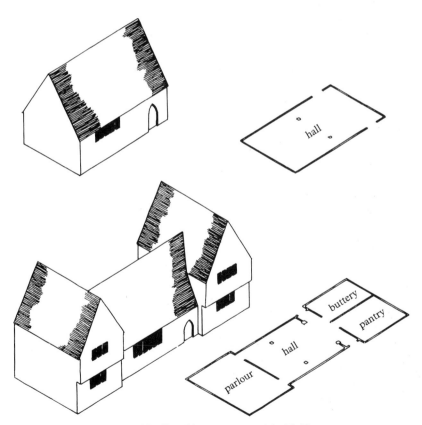

139. Medieval house type, aisled hall

Surrey, to indicate that a two-bay aisled hall without any other rooms was the simplest type of house; it persisted as late as the end of the thirteenth century.

The first development to this unitary plan was the addition of a further bay, built in series with the hall, at its lower end. This was probably at first a single-storey bay, but early in the fourteenth century, when Stanton's Farm was built, this service bay was of two storeys. The lower part of the hall therefore contained upwards of five doors – the entrance door, opposite which was usually a back door, together with up to three doors to the service rooms. Consequently there was a considerable amount of 'coming and going', and to lessen the draught caused by these doorways the end of the hall was screened off.

Screening was achieved by adding a further bay between the hall and service bay, structurally defined by a spere-truss forming a cross-passage known as the 'screens-passage'. At first the separation was only partial, with short 'speres' or screens projecting from the lateral walls into the hall beside each external door. In aisled construction these screens were formed between the arcade post and the external lateral walls, leaving a wide opening, known as the spere-opening, in the centre leading into the hall. This opening was filled with a curtain or a movable screen. (These movable screens are today rare, surviving only at Place House, Ware, Hertfordshire, a fourteenth-century aisled house, and the later Rufford Old Hall.) The service wing contained on the ground floor the buttery and pantry, each with its own door into the hall, and above these a chamber, probably the 'solar', for the private use of the family.

The next development, which occurred in the more important manor houses by the early fourteenth century, was the provision of a bay or cross-wing at both ends of the hall, although the earlier house types certainly persisted alongside it. The earlier examples of these two-storey end bays – late thirteenth and early fourteenth century appear to have been in series, with the hall contained within a larger single-storey building (Stanton's Farm, Lampett's Farm, Fyfield, and Tip-tofts Manor, Wimbish, all in Essex, and Homewood House, Bolney, West Sussex), and it was not until later that cross-wings began to appear in conjunction with halls. In these cases the cross-wings were almost always jettied, as at Baythorne Hall (140), Birdbrook (1360–70), Priory Place, Little Dunmow, and St Clairs Hall, St Osyths, all in Essex.

The lower end adjacent to the entrance still contained on the ground floor the service rooms, while above, the chamber was used according to circumstances, for guests, servants or the adult sons of the family. At the upper end, the ground-floor room was the parlour, used by the

140. Baythorne Hall, Birdbrook, Essex

daughters of the family or as a withdrawing-room after meals. From the often rough and rude square ceiling joists of the parlour in nearly all medieval houses, it is clear that this was not regarded as the 'best room' as it later was. The architectural details bestowed on the hall were not carried on into the parlour and service rooms, the ceiling joists and underside of the floor boards receiving nothing more than a coat of limewash.

Above the parlour was the solar. Sometimes this was of two bays, but more commonly it was of three, the third bay containing a small ante-room and staircase. In all cases the solar or chamber would be open to the roof, with a central open truss. Although separated from the open hall, the partitions to these upper rooms often stopped some two or three feet from the top so that the smoke from the open hearth could pass across both chambers and out through the gable end. With hipped roofs, the gablets at the apex were sometimes positioned above the division wall of the hall, and so this was avoided.

According to the social status of the household, there were one or two service rooms, either a combined buttery and pantry with a single doorway into the hall or a separate buttery and pantry each with its own doorway. In some of the larger houses there was a third door, which gave access to the chamber above or, in a few cases, to an outside kitchen. The main entrance to the house was situated at the lower end of the hall, well away from the central open hearth, separated from the hall by the screens-passage.

Aisled houses are to be found mainly in the South-East and eastern England and are generally thirteenth or early fourteenth century for by the early fifteenth century they were all but obsolete in houses of any importance. Only a few examples date from the fifteenth century: Skinners Cottage, Chiddingstone, and Fairfield, Eastry, both in Kent, Old Manor House, Keymer, West Sussex, and Sawyer's Farm, Little Cornard, Suffolk; but there is even one from the beginning of the sixteenth century at Depden Green, Suffolk. Most of the early aisled houses have been greatly altered.

Outside the South-East and eastern England, the only county in which aisled houses were once built is West Yorkshire, along the eastern edge of the southern Pennines. Although these too had a large open hall with two two-storeyed bays at each end, they were of much later date, being generally constructed at the end of the fifteenth and beginning of the sixteenth century. Being of later construction than those further south, the open hearth had been abandoned, and they had at the lower end a stone reredos against which the fire was laid beneath a firehood. Most appear to have been built of timber and partly rebuilt and clad in stone in the seventeenth century, making it difficult in most instances to know the number and extent of the aisles.

By the middle of the fourteenth century the aisled hall in eastern England and the South-East began to be abandoned, for the arcade posts, which impeded to some extent the clear floor area, proved inconvenient, so to obtain the desired uninterrupted floor space, yet maintain the overall depth of the dwelling, other methods were adopted. At Gatehouse Farm, Felsted, Essex, in the first quarter of the fourteenth century raised aisles were used. This form of construction was subsequently used on a number of buildings in eastern England. A building at Church Farm, Fressingfield, Suffolk, and Wymondley Bury, Little Wymondley, indicate a more advanced use of the same technique.

In many cases, however, the tie-beam on which the posts were supported was hardly more than head-height, destroying the visual effect of height achieved by the old open trusses of the aisled hall. This was overcome around the middle of the fourteenth century at Tiptofts, Wimbish, also in Essex, by the use of a hammer-beam truss which, as it did not require the tie-beams, left the roof of the hall relatively free of timbers, thereby creating the height associated with aisled construction. In some cases formed aisled halls were 'modernized' to provide the desired unrestricted floor; at Thorley Hall, Hertfordshire, for instance, the free-standing arcade-posts were replaced by hammer-beams.

Outside the South-East and eastern England the unrestricted floor was achieved by the use of the base-cruck. As we have seen, the distribution was much greater than that of aisled construction, spreading from Kent into the Midlands and down into the West Country, with the main concentration in Hereford & Worcester. The general arrangement of these base-struck halls was similar to that of aisled constructions. The simplest surviving example is at Manor Farm, Wasperton, Warwickshire, which when originally built comprised a single rectangular block with a two-bay hall and a narrow bay at one end occupied by the screens-passage and divided from the hall by the spere-truss. As arcade posts were no longer used, two stout spere-posts were introduced to support the truss, and a screen was formed between these and the external wall. Most base-cruck houses date from the fourteenth century, although a date of 1250 has been given to Hyde Farm, Stoke Bliss, Hereford & Worcester, by F. W. B. Charles, and dates of around 1300 have been ascribed to Chennell's Brook Farm, Horsham, West Sussex, Rectory Farm, Grafton Flyford, Hereford & Worcester, Moor Hall, Harefield, Greater London, Manor Farm, Wasperton, Warwickshire, and West Bromwich Old Hall, West Midlands. Like aisled halls, most base-cruck halls have generally been greatly altered and mutilated, often clad in stone or brick, so unrecognizable from the outside. The social status of these base-cruck halls is without question, for many bear such names as 'manor', 'manor house', 'hall' or 'old hall', 'court' or 'old rectory'.

With the decline of the manorial system, the importance of the hall also declined, and by the fifteenth century aisled and the various forms of quasi-aisled construction had generally been abandoned for dwellings. Yet the influence of the aisled hall continued to be felt in the medieval house plan right into the sixteenth century, with the hall, still open to the roof, remaining the standard house type in the South-East and eastern England. Although there are a few of late fourteenth-century date, the majority of these open-hall houses are fifteenth century. The simplest open-hall house was that of two bays, one containing the hall and the other the service room, both open to the roof, as at St Mary's Grove Cottage, Tilmanstone, Kent. Slightly larger was a house of two equal bays, one storeyed and the other open and heated by a central hearth. One such example is Winkhurst Farm, which formerly stood at Bough Beech, Chiddingstone, but has been recently re-erected in its original condition in the Weald and Downland Open Air Museum at Singleton, West Sussex. Examples of these single-bay hall-houses discovered so far suggest that this type may be regional, being relatively common in west Kent.

Slightly larger was the three-bay house with a two-bay open hall and the bay containing the service room below and solar above. There were

141. House at Barrington, Cambridgeshire

several variations to this house type: in some cases there was no partition between the open hall and service area, although there was probably some form of removable screen, and in some cases there were opposed entrances with the solar overshot. Next in size was the three-bay house with a single-bay open hall and a single-bay service room at one end with chamber above and a single-bay parlour with solar above at the other end.

By far the most common to survive today are the houses of four bays containing a two-bay open hall flanked at each end by a two-storey bay. Entry to the hall was either direct at the lower end of the hall or, more commonly, by way of a screens-passage. The screens-passage could be situated either within the hall or within the service room with the upper floor overshot. This four-bay house plan could be extended at either the parlour or the service end by an additional bay.

(142) The layout of the basic four-bay house was similar to that of

the earlier aisled construction. The parlour with solar above abuts the upper end of the hall, with the service rooms and a chamber over at the lower end. There was either a single door at the upper end, which gave access to the parlour with a stair leading to the solar above, or, in the larger house, two doors, one at either end of the partition, giving access to the parlour and to the stairs to the solar above. These doors were sometimes flanked by short projecting screens shielding the dais from the doorways. At the lower end of the hall there were one, two or three doors, one clearly indicating a combined buttery-pantry, while two indicated a separate buttery and pantry. When a third door was provided, this gave access either to the chamber stair or, less common,

142. Walnut Tree Farm, Liffenhall, Hertfordshire

to an outside kitchen. When no separate stair access was provided to the chamber above, a stair was located in one of the service rooms.

The open central hearth still remained the most common method of heating the open hall, but at the higher social level there are a few

143. Manor Farm, Brington, Cambridgeshire

instances of open halls which must have incorporated some form of stack – probably a timber and plastered smokehood – to remove the smoke. This must have occurred at Clintons, Little Hadham, Hertfordshire, a fifteenth-century hall house with a fine roof which has no trace of sooting.

Generally these open-hall houses were rectangular in plan with a solar bay, hall and service bay built in line. In many cases the upper storeys of the end bays were jettied sometimes at the service end, sometimes at the solar end but more commonly at both ends; in eastern England this was frequently at the front only, in the South-East to the front and occasionally to the back and ends as well. In the South-East the end-jettied hall-house is almost as common as those jettied at the front. It can also be found in eastern England but is far less common. Not all end bays were jettied, and in some cases similar houses without any jetty at all are predominant. This is true in parts of Sussex, west of the Weald.

In eastern England these jettied end bays were given their own ridged roofs set at right-angles to that of the roof to the hall and so in effect formed a 'cross-wing'. Occasionally these are extended at the rear beyond the face of the hall. This can occur at either the solar or the service end but rarely at both ends to form a U-shaped house. The eaves to the hall still remain lower than the eaves of the cross-wings but, owing to the abandonment of the aisle, not so low as those of preceding centuries.

In the South-East, particularly in the Weald, another house type evolved, known as the 'Wealden' house (144). The basic plan remained the same as elsewhere, although in nearly all cases the screen-passage is clearly defined, often by a separate narrow bay, usually about seven

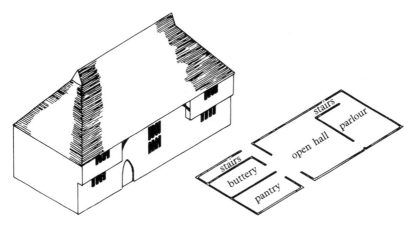

144. Medieval house type, Wealden

feet wide, between the hall and service rooms, and there was often a wide spered opening into the hall. In addition, instead of being roofed in three separate parts with three ridge lines, the complete house was contained under a single steeply pitched roof with one ridge line. The roofs of these houses was traditionally hipped – steep for tiles, slightly less so for thatch, and low-pitched for Horsham flags – rather than gabled, which can be said of most medieval houses in the South-East, especially Kent. Jettied end chambers continued to be used, but the front line of the eaves continued across the front of the halls to produce extra deep projecting eaves. Generally the eaves were coved and carried by means of a pair of arch-braces rising from the jettied walls. The treatment was the same whether the hall had one or two bays, but in some cases of a two-bay hall an extra arch-brace carried on a central corbel was introduced.

The origin of the Wealden house is obscure, but it appears at some date around 1400 – the earliest being Wardes, Otham, Kent (145), said to be of about 1370, while the finest of these early Wealden houses is in the hamlet of Larkfield, Kent – reaching its peak about eighty

145. Wardes, Otham, Kent

years later, and continued to be built for about another fifty years. The high standard of these houses can clearly be seen by the moulded partition beams and cornices and the moulded fascias to the jetties and also the elaborate glazed oriel windows with moulded jambs, mullions and transoms at a time when most houses would have had simple mullioned and shuttered windows without glass.

146. Old Bell Farm, Harrietsham, Kent

These Wealden houses are to be found mainly at East Sussex, Surrey and all of Kent, with the exception of areas of marsh, high down and forest, but with three-quarters of the total coming from the area covered by the extreme east of the Weald, the southern slopes of the 'ragstone' hills and downs and the plains of the north. The highest concentration within this area is to the south-east of Maidstone, which contains every variety of Wealden house. They survive in these regions by the hundred, not only as farmhouses but as village and town houses of the more affluent traders and on a few occasions are of manorial status. They were usually built as detached houses but there are a number of single-ended houses built in terraces, each with a similar recessed treatment of the hall and each borrowing the support from the outer wall plate from its neighbour. In 1977 D. Martin discovered one such terrace at Battle, East Sussex, where the jetties had been underbuilt in brick, and the timbers hidden behind a variety of cladding materials.

Old Bell Farm, Harrietsham, Kent (146), is one of the finest and most complete remaining examples of a Wealden house. Built in the late fifteenth century, it still contains its original front entrance door and four-centred arch, three doors in the screens-passage, its crown-post roof and one of its solid block stairs. The centre recess is coved, the bressummers to the jettied wings moulded, and there is a two-storey bay window to the hall which was probably glazed at one time for its full height.

Although the highest concentration of these Wealden houses is to be found in Kent and East Sussex, they can in fact be found in many parts of the country as far as York – 49–51 Goodramgate (147), in the North and Weobley, Hereford & Worcester, and the George Hotel, Yeovil, Somerset, in the West. Examples occur sporadically in eastern England and in the Midlands, particularly Warwickshire (148).

Some detached Wealden houses are jettied at only one end, and although there must be some that had one end bay removed at some time, as at Pullens Farm, Horsmonden, Kent (149), there are too many examples for this to have been always the case. When Bayleaf Farmhouse (150), a fifteenth-century Wealden house which formerly stood at Bough Beech, Chiddingstone, Kent, was reconstructed at the Weald and Downland Open Air Museum, the evidence was clear that the solar bay was built at a later date than the remainder of the house. Also the chamber over the service rooms is of such a high standard that it seems likely that this end of the house was for a time at least used as a combined solar-service wing. In addition, the solar wing has many details which differ from the remainder of the house, clearly indicating a different building date. These 'single-ended' or 'dimin-

147. 49–51 Goodramgate, York

148. Wealden House, Henley-in-Arden, Warwickshire

149. Pullens Farm, Horsmonden, Kent

ished' Wealden houses were frequently used in towns and in particular in terraced houses, like the group previously mentioned at Battle.

Unlike the aisled house, in the later open-hall house the central open truss was rarely placed centrally; one bay – sometimes the upper bay, sometimes the lower one – was always longer than the other. The overall length of the open hall obviously varied; some can be as little as thirteen feet, as at Pullens Farm, Horsmonden, Kent, which has only a single-bay hall; however, most two-bay open halls vary between twenty-three and twenty-six feet in length.

The type of central truss spanning the hall also differed greatly in various parts of the country. In the East and South-East the crown-post and collar-purlin form of construction was almost universally adopted, while in the West it was the arch-braced collar beam. Both these types, and especially the arch-braced collar-beam roof, which was probably the most ornamental type of roof, were

150. Bayleaf Farmhouse

given special decorative treatment, with the struts and windbraces frequently cusped. In the North the roofs were of the king-post construction with little decoration, probably due to the fact that the open hearth was never a feature in northern England and that the firehood, situated at the lower end of the hall, drew the occupants away from the centre of the hall.

In the West Midlands the medieval concept of a cross-wing was retained, as was the spere-truss supported on two spere-posts, an almost standard design in Hereford & Worcester, while in Cheshire and Lancashire it continued to be a feature as late as the beginning of the sixteenth century. The most famous were in the halls at Adlington, Cheshire, Baguley and Ordsall, Greater Manchester, Speke, Merseyside, and Rufford, Lancashire, where they developed from a simple draught-excluding device into an architectural feature elaborately decorated. The open hall in these areas continued to be built long after it had been abandoned in the East and South-East for houses constructed with two storeys throughout.

Over much of the highland zone open-hall houses of true and jointed crucks construction are fairly common, often comparing in size with those constructed in the South-East and East, but because of the nature of cruck construction these houses were generally less spacious, with a more limited range of internal design. Some of them were originally single-storey throughout and, from the evidence of the soot-encrusted trusses and rafters, were in some cases divided into rooms by only head-height partitions. A few of these open-cruck halls are of fourteenth-century date – for example, Hill Farm, Chalfont St Peter – but most appear to be fifteenth or early sixteenth century. Although in the West Midlands, and particularly in Hereford & Worcester, these cruck houses still retain their timber-frame, most of the external walls have been rebuilt in stone or brick or have always had stone walls.

Post-Medieval Houses
Towards the end of the fifteenth century the importance of the open hall as the dominant and principal room in the house began to decline, being replaced by houses constructed with two storeys throughout. The initial impetus came perhaps from the desire for more privacy that the greater number of smaller rooms provided, coupled perhaps with the desire for making better use of the upper storey, rather than from any inconvenience that the open hearth caused. Certainly in many cases the first stage in the modernization of the existing open hall involved the flooring-over of only part of the hall and the retention of the open hearth in the remaining areas forming a smoke bay from the open hearth on the ground floor to the rafters of the roof. Although houses with smoke bays continued to be built as late as the end of the sixteenth century and were not finally abandoned until the end of the seventeenth century, most of the old open halls probably had a chimney, either of timber and plaster or of brick inserted with the entire hall chambered over from the onset.

This change from the open hall to a house of two storeys throughout first occurred in the South-East and eastern England towards the end of the fifteenth century but elsewhere in the country the abandonment of the open hall occurred somewhat later. In the West substantial timber-framed houses, comparable with the largest to be found in the South-East and eastern England, such as Court Farm, Throckmorton, Hereford & Worcester, were still being constructed during the early part of the sixteenth century with an open hall. Even here, however, the open hall had generally been divided horizontally to give an upper floor during the sixteenth century, but it is clear from inventories that many still remained in use in the late seventeenth century. The room over the hall, in many cases because of the low headroom, became little more than a store and was normally referred to as 'the chamber over the hall'.

In both the South-East and eastern England by the beginning of the sixteenth century, and elsewhere by the reign of Elizabeth, all but those houses built in remote parts of England and for poor farmers and cottagers were being built with two storeys. Yet two medieval features remained: one was the hall, which still retained its medieval distinction of high and low ends, and the other was the screens-passage. This was no doubt due to the influence the open hall, which was not only an old but also a superior form, had on smaller houses long after it had disappeared in larger houses, and so a screens-passage, still flanked by the impressive ornamented timber screens, was often retained. This was so in many late-medieval houses which had a floor and chimney inserted into the open hall at its upper end away from the screens-passage.

With the abandonment of the open hall the jetties of the cross-wings, which, as we have seen, were a feature of so many medieval houses, could for the first time be extended for the full length of the house. The continuous jettied house (151), as this type is known, was probably the first vernacular timber-framed house type to be built with two

151. Smallhythe Place, Kent

152. Whitehall, Cheam, Greater London

storeys throughout. It still retained all the medieval features, with the hall, although no longer open to the roof, remaining the principal room. Above this was a great chamber with an open truss formed above. This chamber frequently referred to as the upper hall, was often treated with all the lavishness of decoration which was once given to the open hall, yet its actual usage is problematical. The external distinguishing feature of these houses is of course the continuous jetty along the length of the building, and in such a building a hall open to the roof would seem an impossibility. However, at the Blue Boar, Winchester, Hampshire, the two have been combined, the continuous jetty being made possible by the provision of a gallery, connecting the rooms at first-floor level at either end of the hall, built along the inside of the hall, the joists projecting to form the jetty. Although examples of the insertion of these galleries connecting the ends of the open hall are not unknown, this is the only case known to date which incorporates a jetty and must be regarded as a rare variant. The distribution of the continuous jettied house is widespread, and later, when such medieval features as the screens-passage disappeared, it still remained a standard

153. Jettied houses, Lavenham, Suffolk

feature in many towns and villages in most timber-framed regions throughout the sixteenth and seventeenth centuries, often incorporating later house plans.

The continuous jettied house was not the only type which succeeded the medieval open hall. At the same time the two-floored hall block between two jettied cross-wings and the two-storeyed L-house also made their appearance, continuing to be built throughout the sixteenth and early part of the seventeenth century. They, like the early continuous jettied house, retained the medieval concept of the hall and screens-passage with a stack either in the rear lateral wall or on a wall between the hall and parlour. Externally these later houses are often indistinguishable from those built in the fifteenth century which have had the roof to the hall raised when the upper floor was inserted, but generally the earlier form of open-hall houses have a steeper-pitched roof than the later ones.

Although the screens-passage or cross-passage remained an almost universal feature of timber-framed houses in much of the

154. Porch Cottage, Potterne, Wiltshire

highland zone, in the lowlands by the seventeenth century a new house type had evolved, brought about, no doubt, by the same domestic pressures that had led to the abandonment of the open hall a century or more before. It was a continuing process of devising a way of providing more specialized rooms and greater comfort. This was achieved by forming a narrow independent bay towards the centre of the building which incorporated the chimneystacks and a draught-free entrance lobby. Although these lobby-entry houses first appeared at the beginning of the sixteenth century, it was not until the end of that century that they became generally accepted, gaining popularity first in south-east England and spreading into East Anglia and then into the South and Midlands. There is evidence that a number of old houses have been converted to incorporate these new concepts either by the insertion of an axial chimneystack in the screens-passage or by the rebuilding of the lower end.

The basic plan of these lobby-entry houses was a simple one. It had an entrance towards the centre of the front lateral wall leading into a small lobby formed between two main rooms, the hall and parlour, by the introduction of a central axial stack, the lobby being in general the width of the stack. This layout had two main advantages over those houses which contained a screens-passage: the lobby reduced draughts, providing greater comfort to the two principal rooms, while it also provided independent access to both rooms, and, unlike those houses with a screens-passage, in which the parlour was rarely heated, the parlour of the central lobby entrance house was always heated, either from its own fireplace or (when only the hall had a fireplace) from heat radiated through the stack from the fire in the hall. In addition they provided some degree of symmetry, although some retained the continuous jettied front elevation.

Most of the early forms of this house type had two ground-floor rooms with only the hall or the hall-kitchen, as it had now generally become, being heated. These two-roomed houses continued to be built during the seventeenth century, although by this time, with the large chimneystack with four fires placed towards the centre of the house, it was usual to heat all rooms on both sides independently. From these two-roomed houses evolved the 'classic' asymmetric three-unit lobby-entry house which in the South-East and eastern England was almost universally adopted for all the larger houses built during the seventeenth century. The house comprised simply three ground-floor rooms – a heated parlour, a heated main room (the hall or hall-kitchen) and at the opposite end to the parlour an unheated service room with the entrance lobby situated between the parlour and the main room. Entrance to the service room was directly from the main room and

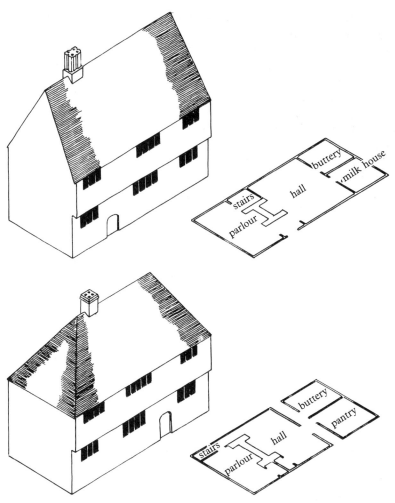

155. Post-medieval house type, continuous jettied

was commonly sub-divided into two, often with a communicating door.

To these basic two- or three-roomed plans there were several variations, and like other house plans these were generally associated with the position of the chimneystack and its relationship with the stairs. Generally the stack could be placed centrally within the depth of the house so that the return wall of the stack formed one wall of the entrance lobby – the one opposite the entrance door – with the stair, either a newel or straight flight, positioned between the stack and the rear lateral wall. In some houses the stair was housed in a separate turret at the rear of the stack. Another layout placed the stack against

156. Church Farm, Church Minshall, Cheshire

the rear lateral wall with the stairs elsewhere. Often it was situated in the entrance lobby, sometimes but not always adjacent to the stack itself, but in the two-roomed unit it was generally in the hall, while in those houses with three rooms it was commonly in the service room. In most of these cases the stairs were a straight flight rather than a newel. In some three-unit houses an additional flight of stairs can be found in the service room to give independent access to the third bedroom without going through one of the other bedrooms.

(157) In some houses the old-fashioned concept of gaining access to the parlour directly from the hall remained popular, and a lobby-entrance house was developed to retain this requirement. These houses were of only two units – the hall-kitchen and parlour, of which only the hall-kitchen was heated by a chimney or firehood situated on the gable wall, with the entrance lobby formed between the side wall of the stack or heck of the firehood and the front lateral wall, with a door from this lobby leading into the hall-kitchen. In some instances the entrance door was placed on the gable wall instead of the front lateral wall. Often the stairs were situated in the hall, sometimes adjacent to

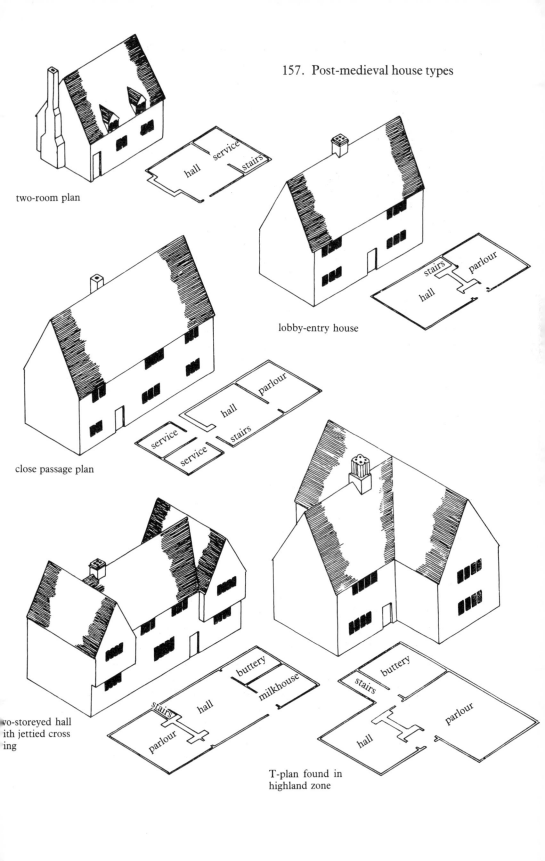

157. Post-medieval house types

two-room plan

hall service stairs

lobby-entry house

stairs parlour hall

close passage plan

service service stairs hall parlour

two-storeyed hall with jettied cross wing

stairs parlour hall buttery milkhouse

T-plan found in highland zone

stairs buttery hall parlour

the stack but commonly elsewhere. Occasionally the end unit would be sub-divided into a parlour and service room.

Not all houses were entered via a cross-passage or entrance lobby; in many cases access was directly into the house. This house type can be found in most parts of the highland and lowland zones, but those in the highlands are generally of later date than those in the lowland zone. In the South-East and East Anglia they are generally of fifteenth- and sixteenth-century date, while in the West and Midlands they are mainly seventeenth and eighteenth century. In the South-East and the East the access was generally at the lower end of the hall in the position formerly occupied by the door to the screens-passage. There is evidence that in some cases, when the medieval open hall was chambered over and a chimney inserted at its upper end, the screens-passage was removed, although both external doors were retained to form a way through. Some new timber-framed houses built in the sixteenth and seventeenth centuries retained these opposed entrances, and this was especially true in East Anglia.

In most cases, however, a single entrance was provided into the hall. In the two-unit house it was situated towards the centre of the house close to the parlour, achieving a certain degree of external symmetry, while in the three-unit house the entrance was at the lower end adjacent to the service rooms. Most halls were heated by a chimneystack in the gable wall or in the rear lateral wall. It was probably the only heated room, although in the three-unit house the parlour was occasionally heated by a gable-wall stack.

Timber-framed houses with cross-wings at either one or both ends are to be seen in many parts of the country, but in many cases these are not contemporary with the main range and are either later additions or possibly the enlarging or rebuilding of a former service or solar bay. There are some, however, in which the medieval concept of a hall range with a cross-wing or wings is retained. They are to be found generally in the southern half of the country, from Derbyshire south- wards, with the highest concentration in the western counties. In nearly all cases they were adaptations of existing house types, but there was a greater variation in the arrangement of the rooms. Unlike their medieval predecessors, these houses were two-storey throughout and often had in addition an attic.

Houses built in an L or T plan are fairly common in many parts of the country. In the lowland zone the main block was generally rec- tangular in plan and comprised the general arrangement of parlour, hall and service room built in line, with the wing placed normally at the rear, at either the solar end or more commonly at the service end. When placed at the service end, the end bay was often the kitchen, with the rear extension becoming the service room. Often, however –

and especially often in Essex and parts of Hertfordshire and Suffolk – the rear extension became the kitchen with an end-gable chimneystack. In some cases a wing was built at both ends to provide additional living and service accommodation and to form a U plan, also known as the half-H plan.

In the highland zone the cross-wing was almost universally located at the upper end to become a solar or parlour wing. This wing was generally of two bays, the parlour to the front projecting beyond the main range, with a service room, usually a buttery, at the rear. In nearly all cases the staircase was also placed in the solar wing alongside the buttery. Very occasionally in a few larger houses there were two parlours – the inner and outer – both heated by a back-to-back fireplace in the wall dividing the two. In the hall range the main variation was its length; occasionally it contained only a two-bay hall, but more often there were three bays, with that at the lower end being the kitchen. The entrance was either in the old medieval position at the lower end of the hall or more commonly into a lobby against the axial stack. In many of the timber-framed houses of Hereford & Worcester this axial stack occupied the upper bay of the hall, serving the hall and the parlour as well as the two upper rooms. They were particularly popular in this area, where the cluster of four chimneys at the junction of the hall and cross-wing is a common feature. They first appeared in about 1600 and continued to be built in Hereford & Worcester and other parts of the west Midlands until the eighteenth century.

The largest of these cross-wing timber-framed houses is the H plan, in which there is a cross-wing at both ends. Many closely resembled the layout of the T plan, with the entrance into a lobby against the axial stack which served the hall and parlour in the cross-wing and at the rear a store and staircase. However, the kitchen at the lower end of the hall was replaced by a cross-wing containing a kitchen at the front and a service room at the rear, with the kitchen usually heated by a stack backing onto the hall. Houses of this type are to be seen in many parts of the country, for their distribution is widespread, although not common.

In Hereford & Worcester another house type, less common than those previously described but still a direct development of the medieval hall plan, was the so-called 'solar' house in which the solar wing was enlarged – usually three bays and two storeys plus an attic range – while the hall now relegated to the kitchen became no more than a single-storey rear wing. Moat Farm, Dormston (158), dated 1663 above the beam to the end gable, is one good example.

In the house types so far described the common feature has been that only the principal rooms were the complete depth of the house, although some, such as the service rooms, may have been divided. In

158. Moat Farm, Dormston, Hereford & Worcester

addition the service rooms were nearly always situated at one end – the lower end. Towards the end of the seventeenth century there began to develop a change to this medieval concept which had lasted for some five hundred years: houses began to be more than one room deep, and for the first time the service rooms were relegated to the rear of the house behind the principal rooms. Even by the first half of the seventeenth century this desire for the service rooms to be located at the rear appeared in the South-East, and houses with a continuous outshut, containing perhaps a back-kitchen and buttery at the rear under a catslide roof, began to be built. By the end of the seventeenth century they had gained popularity throughout southern and eastern England, generally as adaptions of earlier house plans. These houses could be said to be the forerunners of the double-pile house.

Although builders had for many centuries both built and extended houses by means of a wing set at right angles to the main block to form an L- or T-shaped plan, it was not until the seventeenth century that an attempt was made to build a house of two sections, one containing the living-quarters and the other the service rooms, side by side. Each section still spanned the customary eighteen feet or so, each with its own pitched roof forming an M-shaped roof with a gutter in the valley formed between the two. The basic layout of these 'double-pile' houses is four rooms, the two principal living-rooms – dining-room and parlour – at the front, and at the rear the kitchen and another service room. The double-pile house was the ultimate development in house design at the vernacular level, providing a degree of comfort not found in earlier houses and coinciding with the demise of traditional timber-framed house construction. Many older timber-framed houses were adapted to form this house type by the construction of the kitchen and service rooms at the rear.

Town Houses

In all but those areas where there was a plentiful supply of stone, timber-framing was the normal method of constructing houses in towns until the seventeenth century. Then the effect of disastrous fires, such as those at Nantwich in 1583, Dorchester 1613, London 1666, Northampton 1675 and Warwick 1694, dealt urban timber architecture a blow from which it never recovered. It was not so much the effect of the fires as the subsequent regulations which were designed to prevent its recurrence. Town and city councils brought in bye-laws forbidding the use of timber – York, for instance, in 1645. These regulations, coupled with the ever-increasing cost of timber and the increasing popularity of brick, imposing new aesthetic standards, made, by the end of the seventeenth century, the town house built of timber an outmoded form of construction.

(159) Despite the destruction by fire of many towns during the sixteenth, seventeenth and eighteenth centuries and the subsequent redevelopment during the nineteenth and twentieth centuries, there are few towns where pre-eighteenth-century houses survive that do not have some example of timber-framing. Even in Devon, which has no rural tradition of timber-framing (apart from the occasional entrance

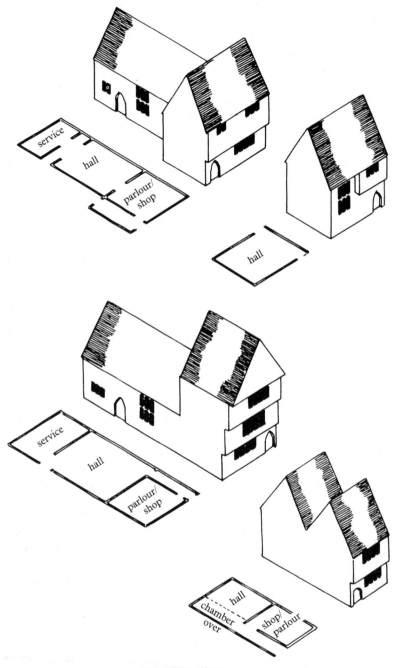

159. Town house types

porch), it is to be found in a number of towns. Here, and elsewhere in England from Cornwall to Cumbria, wherever there was good building stone this was used to provide fireproof walls between houses, and in many cases it seems to have been used for the back wall too, so that only the jettied front was actually of timber, clearly indicating the aesthetic importance that townmen attached to timber-framing. Examples of these 'three-quarter' houses, as they are known, are to be found in many towns of the South-West, such as Launceston (160), Plymouth, Totnes, Exeter and Dorchester, where they are conspicuous by the use of massive corbels carrying the gable end walls forward to match the timber jetties. Where freestone was not available for corbels, as in Herefordshire & Worcester and Cumbria, these houses are less readily recognizable.

Timber-framed town houses did not differ greatly in construction or design from those built in the country, and in most towns where timber-framed houses survive in any quantity can be seen a mixture of what could easily be rural houses. They had the same regional variations as before, but there was often a difference of emphasis in plan arising from their differing function. Aisled houses of timber-framed construction are unknown in towns, undoubtedly because little urban timber construction survives from before the fifteenth century, by which time, as we have seen, the use of aisled construction had generally been abandoned in domestic buildings. The reasons for the absence of timber buildings are to be found in the economic and social history of the country. English towns fall very broadly in two groups; those ancient towns founded before the Norman Conquest, which were centres of local administration in which the Saxon nobles not only owned a considerable amount of property but also lived, and those founded after the Conquest which were centres of trade, incorporating houses of a different kind and belonging to the smaller merchants.

In the first group of towns there are to be found a few large stone houses dating from the thirteenth and early fourteenth centuries which are probably houses of powerful local feudal families or ecclesiastical establishments. By the end of the fourteenth century these towns had some large timber-framed dwellings, comparable in size to manor houses, built either for wealthy merchants or for burghers. In some cases, as at York (the Red Lion in Merchantgate, 28–32 Coppergate and 35 Shambles), these houses incorporated first-floor halls. Others had ground-floor halls resembling manor houses of the period. These houses generally stood well away from the street, forming part of a complex of buildings – house, warehouse and shops – built around a courtyard, reached by a gateway between the row of shops which fronted the road. This typical layout must have been a feature of many medieval towns but few have survived and those that have been rebuilt

160. House, High Street, Launceston, Cornwall

over the centuries. Those of fifteenth- and sixteenth-century date often back onto a river range, as at the Old House, Shrewsbury.

The second group of towns have timber-framed houses, still with an open hall (a feature to be found in almost all types of town houses until the sixteenth century not only in the great town houses of the gentry but in every type of house above the very smallest town house), built not away from the street but parallel to it. Many date from the fifteenth century and are nearly always a simple straight range incorporating a small open hall and a two-storey bay of which the upper part was a solar.

Although throughout the fifteenth and sixteenth centuries, houses continued to be built with their long sides parallel to the street, it then became more common for them to be set at right angles to the street, thus presenting narrow gable-fronted elevations which are a common feature still to be seen in many towns. Their development clearly reflected the growing competition for space in city centres and the importance, no doubt for commercial reasons, of having a frontage on one of the main streets. The result was that in many towns the characteristic 'burgage' plot was not uncommon. Although these plots might be narrow, they were not necessarily small. In Oxford, for instance, in the main streets, where frontages were more valuable, the plots were long and narrow, sometimes two or three hundred feet deep yet only twenty or thirty feet wide. In the side streets the plots tended to be wider and less deep.

With such narrow sites the standard medieval hall-house with an open hall and a two-storey block at one or both ends had to be adapted, and the obvious and most practical plan was to set the hall range at right-angles to the street. In most cases the plan with the two-storey block at both ends seems to have been adopted, for, although the plots were narrow, they were generally deep enough to accommodate the longer house. Over the centuries these medieval town houses have been greatly altered, and it can now be only conjecture as to which end was the solar and which the service. However, it seems from medieval documents that the solar end was to the street, where the ground-floor room could be used as a shop, with the service bay at the far end of the hall, backing onto a courtyard and conveniently placed close to the detached kitchen at the rear.

Where the plot was of sufficient width, the hall range could be lit from the courtyard, even if this was so narrow that it was little more than an alleyway. Independent access to this courtyard was often provided from the street by a narrow through-passage. When the plot was narrow, it was necessary to make use of the entire width, and a problem arose in lighting the open hall in the middle when a two-storey bay was used at the end. In some cases it was possible to get light from

161. Town house, East Grinstead, East Sussex

162. Former Merchant house, Thetford, Norfolk

the neighbouring courtyard or perhaps from a window placed in the side walls, but this was practicable only if the adjoining house was shallow enough or low enough to avoid blocking them in. In many cases, the subsequent rebuilding of the neighbouring premises would have excluded any light to the hall, and there is evidence that in some cases the former end block beyond the hall has been either demolished or rebuilt as a single extension and windows put in to serve the hall. This difficulty in lighting the hall is presumably why in many cases the service end of the house was omitted and perhaps built beyond the courtyard. There was also a similar problem in providing access from the street to the hall, service rooms and courtyard beyond if the plot was entirely enclosed on both sides. To overcome this, a through-passage was provided, running the entire depth of the house from front to back and incorporated within the width of the house. This through-passage, it seems, went through the hall, the top presumably used as a gallery to connect the first-floor rooms at opposite ends of the hall.

Frequently medieval timber-framed houses stood on vaulted cellars which often elevated the 'ground floor' above the level of the street by up to three feet. When this occurred, a flight of steps was necessary to obtain entrance to the house. At Chester these raised ground floors developed into so-called 'rows' which are raised covered galleries at a half-storey position looked at from the street. There is no convincing reason to explain their existence, but A. L. Poole puts forward a theory that the space between the steps was occupied by stalls which eventually became permanent structures attached to the houses, the fronts of these houses subsequently brought forward to incorporate the stalls, narrowing the street by some four or five feet on either side by providing a covered footway at upper ground-floor level. Although these Rows are referred to in the city records of the thirteenth century, in their present form they date chiefly from the seventeenth and eighteenth centuries, with many dating from the half-timber revival which started in the city in about 1850, when many of the houses of Chester were rebuilt. Perhaps the best of the Rows can be seen in Watergate Street, the least commercialized of the main streets where they retain something of a semi-domestic character. Within the Row is Leche House, one of the most notable timber-framed houses in the city, basically a fifteenth-century building on a late thirteenth- or early fourteenth-century cellar which underwent a certain amount of modernization and additions in the seventeenth century and again in the eighteenth century but escaped the restoration which affected the character of so many houses in Chester in the nineteenth century.

The gardens to the rear of these hall-houses were over the centuries filled in, either with further domestic buildings or with workshops, warehouses or other minor industrial buildings. Where the hall-range was flanked by a courtyard or passage, the range could be extended indefinitely with no difficulty, but when the house occupied the entire width of the site, this was not possible and any additional buildings had to be detached and sited beyond the courtyard. In medieval times these 'back-blocks' probably took the form of a detached kitchen or other single building, but this has to be conjecture for they have generally been rebuilt. By the sixteenth and seventeenth centuries one finds more elaborate buildings of two or more storeys, frequently connected to the main house by a passage or gallery, occasionally at both ground and first floor. These galleries still remain a feature of many town houses in Devon, one notable example being the Elizabethan house (70 Fore Street) in Totnes, although this and the staircase have recently been rebuilt. Other examples of these back-blocks linked by a gallery have been found in Chester and Taunton.

As in rural houses, the open hall in town houses began to be abandoned by the end of the fifteenth century in eastern England and the South-East, though it was not until during the sixteenth century that it was superseded elsewhere. Medieval houses were modernized and altered by the insertion of floors in the open hall and the provision of enclosed fireplaces and chimneystacks. New house-types were also evolved, with those improvements in rural houses also to be found in town houses. One noticeable change was the use of the top floor, which in the medieval house was originally unceiled and open to the roof but towards the end of the sixteenth century usually ceiled to provide greater comfort and at the same time boarded to provide additional accommodation, the rooms being lit either by windows being inserted in the gable or by the insertion of dormer windows. At the commercial heart of the town, where space was expensive, the houses on the street front could be extended only upwards, with the result that in some towns houses which had up to this time been of two storeys were constructed of three. In such towns as London, Bristol and Exeter it was not uncommon for houses to be four or even five storeys in height, as well as having an attic. Given the width limitation imposed on many building sites and the continuing need to gain access to the rear, the side-passage house continued to be the most convenient urban plan. Within it the stair was of considerable importance, often situated in the centre of the building and providing access to more intensively used upper chambers which were now heated by one good chimneystack. Gable-end houses continued to be built; some were only one room deep on each floor but the majority were two-rooms deep, as in the earlier examples, often had a back-block at the rear to form a kitchen or perhaps a parlour with a kitchen beyond that.

Away from the prime sites, town houses continued to be built with their long sides to the street. Unlike the end-gable houses, these houses varied enormously in lay-out according to the width of the plots available, and all post-medieval house plans are represented, but certain variations of design obviously proved more suitable than others. The two-storey lobby-entry house with a continuous jetty became the standard house type almost universally adopted in many of the smaller towns, particularly Suffolk, while houses with a cross-passage are to be found in the west Midlands.

The largest of the timber-framed town houses which survive in England were frequently the residences of successful merchants and are generally to be found in the towns of the West. Shrewsbury has a number of such buildings, of which the finest is Ireland's Mansion, a three-storeyed jettied building with attic, built in about 1575, of four

RJBROWN '84

163. Rowley's Mansion, Shrewsbury, Shropshire

bays, each having a projecting bay-window to the two principal upper storeys. The centre two bays were Ireland's own house, flanked on either side by a single-bay house. Of slightly later date is Rowley's House (163), equally large but less flamboyant.

In a number of English towns, rows of small houses, each standing on a small plot, were a feature, tending to be long, narrow ranges often sited with their longer sides parallel to the street and only one room deep. At York such development had begun by the fourteenth century at Goodramgate and at St Martin's Row in Coney Street. The Goodramgate terrace, known as Lady Row, was built in or shortly after 1316 and originally contained nine or ten houses each consisting of one room, about ten by fifteen feet, on each floor. They are built on the edge of the churchyard, the rents collected from them being used to endow chantries in the church. It is an early example of a continuous jettied range of buildings and, unlike other, slightly later rows of houses built along and parallel to the street, did not incorporate a small hall open to the roof. At St Martin's Row, for which a contract survives dated 1335, each house was to have been built with a ground-floor chamber, with an open hearth, with a door and window towards the lane with the chambers jettied over the lane at the front and with a window on the opposite side overlooking the churchyard. The overall length of the row was a hundred feet, and it was eighteen feet wide at one end and fifteen feet at the other. Ranges of identical small houses are a feature of a number of towns, and the existence of these, which often incorporated a shop on the ground floor, implies speculative development for letting. The exceptionally complete range at Spon Street, Coventry, may be taken to illustrate the type that must have been typical in many towns. Each cottage consisted of a ground-floor hall, half of which was open to the roof, with an upper chamber over .the other half jettied onto the road and with possibly a cross-passage beneath the chamber from the street entrance to the yard at the back. These houses had recessed-bay open halls with jettied chambers facing the street or a two-storey range facing the street and an open hall behind.

Country Houses

The majority of rural timber-framed houses that survive today are relatively small, and apart from those of manorial status generally belonged originally to yeoman farmers and smallholders. During the latter part of the fifteenth and early part of the sixteenth century, however, a number of timber-framed houses appeared that were much larger than any previously seen, built or enlarged for the gentry who were at that time amassing large country estates. Why these landowners continued to build in the timber-framed tradition when many could undoubtedly have built their houses of the then fashionable brick or stone has never been satisfactorily explained. Without doubt, however, a man could, for the same capital outlay, construct a more commodious house in timber than he could in either brick or stone.

The finest of the houses are to be found in the North-West. The group comprises such notable houses as Rufford Old Hall and Samlesbury Hall, both in Lancashire, Speke Hall, Merseyside (164), Smithills Hall, Bolton, Ordsall Hall, Salford (165) and Bramall Hall, all in Greater Manchester, and Little Morton Hall (166) and Adlington Hall (167) both in Cheshire, all of which have quite rightly long been famous for their size and exuberant decorative framing, with an abundance of Renaissance detailing. The halls in these houses did not differ greatly from those in the rest of England: the usual entrance door led into a screens-passage divided from the hall itself by the spere-truss, as in so many houses in Lancashire and Cheshire. At the

164. Speke Hall, Merseyside

upper end of the hall was the high table, lit by an oriel window and
protected by a coved canopy above and on either side by screens from
the doorways to the parlour and chamber wing. Leading from the
screens-passage where the customary doorways to the kitchen, buttery
and pantry. However, in most cases this is where the similarity stops,
for these houses of the North-West are often distinguished by an
unusually long two-storey range of rooms at right-angles to the hall
and sometimes forming one wing of a courtyard enclosed on three or
perhaps four sides. Some, such as the range at Denton Hall, Hyde,
Cheshire, now used as a barn, were completely detached from the
upper end of the hall. A characteristic feature of these long wings is
the incorporation of an internal corridor on the courtyard side, as at
Speke Hall, from which the rooms are reached. The use to which these
rooms were put is not clear for they seem too large for servants and
were probably reserved for guests.

The visual unity of these buildings of the North-West often disguises
their complex and protracted building history, for seldom are they of
one build. Little Morton Hall is one excellent example. The earliest
part of the house is the north range together with the great hall which
was completed in the late fifteenth century. The first-floor room in the

165. Ordsall Hall, Greater Manchester

166. Little Morton Hall, Cheshire

north-west corner was probably the principal solar, the rooms beneath
being the buttery, pantry and kitchen linked by the screens-passage
to the hall. Further rooms must have stood to the east of the hall
but these were undoubtedly remodelled when the parlour and
withdrawing-room were built. In the mid-sixteenth century the now
unfashionable great hall was sub-divided by the insertion of a floor.
At the same time the sleeping accommodation to the east was transformed, and two large bay windows were inserted overlooking the
courtyard to light the hall, the new withdrawing-room and the rooms
above. This work was carried out in 1559 by Richard Dale. Later in
the century the building was further enlarged; a chapel was provided
and finally the south wing, with its long gallery which looks like an
'after-thought', but there is no structural evidence that the gallery was

167. Adlington Hall, Cheshire

superimposed on an already completed first floor. Other halls also show this continuing development: at Bramall, for instance, the south range with the chapel is of fifteenth-century date while the remainder is late sixteenth or early seventeenth century (the dates 1592, 1599 and formerly 1609 are inside) while at Samlesbury the hall is fifteenth century, with the long south range, except the west end which was added in 1862, built in about 1545.

These houses are famous not only for their external decoration: internally they were often equally elaborate. Needless to say, the great hall received most of the decoration. The spere-truss within the hall developed from the simple draught-excluding device found in the South into an architectural feature elaborately decorated. Undoubtedly the two finest are those at Adlington and Rufford, almost identical, with each of the posts worked in a series of trefoil-headed panels and separated from the adjoining one by a roll-moulding with the posts linked by a four-centred arch formed in two braces. Similar spere-trusses are to be found at Little Morton Hall and Ordsall Hall. At Adlington a battlemented moulded beam, which spans the hall above the dais, provides the springing for the great panelled canopy upon which are displayed the arms of many Cheshire families. While unique in both heraldic display and size, many of the halls of the North-West possess more modest versions of it. The roof structures too received this elaborate detailing. The finest roof is undoubtedly at Old Rufford Hall with its splendid five hammer-beam trusses. The hammer-beams have carved angel figures and the arched braces up to the collar-beam have bosses in their centres. In addition there are three tiers of windbraces forming quatrefoils and in their centre concave-side square paterae. Adlington too has a hammer-beam roof plastered between the purlins with a dormer window on the south side.

Besides these notable examples already mentioned there are other large timber-framed houses of note in the area. In Cheshire, for instance, there is Gawsworth Old Hall, now with 2½ ranges but originally of three or four. The original planning and function of the remaining rooms are not clear. In Greater Manchester one can cite Baguley Hall, Wythenshawe, the earliest of the great halls of the North-West of early fourteenth-century date. Near Baguley is Wythenshawe Hall, of early sixteenth-century date, while Hall i't Wood, Bolton, is certainly one of the most attractive of all the timber-framed houses in the North-West. In Shropshire there is Pitchford Hall undoubtedly the most splendid of all the black-and-white buildings in the county. Built by Adam Otley, a wool merchant of Shrewsbury, in about 1560–70, the house is on the E plan but with square projections in the re-entrant angles between the wings and centre. Unlike many of the larger houses further north, the decoration here is obtained only

168. Preston Court, Gloucestershire

by the use of diagonal struts forming lozenges within lozenges with none of the concave cusped lozenges and other elaborate designs to be found except for the quatrefoils in the porch. In Staffordshire one can cite Broughton Hall of 1637, the most spectacular black-and-white building in the county, made even more so in 1926–39 when the size was doubled. However, more delightful is Hall o'Wood, Balterley.

In the South-East and East large timber-framed houses are also to be found, although none compares in size with those in and around the North-West. Many, such as Crowhurst Place, Surrey, of about 1725 and the slightly later old Surrey Hall, near Lingfield, owe much of their present size and appearance to later 'restoration', in these cases by George Crawley between 1918 and 1922. In Sussex one can cite Horselunge Manor, Hellingly, one of the most spectacular houses in the county, due to some extent to Walter Godfrey who in 1925 transformed the house as near as possible to the original built early in the sixteenth century, and Great Dixter, which Lutyens enlarged in 1910 with a complete timber-framed building from Benenden.

Gatehouses

Houses built around the gate of many castles and manor houses were originally a defensive feature of some importance. Later, though no longer used for defensive purposes, many manor houses, farms and moated sites retained these gatehouses in a modified form until the beginning of the seventeenth century. Many of these later gatehouses

169. Gatehouse, Cheylesmore Manor, Coventry

were constructed of timber and, although unfortunately most have now disappeared, a few still survive.

Several, such as those at Ashby-St Ledger, Northamptonshire, Wigmore Abbey, Hereford & Worcester, and Bromfield Abbey, Shropshire, have a lower storey of stone, while others, such as the Old Hall, Mavesyn Ridware, Staffordshire, have been underbuilt in brick. The majority, however, are of timber throughout, some such as those at Little Morton Hall, Cheylesmore Manor, Coventry (169), and West Bromwich Manor House, West Midlands, forming, or

170. Gatehouse, Abington Piggotts, Cambridgeshire

formerly forming, part of a courtyard complex, their purpose to control access into the courtyard from which the house was reached. Most, however, are isolated structures belonging to farms and manor houses, many of which were moated sites.

These gatehouses are usually of two storeys, often jettied on two or more sides. The majority have a single large opening on the ground floor for waggons and horses but some, such as the one at Down Hall Farm, Abington Piggotts, Cambridgeshire (170), have a separate pedestrian entrance. Sometimes, at the more substantial ones, there is a room to one side of the entrance, while in all cases there was a room above running the full length of the building, sometimes, as at Stokesay Castle, Shropshire, incorporating an oriel window. This gatehouse at Stokesay is without doubt one of the finest examples remaining, built towards the end of the seventeenth century, when the crenellated outer walls were reduced. Of equal charm is Lower Brockhampton Manor, Hereford & Worcester (171), late fifteenth century with an upper floor projecting on all four sides. Other timber-framed gatehouses of note

171. Lower Brockhampton Manor, Hereford & Worcester

172. Gatehouse, Rectory Farm, Northmoor, Oxfordshire

that still survive are at Frocester Court, Gloucestershire, with four gables, and Rectory Farm, Northmoor, Oxfordshire (172). Only one of these small timber-framed gatehouses survives in the north of England, at Bolton Percy, near Tadcaster, North Yorkshire, an early fifteenth-century structure with fine detailing restored with the aid of Avoncroft Museum of Buildings in 1974.

Porches

Porches with a small room over are a feature to be found on many Elizabeth and Jacobean timber-framed houses. These structures, frequently jettied on the first floor, first appeared at the end of the sixteenth century and were often the first part of the house to exhibit the new Renaissance ornamentation and detail. The reason for their introduction is not clear but certainly the main practical reason was to reduce the draught from the main doorway, consequently increasing the comfort of the inhabitants of the house and in particular those using the hall. Even so, it is not uncommon for porches to have open balustered sides to the ground floor which would undoubtedly reduce

173. Woundale Farm, Woundale, Claverley, Shropshire

174. Dairy Farm, Tacolneston, Norfolk

175. House, High Street, Castle Donington, Leicestershire

their effectiveness in this respect. At Woundale Farm, Woundale, Claverley (173), Shropshire, the upper floor is also open, and the purpose of this structure must have been ornamental rather than practical. Certainly timber-framed porches were regarded as being of high social standing, for even in those areas where timber-framed construction had little or no significance – for instance, in Devon and Cumbria – timber-framed porches were constructed on houses where the main structure was cob or stone.

Two-storeyed porches are of course to be found on many of the larger timber-framed houses in the country, but it is probably those on smaller buildings that are seen to their best effect. They are to be found on some village houses, the most notable being Porch House, Potterne, Wiltshire, but it is on farmhouses and similar buildings that most occur. The most unusual of these is the three-storeyed porch at Dairy Farm, Tacolneston, Norfolk (174), the first and second floors set back from the one below, each with its own gable.

Although most two-storey porches are in rural areas, they were at one time equally fashionable in towns. Now almost all have been totally removed – if not by the Georgians in their desire to produce regular elevations, then by two centuries of road-widening schemes. Evidence of the former presence of porches in towns comes largely from fines imposed and recorded in borough accounts for encroaching on the pavement and from the existence of the empty mortices in timber-framed houses particularly of the Jacobean period. In some of the smaller towns these porches still remain, as at Castle Donington, Leicestershire (175).

Farm Buildings

Of all timber-framed buildings, those connected with the farm are perhaps the most vulnerable. In most cases these buildings have no future, for all – barns, granaries, cattlesheds, stables, cartsheds and other traditional farm buildings – were functional buildings designed for a specific purpose which few can now satisfactorily serve. The usefulness of the barn – which in its true sense was designed exclusively for storing unthreshed corn and for winter threshing by manual labour – began to decline as far back as 1788, when Andrew Meikle patented the threshing machine. Old cattlesheds no longer met the requirements of modern dairy farming or the hygiene regulations in force today. With horses no longer kept on farms, other than those for riding, which are more likely to be kept in loose-boxes, the stable is rarely used. The dovecots that still survive are more often than not picturesque garden ornaments, with the doves kept for pleasure rather than for meat and manure. Granaries have been replaced with silos and hoppers, while cartsheds and other implement stores, although still often used, are generally too narrow and low for much of today's machinery.

These traditional buildings, no longer meeting the needs of modern farming, have been either put to some new use or allowed to remain under-used and partially empty, or, because they are expensive to repair and conserve, have become derelict, finally to be demolished. Although an ever-increasing number of these buildings are disappearing from the English landscape, many still survive. Some have been put to other uses, often converted to dwellings. This is not only true of barns but also applies to other farm buildings. Granaries – for instance, one at Felsted, Essex – and dovecots have been successfully incorporated into new houses.

Barns

The barn is the most obvious and familiar of all farm buildings. It has for some six hundred years dominated many farmsteads, not only by its sheer size but also in that it was the building in which the corn crop was housed, on which the farmer depended for his continuing livelihood, where the threshers worked throughout the winter and in which the threshed straw was kept prior to its use as litter or fodder

294

for the cattle. It may also have housed pulse crops grown on the farm such as peas and beans. The barn was therefore the most important of all the working buildings on the farmstead, taking pride of place amongst the farm buildings.

The size and distribution of these barns reflect not only the wealth of the farmer but also the national and local farming patterns. In areas where pastoral farming predominated or where the land was enclosed at an early date or where gravelkind, the system of inheritance by which land was shared equally among sons, was common, the barns were generally small, but where arable farming predominated or there was a late enclosure of the land, resulting in larger farms, the barns were generally large.

No matter what size the barn, a standardized pattern evolved over the centuries for storing and processing grain. In its simplest form, and what could be considered the standard English barn, it was divided into three bays, the central bay containing the threshing floor, which in England was traditionally placed transversely across the barn and not, as in some parts of Europe, along the length, with the two end bays used for storage. The threshing floor was generally in the middle but not necessarily so, for there are examples of their being off-centre with the side bays of differing lengths. Why this was so is not clearly understood. The central bay was served by a pair of large double doors in opposite walls, the waggons from the fields entering one door, unloading the corn, which was either loose or bound into sheaves, and leaving by the other door. Larger barns, usually of five bays, are simply an enlargement of this basic plan, comprising three storage bays and two threshing floors, each with a set of doors. On many of the large farms, as an alternative to the large barn, two smaller barns were often provided. Very occasionally one finds barns with three threshing floors, as at Leighs Lodge, Felsted, Essex. All barns were, however, built on the same principle and fulfilled the same function.

The barn was completely filled with crops, leaving only the threshing floor clear, with the crops being stacked up as high as possible, well into the roof space. The practice of using half of the barn for the storage of threshed straw, filling one side only with the unthreshed corn, is, it seems, a later development. During the winter months the corn was threshed by hand with the use of a flail, an implement which is basically two sticks joined by a flexible knot, the smooth wooden handle about three feet six inches long, and the swingel, the part that strikes the straw to shake out the grain, about two feet. This laborious and extremely arduous work was carried out by five or six men at a time, in the threshing bay. The threshing floor needed to be hard, and various materials were used. Stone flags were a popular material in those areas where stone was readily available, as was rammed chalk.

Bricks laid on edge was another type and can still be seen (at Grange Farm, Coggeshall, Essex) but the wooden boarded floor, though once a traditional form of covering, is now rare because of its susceptibility to rot.

After threshing, the winnowing of the corn could begin. This entailed the cleaning of the corn to remove the dust and chaff; the grain was collected together into a heap on the floor, the doors to the barn were opened to ensure a through draught, and the grain was thrown into the air. This blew away the light dust and chaff whilst the heavier grain fell to the ground. The grain was cast into the air by means of wooden shovels – casting shovels – and often thrown into wooden sieves to assist in removing foreign material. The barn was so orientated that the doors opened into the prevailing winds, thus enabling the maximum of through draught. In the nineteenth century a winnowing machine, called a blower, was introduced, enabling the chaff to be more readily removed. This machine comprised five fans fixed to a central spindle turned by hand and placed with its tail to the barn door so that any wind assisted in blowing the chaff away. Once dressed, the grain was either stored in a granary or measured into bushels – the standard measure – and taken to the mill or sold. The chaff from the corn was stored and used as fodder for cattle, either by itself or mixed with chopped root crops, while the straw was stacked and used later for litter, fodder or occasionally thatching.

Barns, like other traditional buildings, were constructed with materials prevailing locally, so in all those areas where timber was available – in eastern England, the South, the South-East, the West and the west Midlands – there are still plenty of timber-framed barns to be seen despite the fact that they are being destroyed at an increasing rate. In construction they are as good as any of the houses within the area, for the barn was of high social standing and was given as much architectural detail as could be afforded.

In the South-East and eastern England many of the early barns were clad with vertical, square-edged boarding which was housed in grooves in the underside of the eaves-plates, pegged to cross-rails, usually at midway, and to the outer edge of the sill-plate. The enduring qualities of this type of boarding are evident by the fact that examples, for instance at Frindsbury, Kent, dating from about 1300, and Upminster, Essex, from about 1430, still survive, although now much at Upminster has been replaced with horizontal boarding. That many early barns originally had an infilling of wattle-and-daub can be proved by the presence of wattle grooves. Little now survives, having been generally replaced in these areas with weatherboarding. In some instances wattle-and-daub can be found beneath the later weatherboarding. Today black horizontal weatherboarding is by far the standard cladding material, and it is to be found throughout the South-East, southern and eastern England, the large, sweeping red tiles or occasionally thatched or pantiled roofs still a joy to be seen. Only occasionally in these areas does one find a barn which has been clad with plaster, and in some cases weatherboarding and plaster finish can be seen together, particularly in Essex and Hertfordshire, with the plaster above the weatherboarding being more common than the reverse arrangement. Brick nogging has survived in a few cases but those that do are usually much repaired. It was sometimes used, as at Wheat Barn, Cressing, Essex (176) as a replacement of an early infilling material, although some good examples are to be found, among the most notable being the barn at New Hall, High Roding, Essex, and the Old Hall, Tuddenham, Norfolk.

In the western half of the country weatherboarded barns are less common, although they can be found, and those with wattle-and-daub and later brick infilling are far more common. A feature that was at one time common in the West, particularly in Hereford & Worcester and Shropshire, was the infilling of the open panels with split oak

RJBROWN '85

176. Wheat barn, Cressing, Essex

pales woven around vertical oak staves and left undaubed to permit air to ventilate the stored crops. Although most of these panels have now been replaced with brick, a few are still to be seen, for instance at Wichenford, Hereford and Worcester.

Barns clad with weatherboarding needed no provision for ventilation, for the boards rarely fitted closely, but when brick-nogging was employed, air vents were provided by omitting bricks to form various patterns.

No matter what the size, the working arrangement of these barns was the same, although many features differed. Externally the most prominent features were the doors to the threshing floor. The most common type was the pair of hinged, ledged, braced and battened doors, those to the entrance being larger than the one at the rear to allow access of a fully laden waggon into the threshing floor for unloading. In some instances there was only one door to the threshing floor, preventing a through draught essential for winnowing which meant that carts had to be backed out. This arrangement was not common in timber-framed barns. Sometimes the large double doors were cut horizontally, dividing the doorway into two pairs, the lower pair some five feet high, the upper pair slightly higher, generally between seven and ten feet. This arrangement enabled a man to enter without opening the whole door. These large doors were designed so that they could be swung open 180 degrees and hooked back against the wall; when closed they were held in position by a removable vertical timber, known as a 'middlestree', square in section, which fitted into a pocket in the door lintel at the top and a hole in the floor below. In many cases the barn doors stopped a foot or two above the ground, and the space between the bottom of the door and the ground was filled in with a series of separate boards held in position by timber battens fixed to the door frame. The lift, as these boards are known, stood in front of the middlestree, both of which were removed when the waggons entered. The purpose of the lift was that it enabled the doors to clear the manure in the yard, to stop animals, especially pigs, from entering when the doors were open; it also had the advantage of stopping any grain which might fly out during the flailing.

Waggon porches too are to be found. They are a feature on many surviving medieval barns as well as some of later ones built in parts of southern and eastern England. Their advantage was that they provided an additional threshing area and gave protection to it when the doors were open during the winnowing. In Suffolk a small lean-to addition, known as a 'cornhole', was often provided at the angle between the barn and porch. Its purpose was to store the grain and chaff after it had been flailed until sufficient had been collected to enable the winnowing to take place. In most cases they seem to be

177. Barn, Mutlow Farm, Wendens Ambo, Essex

later additions and were undoubtedly in connection with the later machinery for this operation. When the barns were of aisled construction, resulting in low eaves, a gable within the roof had to be provided to enable the loaded waggon to enter the barn. A porch as such was not provided, for generally it did not project beyond the lower walls but a dormer-like structure was built, enabling the loaded waggons to enter in the normal way. Sometimes the dormer roof extended over the doors to form a canopy supported on timber brackets, a common feature in Kent and other parts of the South-East. Small doors were also often provided at high level to the sides and sometimes to the ends of many barns. These were used for pitching corn or hay into the barn from a cart standing outside and were often essential when the barn was getting full. They also provided light and air when the barn was not full. These doors often gave access to the high-level platforms provided within some barns.

Internally barns were generally open from end to end, there being no sub-divisions, with the exception of some aisled barns which had a tie between the arcade post and the outer wall framing, this remained so in most parts of the country. In the Welsh border counties and those of the west Midlands, however, from the seventeenth century until well into the nineteenth century, timber-framed barns began to be divided into bays. At first the most usual arrangement of this sub-division was to provide a tie-beam some two or three feet above the floor framed at both ends into the main posts of the wall frame. Between this and the tie-beam to the roof truss a vertical post was framed with two curved braces between the lower tie-beam and the main posts. In later examples the vertical post and curved braces were replaced by two raking struts. The advantage of this arrangement was both structural and practical. Structurally it strengthened the walls against pressure from the wind externally and the weight of the crops internally, as well as strengthening the doorposts against the weight of the doors, which were often vulnerable. Practically it helped to separate the loose crops or straw from the threshing floor. Sometimes the lower section was boarded, which helped to retain the grain which flew about when being flailed.

The majority of traditional timber-framed barns date from the seventeenth and eighteenth centuries. There survive a few, however, which belonged to medieval monastic granges dating from the twelfth and thirteenth centuries, and these, together with other large barns, are sometimes called tithe barns. The name is correctly used to describe those barns built on ecclesiastical estates to store tithes – a form of tax paid to the Church in kind, generally corn and not in money – but while there seems little evidence that many of these barns survive, the payment of tithes was for many centuries an important part of village life. Undoubtedly many of the early, large barns were of manorial status and were obviously used to store tithes as well as the produce from the demesne farm itself.

The majority of these early barns are of aisled construction (178). There are many splendid examples, and to those with timber-framed walls can be added cathedral-like barns which have timber aisles and external stone walls, such as those at Great Coxwell, Oxfordshire, and Bredon, Hereford & Worcester.

The earliest of these aisled barns is the Barley Barn, Cressing, which is considered by Mr C. A. Hewett to date from around 1130 (he has obtained radio-carbon dating of the timbers as about 1000–1060 but this of course indicates the age of the wood, not the date of construction). Close by is the Wheat Barn thought to be late thirteenth century. Both have aisles and scissor bracing, and it was here that the historical significance of this feature was first recognized. These two barns, together with a third, dated 1623, form an exquisite group. Essex is rich in medieval barns, and others of early date are those at Grange Farm, Coggeshall, which is twelfth century and Prior's Hall, Widdington, built around 1300 (179).

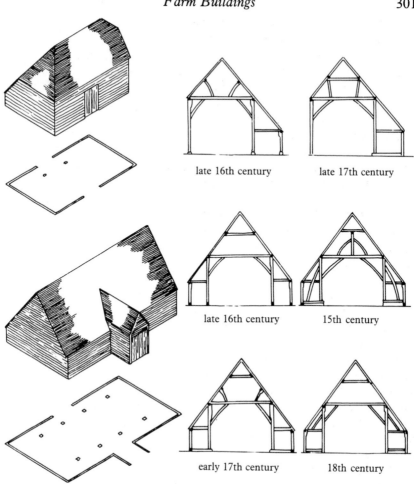

late 16th century   late 17th century

late 16th century   15th century

early 17th century   18th century

178. Farm buildings, aisled barns

Because of the increased width that aisled construction permitted, it remained popular in the construction of barns long after it had been abandoned in the construction of domestic buildings. Aisled barns continued to be built in some parts of southern and eastern England throughout the seventeenth and well into the eighteenth centuries. The distribution of aisled timber barns as given by S. E. Rigold clearly indicates that they are found mainly from Wiltshire and Hampshire across to Suffolk and Kent, with the highest concentration in three areas – East Kent, West Suffolk and the downlands of Hampshire and Berkshire. All these areas are predominantly chalk. Yet in the rich arable part of Norfolk, where there are many large barns comparable with any elsewhere, there is a complete absence of aisled barns. This

179. Priors Hall barn, Widdington, Essex

is confirmed by the work carried out by Sheridan Ebbage in that county.

Aisled barns are also to be found in South Yorkshire, the Pennines, especially in the Aire and Calder Valleys to the east and the Ribble Valley to the west, and parts of central Lancashire. These barns, like most of the timber-framed buildings in the area, have had their external walls rebuilt in local stone. The most notable example is the Long Barn, Whiston Hall, South Yorkshire; claimed to be the earliest secular building so far identified in Yorkshire, it may well, from the number of early timber features, be fourteenth century or even earlier. Another notable aisled barn is at Gunthwaite Hall, South Yorkshire, a barn comparable in size with those in the South and East. It is thought to be of sixteenth-century date; the lower part of the aisle walls are of stone with studwork above with diagonal framing to give a herringbone pattern. Another of note is at East Riddlesden Hall, Keighley, West Yorkshire. Examples of aisled barns are also known in Leicestershire – for instance the tithe barn at Newhouse Grange, Sheepy, probably early sixteenth century.

Most aisled barns follow the standard form of construction, with the aisle to both sides, but sometimes an aisle was provided along one side only. In many of the later aisled barns in Yorkshire, for instance, the wide side aisles, often as wide as the nave and with a separate access from the outside, housed cattle, it is believed. A similar

180. Rogate tithe barn, West Sussex

arrangement can be found in Lancashire. In Sussex and Surrey too some barns appear to have been designed to house cattle. In West Sussex and east Hampshire another type of aisled barn was common, in which the aisles continued around the ends as well, forming a continuous eaves broken only by the tall barn doors. Generally these barns were of three bays with a central threshing floor and because of their plan and construction could not be extended as other types of barn could by simply adding a bay.

Barns comparable with those of aisled construction were also built of cruck construction. Pride of place must go to the early four-teenth-century barn at Leigh Court, Hereford & Worcester, with eleven cruck trusses – the gable trusses reaching only to collar level, so the roof is half-hipped, making it the largest cruck building known to survive, with a width of some thirty-four feet and a length of over 150 feet. The two waggon porches are also of cruck construction. Siddington tithe barn, near Cirencester, Gloucestershire, may well have the oldest timber frame in England, being thought to date from the twelfth century and having all the features, the lap-joints and scissor-braces, associated with the earliest timber-framed buildings. Originally there were seven bays and eight trusses, two of which were aisled and the rest base-cruck. The walls of the barn are stone, with

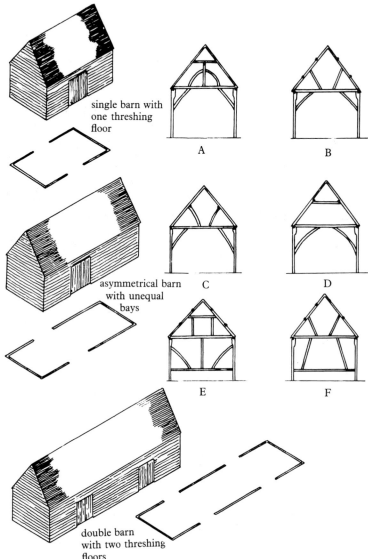

single barn with
one threshing
floor

A

B

asymmetrical barn
with unequal
bays

C

D

E

F

double barn
with two threshing
floors

181. Farm buildings, barns

the east gable having certain details which can be ascribed to the
Anglo-Saxons. Middle Littleton tithe barn, near Evesham, which
dates from about 1300, has, like Siddington, two end bays of aisled
construction with eight intermediate base-crucks. Again as at Siddington, the walls are of stone. Unfortunately one of the base-crucks has
been replaced, and the others are supported by posts and cross-beams
which tend to destroy the visual scale of the barn's interior. Other

182. Barn, Old Manor Farm, Ashton-under-Hill

183. Lenham tithe barn, Kent

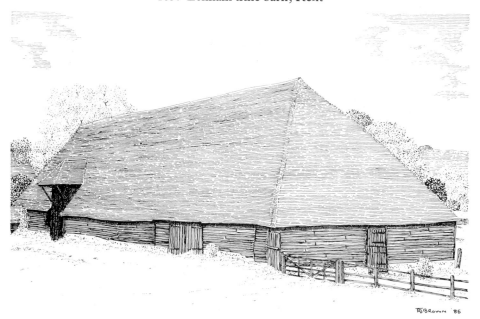

notable cruck barns are at Holiday Farm, Berrow Green, with five crucks, and Rectory Farm, Grafton Flyford, both in Hereford & Worcester and both fourteenth century. For obvious reasons many of these medieval cruck barns tend to be of base-cruck rather than true cruck.

Smaller cruck-frame barns are a fairly common feature over a very wide area of England and continued to be built in parts of the North well into the eighteenth century. The highest concentration is in the Welsh border counties, with Hereford & Worcester having the most. A typical sixteenth- or seventeenth-century cruck-framed barn can be seen at the Avoncroft Museum of Buildings. It formerly stood at Cholstrey Court Farm, Leominster, and has been re-erected in its original form; it embodies the essential structural elements common in cruck construction and is three bays long with a thatched roof and wall panels infilled with riven slats woven between staves set in the frame.

Barns vary considerably in size; some of the early examples with one entrance could vary from between fifty and a hundred feet in length. However, the length of most three bay barns is between forty and fifty feet. The largest barns are those of aisle construction: the barn at Manor House, Frindsbury, Kent, which is over 210 feet, is the longest entirely roofed barn in England; that at Court House Farm, Alciston, East Sussex, is 170 feet; the one at Leighs Lodge, Felsted, Essex, is 159 feet; that at Great Coxwell, Oxfordshire, is 152½ feet, and the Wheat Barn, Cressing, Essex, is 140 feet. Barns of cruck construction can also be of considerable size. The barn at Leigh Court, for instance, is over 150 feet, while the one at Middle Littleton is 136 feet. Generally the width of aisled barns was between twenty-five and fifty feet, those constructed with base crucks between thirty and thirty-six feet, while the width of an ordinary timber-framed barn was around twenty feet.

Another type of barn, now rare, had open sides and open ends. These structures consisted of an elementary box-frame with a raised floor supported on joists resting on staddle-stones with a pitched roof, usually of thatch to reduce the weight on the structure. The central bay – the threshing bay – did not have a raised floor, so enabling carts to be driven through in the usual way. This type of barn originated in the sixteenth century and became popular through southern England in the eighteenth century. Few survive, among them that at Oak House Farm, Hampstead Norreys, Berkshire.

Granaries

Grain was the most important of all farm produce for it was essential in the production of bread and ale, for the feeding of livestock and

above all for use as seed for the following year's harvest. At first, due
to the inadequacies of traditional farming methods, the yields produced
were small – each grain sown would only produce a three- to five-fold
increase – and so precious to the livelihood of the farmer and his family
that on many small farms the grain was stored within the farmhouse,
often in an upper room. Although on some of the larger farms separate
buildings were built to house the grain from as early as the fourteenth
century (the granary at Grange Farm, Little Dunmow, Essex, is
thought to be early fourteenth-century date), it was not until the
eighteenth and nineteenth centuries, with the improvement of farming
methods and the increase in size of many farmsteads, that this became
common. These specialized stores could be either a first-floor room
within a larger building or a separate purpose-built building (184).

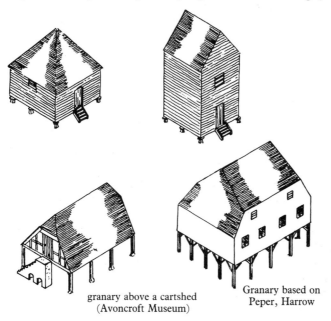

granary above a cartshed
(Avoncroft Museum)

Granary based on
Peper, Harrow

184. Farm buildings, granaries

Those situated at first-floor level were generally placed over a
cartshed, the air circulating beneath the partially or often whole open
ground floor, helping to keep the place dry. There are many examples
of these to be found: undoubtedly the finest is the large granary at
Peper Harow, Surrey, built in about 1600, tile-hung above and open
below, resting on twenty-five oak posts and said to be one of the best
vernacular buildings in the South-East. At the Avoncroft Museum of
Buildings there is one which formerly stood at Temple Broughton
Farm, near Hanbury. The timber-framed granary is supported on

brick columns and is thought to date from the last quarter of the eighteenth century. Its unusual features are the dog kennels under the external steps (for protection against theft of the precious grain) and the ladder stored under the eaves on the same elevation. In some cases access to the granary was by means of a ladder and trapdoor, as at Peper Harow. In some areas, such as Hereford & Worcester, the granary was frequently placed over the stable or cowshed, producing conditions in which the ventilation and humidity were detrimental to the grain.

Free-standing purpose-built granaries, usually square or rectangular, placed on staddle-stones to raise them off the ground, giving the building some protection against damp and especially vermin, are to be found in many parts of the South-East and eastern England, and even in the South-West. They first appeared in the sixteenth century or earlier, and by the eighteenth century their use was widespread. They are constructed of timber – oak, elm and softwood were all used, the earlier ones usually having brick infilling, while later weatherboarding became more and more popular until in the nineteenth century its use was universal. In the South-East they were sometimes tile-hung, like that at Peper Harow, and even, as has already been mentioned, clad with slates. The number of staddles or piers varied according to the size of the granary; some have only five, while others have sixteen or so; however, nine or twelve seem to be most common, particularly in the South-East. These were generally between six and seven feet six inches apart. The staddle-stones range from the more usual round mushroom type to flat-headed or square forms. Less common was the use of brick piers and arches usually associated with brick-built granaries. Local stone, where available, was used for these staddles; however, where it was not readily available, it seems that it was often imported from quarries well outside the area. In the nineteenth century slender cast-iron imitations of earlier staddle-stones became popular.

The size of these timber-framed granaries varied greatly: they could measure as little as twelve feet or so square on plan up to some twenty feet square, such as the one at Littlehampton now re-erected at the Weald and Downland Open Air Museum, Singleton. An unusually large example is to be found at Cressing, Essex, a ten-bay building and as wide as many aisled barns of the same date (early seventeenth century); such was the span that two bridging-joists were provided between each pair of successive binders. The building could be either one or two storeys, with access to the upper floors by either an external stair or an internal ladder. Occasionally in the loft above the first floor a small dovecot was provided.

Windows in granaries were generally provided, more for ventilation than for light, and so these were either shuttered or more commonly

185. Slate hung granary, Trewithick Farm, Launceston

louvred, which could be either fixed or adjustable. In some instances the windows were filled in with a lattice of timber slats providing both light and ventilation yet excluding birds. Although the grain could be stored loose or in sacks, it was more common, particularly in the smaller, separate buildings, for it to be stored in bins built of timber and so constructed as to form low partitions. The walls and ceilings were often plastered, presumably to reduce the amount of dust collecting on surfaces, although sometimes, especially where those external walls formed part of the bins, they were boarded. In some areas plastered floors were provided instead of the more usual boarded ones, providing a smoother, cleaner surface which was better for shovelling. Access to the granary was usually by means of timber steps.

Cattlesheds

Cattle were important to the well-being of the farmer and his family. They kept oxen for haulage, milk cattle for producing milk and consequently butter and cheese, and store cattle for meat. During much of the year they would be kept, except for milking, in the

open, but in the winter accommodation, either partially or completely
enclosed, was needed. The number of cattle which could be wintered,
and consequently the size of the accommodation, depended entirely
on the amount of fodder available, and it was not until the eighteenth
century, with improved farming techniques producing greater winter
feed, that any great numbers of cattle were kept during the winter
months.

Enclosed timber-framed cattlesheds are, or at least were, a common
enough feature and are mainly of eighteenth and nineteenth century
(186). Oak was as always the traditional material, but elm was also
popular, as was softwood in the nineteenth century. Like other farm
buildings, particularly in the South-East and eastern England, these
were generally weatherboarded. The layout and size obviously depended on the number of cattle to be kept and also the provision for
feeding and mucking out. Generally the cattle were arranged in double
stalls, divided from one another by a low, timber-framed partition and
so tethered that they faced a wall or onto a central feeding passage
which ran the full length of the shed. The cattle were fed from a manger
or loose feeding-box and usually a hay rack. The floor comprised brick
paviors or stone slabs sloping down to a wide drainage channel. Until
the nineteenth century sheds were low, a hay loft often being provided
above, and in many cases the only light and ventilation came from the

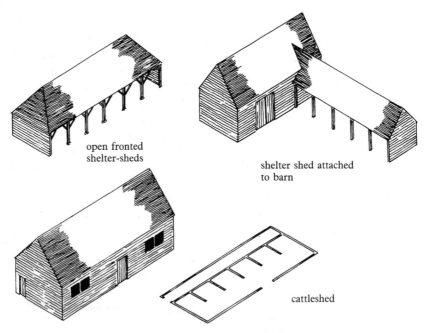

open fronted
shelter-sheds

shelter shed attached
to barn

cattleshed

186. Farm buildings, cattlesheds

split door. From the middle of the nineteenth century onwards more importance was given to the housing of cattle, and legislation, particularly that of 1885 and 1926, laid down that more hygienic accommodation was to be provided, with more windows and ventilation. In addition, as hay was at this time only part of the winter diet, the cattleshed became open to the roof, the hay being kept in stacks or hay barns.

Another method of housing cattle, and one commonly employed, was the open shelter opening up onto a foldyard. Foldyards became a feature from the late eighteenth century onwards with the increasing number of cattle being kept over winter. In many cases young heifers and bullocks could be kept in the open the whole year, although they could not necessarily be left in the open fields where they would damage the pasture for the coming spring and summer. The answer was to house them in a yard providing some shelter and where food and water could easily be provided.

Open-fronted shelter-sheds or 'hovels' were provided in these fold-yards, giving additional protection to the cattle during the worst of the winter and providing a place where the cattle could be fed and watered by means of mangers and hay racks as usual. These shelter-sheds provided a cheap and satisfactory way of housing young cattle and were particularly common in eastern England and the South-East, where rainfall was relatively low. The structures were simple: the roof was carried above the open front on timber posts generally built on a stone or brick foundation, the frame to the end and rear walls being usually weatherboarded. Unlike the cattleshed, there were no stalls and no means of tethering the animals. The form of these timber-framed shelter-sheds appears to be almost completely standardized since the eighteenth century with very little difference in the lengths of the bays or their construction. The number of bays actually varied considerably, from three up to as many as eight, although four or five appear to be most common. In most cases there was one row nearly always forming part of an enclosed or partially enclosed yard, frequently being built at right-angles to and attached to the barn.

Although foldyards and shelter-sheds were generally located in the farmstead, this was not always so. In parts of the South-East, particularly on the Downs, timber-framed, weatherboarded outfarms were provided, generally comprising a barn for the storage of hay, a foldyard with a shelter-shed or cattleshed and perhaps a stable. Most date from the nineteenth century, when they were recommended because of the saving in transport and time.

Stables

Unlike the cramped, ill-lit cattlesheds of the eighteenth and nineteenth centuries, the stable was a more spacious, better lit and ventilated building. This was due undoubtedly to the importance given to the horse, an expensive animal to buy, rear and feed. In construction timber-framed stables are similar to the cattleshed, generally being constructed with an oak frame and generally weatherboarded, although some are infilled with wattle and daub or brick-nogging. The majority date from between the late seventeenth century and the beginning of the nineteenth century, after which most were constructed of brick, although some are obviously earlier, perhaps of late sixteenth- or early seventeenth-century date.

Most of these timber-framed stables generally housed between three and five horses and incorporated a harness room and perhaps a loose-box. Each horse was given an individual stall (divided by a stout, high, timber stall partition) with a manger and hay rack. The floors, like those of the cattlesheds, had to be impermeable and were of stone, or of brick paviors specially designed to give a good grip to the horses hoofs. In many instances a loft was provided over the stable either for the storage of corn or more commonly for the storage of hay.

Cartsheds

Prior to the nineteenth century farm equipment comprised mainly carts, waggons, ploughs and harrows, and on most farms some form of shelter was provided to protect these items which were usually made of wood with only the moving parts of iron (187).

The most common form of timber-framed cartshed was an open-fronted building, resembling in many ways the open-fronted shelters for cattle, with the front supported on timber posts and the sides and rear usually clad with weatherboarding. Internally there was no division between the bays, enabling easy access to all the equipment. The length of these cartsheds varied greatly from a single bay to over ten, although generally they were four or five bays long. Most cartsheds were open along their long side but some, particularly those of a later date, were entered from one or both ends, those opening at both ends permitting easier access for the carts and waggons, enabling them to be pulled in one side and out the other. Generally these cartsheds were single-storey but it was not uncommon to provide a loft above, usually for use as a granary. In these cases it was not uncommon for the ground floor to be completely open, as at Peper Harow, providing excellent ventilation to the produce stored above but giving only limited protection from driving rain or snow to the equipment below.

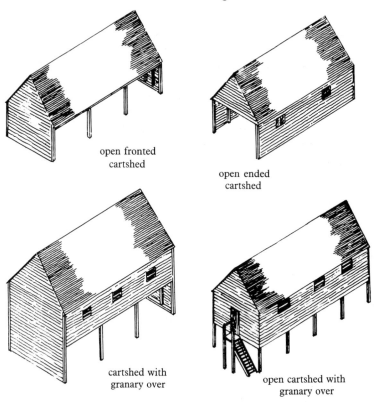

open fronted
cartshed

open ended
cartshed

cartshed with
granary over

open cartshed with
granary over

187. Farm buildings, cartsheds

Dovecots

Until the eighteenth century, with the introduction of root crops, the wintering of animals was restricted to those required for breeding, the others being killed either for immediate consumption or salting for eating later. To supplement the limited diet, fresh meat was provided by keeping pigeons, not wood pigeons which breed only twice a year but domesticated pigeons which have an exceptionally short breeding cycle. Every six weeks for nearly the whole year they are capable of laying a pair of eggs, hatching them out, fattening up two squabs on pigeon milk and then laying two more eggs. Evidently, to maintain the numbers at full strength indefinitely, it is only necessary to keep back one pair from each nest every seven years – the useful breeding life of a pair.

In medieval times the keeping of pigeons was restricted to the lord of the manor, and it remained the sole province of major landowners up to the eighteenth century, when smaller freeholders and even tenants, if they gained the landlord's permission, were allowed to keep them. As farming developed, the importance of pigeons decreased and, because they fed on standing crops, the harm they caused to crops outweighed their value in meat and manure.

Dovecots, the buildings in which the pigeons were housed, constructed of stone, brick or timber, can be found in various states of preservation, decay and antiquity in many parts of the country (188).

| Typical Hereford & Worcester dovecot (based on Luntley Court) | Typical Essex dovecot (based on Great Yeldham) | section through Hill Croome dovecot restored by Avoncroft Museum |

188. Farm buildings, dovecots

The best-known type is the free-standing one, either circular, square, rectangular or multi-sided in plan. Means of access for the birds varied, but probably the most common was the glover, an open-sided structure on the ridge, while access into the dovecot for people was by means of a small door. Internally around the walls were rows of L-shaped nestboxes which could vary from a hundred or so up to two thousand.

Nowadays pigeons are no longer kept on farms for food but many dovecots, often used as stores, still survive. Amongst the most attractive are those constructed of timber. In Hereford & Worcester the National Trust own two excellent examples in the county – one at The Grange, Hawford (189), and one at Wichenford (190), both of seventeenth-century date. Two more in the county owned by or leased to the Avoncroft Museum of Buildings stand at Moat Farm, Dormston (191), and Glebe Farm, Hill Croome. The former is also seventeenth century and stands adjacent to the farmhouse of similar date. The latter dovecot probably dates from the fifteenth century and is rare because it is of cruck construction.

Lofts were also used as dovecots. Some are built over porches or gatehouses, but normally they are in the gable end of farm buildings – barns, stables and even granaries were all used. These were often small, restricted to the area above the collar-beams. Access for the birds was by means of rows of holes, varying in number from one up

189. Dovecot, Hawford, Hereford & Worcester

190. Dovecot, Wichenford Court, Hereford & Worcester

191. Dovecot, Moat Farm, Dormston, Hereford & Worcester

192. Dovecot, Pimp Hall Farm, Chigwell, Greater London

to eight or so depending on size, fitted with either a separate or more
often a continuous landing platform. Access into the dovecot was
usually by means of a door into the back from the inside of the farm
building.

Industrial Buildings

The use of timber framing in the construction of industrial buildings was at one time a common feature in many parts of the country. Of these, undoubtedly the finest to survive are the windmills – post and smock – which still grace the countryside in eastern England and the South-East as well as the odd example in the Midlands. Of almost equal charm and more numerous are the timber-framed watermills which are still to be found on the many rivers over much of the same area. Also within the group are warehouses, storage sheds, maltings, workshops used for local crafts (for instance, blacksmiths, wheelwrights and the like) and even toll cottages.

To these buildings must be added the numerous timber-framed cottages used for the many cottage industries prior to the Industrial Revolution, particularly those relating to wool and weaving. These

193. Southfields, Dedham, Essex

319

cottages would have differed little from other houses, although in many cases a workroom would have been provided. Former weavers' cottages can be seen in many parts of the East in such places as Lavenham (the weavers' cottages, Water Street) and Kersey. The most interesting of these buildings is undoubtedly Southfields, Dedham, Essex (193), said to have been originally a 'bay and say' factory. Built by a rich clothier in about 1500, it comprised living-quarters, workrooms or offices and a warehouse around a courtyard. The layout is not now clear but the south-west wing was called the master weaver's house, while the upper floor of the east wing was one long room.

Windmills

The origin of the windmill in this country is now lost in history; whether they were an imported idea or the product of natural development is no longer certain. It is known that no windmills are recorded in the Domesday Book for the mills referred to in that document were either water- or horse-mills, with the first authentic reference being from 1185, when a windmill was let in the village of Weedley, Yorkshire. The earliest illustrations of windmills are those of the postmill in the English Windmill Psalter written in about 1260 and on the memorial brass in St Margaret's Church, King's Lynn, Norfolk, which commemorates a mayor of the town who died in 1348. The appearance of these and the representation of other postmills that have survived differ little from the mills of centuries later.

Postmills were the earliest of all the types of windmills deriving their name from the great post on which the body containing the machinery turns to face the wind. They were a feature of the fairly flat corn-growing counties of Kent, Sussex, Surrey, Essex, Suffolk, Cambridgeshire, Norfolk, Lincolnshire and the east Midlands as well as in the Lancashire Fylde. Postmills probably reached their zenith in the eighteenth century with the construction of those in east Suffolk described by Rex Wailes as 'the finest of their type in the world'. Of these, the finest one surviving and still in working order, is at Saxtead Green, built at the end of the eighteenth century and now owned by the Department of the Environment. The earliest surviving postmill dates from the beginning of the seventeenth century: Bourn Mill, Cambridgeshire, is generally regarded as the oldest, but that at Great Gransden in the same county may well be older. The mill at Pitstone, Buckinghamshire (194) is the oldest dated example – 1629 on a side girth, while the postmill at Outwood, Surrey, is the oldest working example, built in 1666. Working examples are to be found at Nutley, Sussex, which has been restored to full working order by the Uckfield and District Preservation Society, Wrawby, Humberside, the sole surviving postmill in Lincolnshire and Humberside, and Danzey Green

194. Pitstone Windmill, Buckinghamshire

Mill, which has been re-erected at the Avoncroft Museum of Building.
There are several others which have been restored in recent years,
among the finest being those at Stevington, Bedfordshire, Brill, Buck-
inghamshire, Great Chishill, Cambridgeshire (195), Cat and Fiddle
Mill, Dale Abbey, Derbyshire (196), Aythorpe Roding, Bocking,
Mountnessing and Ramsey, all in Essex, Cromer, Hertfordshire, Chill-

195. Great Chishill Mill, Cambridgeshire

enden and Rolvenden, both in Kent, Kibworth Harcourt, Leicestershire, Drinkstone, a typical west Suffolk mill, Friston and Framsden,
both in Suffolk, Reigate Heath, Surrey, and in Sussex those at Clayton,
Argos Hill, Hogg Hill, Icklesham and Cross-in-Hand.

The construction of the postmill varied little in principle from other
timber-framed buildings but greatly in detail. Oak was the principal
timber used, although in Sussex pitch pine was a popular alternative

196. Cat and Fiddle Mill, Dale Abbey, Derbyshire

(Clayton and Argos Hill). The body of a postmill is carried and pivoted on a massive central post called the 'main post', about which the body of the mill revolves. Supporting the main post in its vertical position are four raking 'quarterbars', each morticed and tenoned into the main post at one end and generally framed at the other end to the 'crosstrees' by means of a birds-mouth joint and iron straps. The main post is quartered over the crosstrees but is not supported by them, being kept an inch or two above. Those crosstrees were first laid directly on or more commonly buried beneath the surface of the ground to give the mill greater stability. Later they were raised on brick piers but not fixed to them. Most postmills were constructed with two crosstrees set at right-angles to each other, but a few mills had three crosstrees and six quarterbars. These were at Chinnor and Stokenchurch, both in Oxfordshire, Bledlow Ridge, Buckinghamshire, Costock, Nottinghamshire, and Moreton, Essex. All of these have now either collapsed or been demolished.

The top of the post terminates either with a 'pintle', turned out of the solid, or an iron gudgeon or 'Sampson head', a cap and bearing of iron. Pivoting and rotating on top of this is a great transverse beam, called the 'crowntree', on which the weight of the body of the mill rests. The framing varies greatly: generally on each end of the crowntree, are fixed the 'side girths' which are jointed and pegged to the four corner posts, and about these timbers the mill is formed. The top and bottom side girths, at the eaves and the lower ground floor, run parallel to the side girths, and between these are vertical studs with diagonal bracings. At the breast and tail, cross timbers, called 'the breast' and 'tail beams', are secured to the top side girts to carry the neck and tail bearings of the windshaft respectively. In addition the breast beam is supported in its centre by a vertical member, called the 'prick-post'. The breast beam is sometimes curved, while others are splayed to form an obtuse angle at the centre. Two large horizontal timbers, called 'sheers', are fixed either side of the main post, the full length of the body and beneath the lower floor, to support the mill about the post. Beneath these is a 'collar' or 'girdle' – a heavy wooden frame around the main-post – which steadies the mill in rough weather, relieving the strain from the main-post. Occasionally other methods have been used to steady the mill: at Sprowston Mill, Norwich, a ball-bearing collar was used, and this is now at the Bridewell Museum, Norwich. At Argos Hill a vertical iron track is fitted around the main-post with iron rollers on brackets fixed to the underside of the lower floor.

Early mills had a simple pitched roof, as at Bourn, but later curved rafters were generally used to accommodate the larger brake wheel. At Cromer Mill, which dates from about 1720, an ogee roof can be seen, the rafters shaped to follow a reverse curve to a point at the ridge. The whole of the framing is usually covered by horizontal shiplap boarding either painted white or tarred, but some postmills in Yorkshire were covered with vertical boarding, while in Sussex mills were occasionally partly or almost completely covered with flat galvanized iron sheets painted white. This can still be seen – for instance, the mills at Argos Hill and Clayton are clad on the breast only, while the mill at Cross-in-Hand has the breast and sides clad. To make the mill waterproof, the boarding to the breast is extended beyond the sides, with the sides and the roof carried beyond the rear boarding. A number of mills had the weatherboard to the breast carried down below the lower floor in a shield-like extension, as at Chillenden Mill, to give protection to the mill's substructure. Some mills had the weatherboarding lath-and-plastered inside to keep the interior dry and free from draughts. At Aythorpe Roding, the interior of the roof, with part of the walls of the floor below, was similarly treated.

Access to the mill body is gained by means of a wide ladder from the ground up to the platform at the rear of the lower floor. Above this ladder many mills had a porch canopy over the door, and this varied greatly from mill to mill. Some had a simple lean-to (Great Chishill, Cambridgeshire), some a pitched roof, some a flat curve, while others were bonnet-shaped. Some postmills had balconies at the rear, as at Holton, Suffolk, and a few even had galleries around the eaves.

The early postmills were the open-trestle type, and these can still be seen (Nutley, Great Chishill, Bourn and Chillenden, are good examples) but in the late eighteenth and early nineteenth centuries roundhouses were added to many mills to give protection to the substructure and to provide extra storage space. These roundhouses are not attached to the mill in any way, the main-post passing through an opening at the apex of the roof. Later, many mills in east Suffolk had the roundhouse built at the same time as the mill itself, and some had as many as three floors and were as high as the body of the mill proper. Mills were sometimes raised when the roundhouse was constructed, and the mill at Saxtead Green (197) was raised three times altogether, the last time probably in 1854. The roundhouse at Holton has two floors, one of which is below ground level. The walls are generally built of brick, stone or flint, but in Sussex timber walls were sometimes used. The roofs are now always boarded and felted, but a few had tiles (as can still be seen at Stevington Mill), slates and even thatch. The weatherboarding of the mill body is generally extended down and shaped to clear the roof of the roundhouse. Some mills had a small petticoat, attached to the underside of the lower floor of the mill, to protect the opening in the roof of the roundhouse. Occasionally the roundhouse has no roof, and in this case the petticoat is built out to form the top of the roundhouse as at Kibworth Harcourt. Two doors were provided, on opposite sides of the roundhouse, so that access could be obtained wherever the sails were positioned.

In the Midland-type postmill the roundhouse roof is attached to the body of the mill with support gained by timbers set at right-angles to the sheers, called 'outriggers'. Cast-iron rollers are fitted to the ends of the sheers and outriggers which run on a curb on top of the roundhouse wall. This arrangement can be seen at Cat and Fiddle Mill, Dale Abbey, probably built in 1788 (a date carved on the crosstree) and Danzey Green mill.

Tower mills were a logical development from the postmills. They consisted of a fixed tower with a timber cap which contained the windshaft with the cap being the only part which turned to face the wind. The tower was built of brick, stone or timber, those of timber being clad with weatherboarding and known as 'smock mills' because of their likeness to the linen smock that was once the traditional dress

197. Saxtead Green Mill, Suffolk

of the British countryman. Generally smock mills are octagonal in shape but six, ten and twelve-sided smocks have been constructed. Most smock mills are on a brick base which varies from a few courses high, as at Stelling Minnis, Kent, to one, two or even three floors.

The main structural framing of a smock mill has large timber 'cant' posts at each corner, which extended for the full height converging to give the body of the mill its batter. These cant posts are secured to timber sill-plates on top of the brick base. The inherent weakness is that it was difficult to provide satisfactory fixing between the cant post and the sill and there was a natural tendency for the feet of the cant posts to move outwards, allowing the structure to collapse. The cant posts could be either secured with iron straps bolted to oak blocks on the inside of the sills, or mounted on iron shoes bolted to the sill. At the top, the cant posts are framed into the timber track or curb on which the cap rotates. Between and housed to each cant post are horizontal ledges, with a vertical central post fixed between these, strengthened with diagonal braces and filled in with vertical studs to ensure a strong and stable structure. Two large beams, called 'binders', carrying each floor are partly framed into the cant post and rest on the horizontal ledges. These binders are arranged at right-angles to those of the floor above, so spreading the load around the mill.

Smock mills are generally covered by horizontal weatherboarding, although in Cambridgeshire vertical boarding was sometimes used and can still be seen at the derelict mills at Swaffham Prior and Sawtry. The corners were always vulnerable, and to overcome this problem the alternate horizontal boards to each side are extended over the adjoining boards of the other side. These corners were often protected by lead or zinc to make them weatherproof. The boarding of the smock mill, like that of the postmill, is either tarred or painted white.

The taller smock mills have a stage, usually fixed to the brick base at the first floor or the meal floor, enabling the miller to load up the grist waggon or regulate the sails with ease. These stages are generally of wood, supported by brackets built out from the brick base, but for the odd stage, usually in Kent (for instance, Stelling Minnis), vertical uprights are provided. Two doors were provided onto the stage, opposite each other, so access could be obtained no matter where the sails were positioned, and this also applied to the doors on the ground floor whether the mill had a stage or not. The smock mill varied greatly in size, from several floors, as at Cranbrook, Kent, to a few floors, as at West Wratting, Cambridgeshire.

There are still a number of smock mills surviving today in Kent, where brick towers were never as popular as elsewhere. The finest in the county is undoubtedly Union Mill, Cranbrook, which dominates the skyline of the town. It was built in 1814, is now owned by Kent County Council and is open to the public. Others of note in the county are Herne Mill, built in 1789, Draper's Mill, Margate, built in the 1840s, Meopham Mill, built in 1801 (from, it is said, an old broken-up battleship from Chatham), Stelling Minnis, built as late as 1866, and West Kingsdown Mill, built at the beginning of the nineteenth century. Other smock mills of note are those at Lacey Green, Buckinghamshire, the oldest surviving one in the country, reported to have been built in 1650, West Wratting, Cambridgeshire, with the date 1726 on the brake wheel, Upminster, London Borough of Havering, dated on the beam below the fantail as 1799, Dalham Mill and Great Thurlow, both in Suffolk, and in Sussex those at Chailey, built in about 1830 and moved to the present site in 1864, Blackdown Mill, Punnetts Town, Rottingdean and, the finest in the county, the one at Shipley (198) built in 1879. All these mills are preserved, some still in working order, and most open to the public on certain days.

Most mills were generally used for grinding corn or other cereals, or on occasions snuff, pepper, mustard and vegetable oil, but there were also a number whose function was the drainage of land, generally in the Fens and the Broads. Those used to drain the Fens were usually smock mills, with the exception of the small mill at Wicken Fen, Cambridgeshire, have now largely disappeared. The mills of the Broads are far more numerous, being generally of bricks. These often replaced earlier smock mills, the only one of these to survive is at Herringfleet, Suffolk (199), built in 1830, its survival undoubtedly due to the fact that it belonged to the Somerleyton Estate which kept it working until 1956 when the county council agreed in principle to its preservation. Another but much smaller mill owned and worked by the Somerleyton Estate until 1957 stands nearby, at St Olaves, Norfolk. Built in 1910, it is the only surviving smock drainage mill with patent sails and fantail.

Other types of mills were used; the composite mill was a combination of a postmill and tower mill. The mill had the body of a postmill with the post removed, and was mounted on a short tower, in the same way as a cap, which ran on casters or tram-wheels with the whole body turned into the wind by a tail pole or a fantail mounted on the roof. There were only a few of these mills built and, with the exception of the one built at Monk Soham, Suffolk, they were all adaptations: the only advantage seems to have been that of economy – using a sound body of a postmill rather than having it demolished.

An unusual design was the hollow postmill, a Dutch invention, which was first used for drainage. It had a small post-mill-type body, which contained the windshaft, brake wheel and wallower, and an upright shaft which passed down through a hollow post to drive the

198. Shipley Mill, Sussex

199. Herringfleet Mill, Suffolk

machinery below. Only a few of these mills were built in England, the most famous being the mill at Wimbledon Common built as a hollow postmill in 1817 but later rebuilt as a composite.

A variation was the small, skeleton, hollow postmill often used for drainage in the Fens and the Norfolk Broads. These windpumps were skeleton framed, winded by a large weather vane and driving the pump, by common sails, through a crank in the windshaft.

Water- and Tide-Mills

Unlike those constructed of brick or stone which have no distinctive architectural or structural style apart from the 'Lucan' (the protective loading gantry, a feature of most water-mills), those constructed of timber and clad with weatherboarding and often crowned by a red tiled roof are features of many of the riverside towns and villages in the South-East and eastern England. Like the windmill, they were an important feature in the structure of the medieval village, but although many stand on sites where mills have stood since the Domesday Survey was made, the majority that survive today date from the seventeenth and eighteenth centuries, some being built as late as the nineteenth century.

Oak was the traditional material used for the construction of watermills, although towards the end of the eighteenth century soft-wood was the timber often employed. A feature of many mills is the use, long after it had been abandoned in domestic buildings, of the gambrel or mansard roofs which provided additional space for the housing of corn bins and other equipment. The frame was almost always clad with horizontal weatherboarding, although in parts of Cambridgeshire vertical boarding was the traditional covering and can still be seen at the watermill at Lode. Generally the boarding was painted white, although presumably at one time there was a fashion for blue colour work, which may account for the number of 'blue' mills about. In many instances sides and back were often tarred but in most cases even here the front was painted white. Occasionally one finds a mill which is clad not in timber but in tiles, the most famous being Shalford Mill, Surrey (200).

Water-mills varied greatly, not only in size but in the method by which the water drove the wheel. The various types can be identified by the position at which the water strikes the wheel. An undershot mill is turned by water flowing through the floats at the bottom of the wheel first, while with an overshot wheel the water strikes the top first. An overshot wheel – usually placed on a man-made or natural weir – is the more expensive but far more efficient of the two, needing only around a quarter of the volume of water to produce the same amount of power. Some mills are built across their streams with internal

200. Shalford Mill, Surrey

201. Coggeshall Mill, Essex

wheels, a more sophisticated arrangement than those built beside their streams with the wheel outside.

While corn-milling was the primary function of most water-mills, in some areas from the thirteenth to the eighteenth century the fulling trade was equally important. A large number of the water-mills were built or rebuilt as fulling mills to be converted to cornmills by the end of the eighteenth century as the cloth industry died out and the demand for bread increased. Some water-mills carried out both trades. Although corn-milling and fulling were their principal uses,

202. Colne Engaine Mill, Essex

mills were often put to crushing seeds for oil and the pulping rags for paper.

Not all water-mills used rivers to drive the wheels: in some coastal areas tidal-power was used. The South-West, parts of the south coast and the low-lying coastal regions of Essex and Suffolk were amongst the limited number of areas in England suitable for this type of mill. Tide-mills, as this type of mill is known, were usually situated along shallow creeks, often some miles from the coast, and on large ponds constructed to hold the water of the incoming tide. The ponds

203. Woodbridge Tide Mill, Suffolk

varied greatly in size: one at St Osyth's, Essex, was over thirty acres in area; another, at Birdham, Sussex, was thirty acres, although the majority seem to be less than ten acres. The disadvantage of these tide-mills was that they could be used only on the ebb tide as the millpond emptied, but they had one advantage over river mills in that they did not suffer from the effects of drought. These tide-mills were once a familiar sight around the coast, but today only two survive. The most famous is the one at Woodbridge (203), built probably in

204. Houghton Mill, Cambridgeshire

the eighteenth century on the site of an earlier mill and continuing to be worked commercially by water power until 1957 when the main wheel-shaft broke. At one time the mill seemed destined to follow the fate of the tide-mill at St Osyth's which, despite much concern by local people, fell down in 1962. Fortunately the mill at Woodbridge was finally saved and work commenced in 1971, when the estimate for the repairs was £50,000. The final cost was over £70,000. The only other surviving timber-framed tide mill stands at Thorrington, Essex. The present building dates from 1841, but it is on the site of previous mills which can be traced back to 1675. The mill worked by water until 1926 when the iron wheel failed, after which it was driven by a portable steam-engine. After ceasing work it was used for many years as a seed store before being purchased in 1974 by Essex County Council with the intention of restoring it to full working order.

Warehouses
Warehouses and storage buildings from another group of timber-framed buildings which must at one time have been common, particularly in parts along the east coast. The most famous perhaps is the Haseatic Warehouse, King's Lynn, Norfolk, a jettied building dating from the fourteenth century, now converted to offices. A large sixteenth-century warehouse, until recently used by a firm of local brewers as a bottle store, has recently been discovered at Ipswich, Suffolk. Unfortunately it has been dismantled to make way for road improvements, but it is hoped that it will be re-erected when a suitable site has been found. A former timber-framed warehouse also survives at 32 Close, Newcastle-upon-Tyne, but this, like so many, has been converted to other uses. The largest timber-framed warehouse is undoubtedly the one at Faversham, formerly known as Provender Mill; it stands on the creek and is still used to store grain and animal feed. The building dates from the seventeenth century and, although now largely underbuilt with bricks and stone up to the first floor, was undoubtedly timber-framed throughout, for full height posts and wattle-and-daub infilling remain at the rear. Above first-floor level the building has exposed timber with brick infilling. Its overall length is about 160 feet, the main range being of twelve bays, with a separate three-bay building of later date at the south-west end, while at the other end is a Victorian bay.

As previously mentioned, warehouses often formed part of one side of the courtyard of a merchant's house. Few such arrangements now survive; the one at Southfields, Dedham, has already been mentioned, but this has long since been converted into tenements, but at Fore Street, Ipswich (205), a private warehouse leading onto the quay forms part of an inner courtyard of a Tudor merchant's house. This

RJBrown'84

205. Isaac Lord's Warehouse, Ipswich, Suffolk

arrangement must have been a common feature in many parts in Tudor England.

Maltings

In eastern England maltings are a familiar sight, although they, like other such buildings, are being either demolished or converted into other uses. Although the majority are of brick, there were some that were constructed of timber. Most of these would have been nineteenth-century, but at Myddlyton Place, Saffron Walden, Essex (206), there still survives a building which at one time was used as a malting. Its original purpose is unknown for it is not characteristic of any building type so far recognized in Essex. One suggestion is that it was originally a guildhall, the shop to the front let to provide additional

206. Former malting, Saffron Walden, Essex

income, as at Felsted. Another hypothesis is that it was built as the house of a wealthy merchant, with extensive accommodation for trade, which, of course, would have been in saffron. The building is of early sixteenth-century date and certainly by the beginning of the eighteenth century was converted into a malting. The property now belongs to the National Trust and is leased to the Youth Hostels Association.

Workshops

Timber was frequently used in the construction of workshops connected with local crafts or trades but, like other buildings which have now no practical use and being more vulnerable than those constructed of brick or stone, these old buildings have been rapidly disappearing or occasionally converted to other uses.

Of these buildings the smithy was the most important, as essential as the mill to the economy of even the smallest community. Close by the smithy, or in some cases forming part of the same building, was the wheelwright's shop. Over most of eastern England and the South-East these buildings were constructed of timber, weatherboarded externally. A technique commonly employed on these simple structures was the use of wide planks set vertically, the joints being covered with off-cuts of timber. This was a feature in parts of Sussex and can be seen at the smithy from Southwater re-erected at the Weald and Downland Open Air Museum, Singleton. Although many of the early ones would have been well constructed of oak or elm, those from the nineteenth century, of which most remain, were generally rough and simple structures, using materials that were both cheap and close at hand, often secondhand oak or elm but generally softwood.

Toll Cottages

At one time toll cottages, numbering many thousands, mainly built between 1750 and 1810 for the network of roads administered by some 1,100 separate turnpike trusts, were a feature throughout the country, but most have fallen casualty to either road-widening or roadside improvement schemes. Most of these humble dwellings were built of brick or stone but some were of timber, particularly in Suffolk and Cambridgeshire and parts of Sussex. Generally these cottages were small, often only two rooms – a bedroom and living-room-cum-kitchen – although many were later extended, probably after the 1870s when most of the turnpike trusts were wound up. A few of these timber-framed structures have been saved. The one now at the Weald and Downland Open Air Museum at Singleton was originally situated at Upper Beeding and is the sole survivor of a group of weatherboarded toll cottages that once existed in the Worthing–Horsham–Shoreham area of Sussex. Another, rescued from the main Ipswich to Norwich road at Mendlesham, known as 'the Mustard Pot', has been re-erected at Needham Market. This, like others, was built in picturesque style, octagonal in plan with a thatched roof.

Repair of Timber-Framed Buildings

Although some repair work is undertaken under the supervision and direction of an architect or building surveyor with knowledge of the repair of timber-framed structures, most of the repairing and adapting of these buildings is undertaken, with little or no professional assistance, by local builders who in many cases follow the instructions of their clients. Before leaving the subject of timber-framed buildings it might, therefore, be appropriate to say something about the repair of these structures to assist those people contemplating such work either by themselves or with the aid of a builder.

First, one must distinguish between the terms 'repair' and 'restoration', both frequently used in connection with old buildings but meaning very different things and having very different effects on the building. The term 'restoration' implies an attempt to revert the building to a precise period in its architectural history. In a misguided attempt to restore an old building to an original form, it might be necessary to destroy other, later and important features, and this constitutes in many cases at least as great a threat to our heritage as decay and redundancy. It must be remembered that the form and character of an old building are a result of a long historical process in which the many changes which have occurred throughout the centuries are as much a part of the building as any old feature. Restoration work should only be undertaken when the building is unique and the work is carried out to enhance the architectural and historic value of the building. Any such restoration work should be approached with great caution and carried out under the supervision of an expert and is perhaps best left to one of the museums, such as the Avoncroft Museum of Buildings or the Weald and Downland Open Air Museum.

The repair of an old structure is another matter and is restricted to the repair of the structure made necessary by lack of maintenance and subsequent decay. It does not demand the replacement of a decayed feature – for instance, a moulded medieval beam too decayed for repair – with a replica but with something in the modern idiom which may compete, by comparison, with the old and so form a continuation of the building's architectural development which is a fundamental part of its beauty and interest. It is the repair of the timber-frame and in particular the frame and roof structure that are dealt with in this chapter.

Before carrying out any repairs to a timber-framed structure, it should be carefully surveyed, for no repairs will be successful unless the building is fully understood both technically and aesthetically. The internal finishes need to be stripped away, and this should be done with great care, for often much important information about the building's history is lost by their careless and sometimes needless destruction. Beneath the layers of wallpaper, which may themselves be rare, may well be the original wall and ceiling paintings, and although these and other details may not be suitable for preservation, all should be recorded.

It is, however, the timber-frame and its condition that must be most carefully examined. It is important to understand the bay system and the method by which the rigidity of the building is ensured. Timber-framed structures were, as we have seen earlier, nearly always triangulated against racking by means of diagonal braces between the various beams and main posts and roof trusses and purlins. Mutilation of these and other structural members over the centuries has been caused, in many instances, by a complete ignorance of the structural relationship between these members. The cutting of these structural members often transfers excess stress to the joints, particularly where new doors and enlarged windows have been provided or where braces have been removed in order to provide additional headroom, particularly in roof spaces where new doorways between attic rooms have been formed. In some instances the tie-beam of the roof truss triangulating the roof members has been cut away. Another source of weakness often arises with the insertion of a chimneystack cutting through bridging joists, binders and roof members. Again structural failure often occurs in a building whose upper floor had originally been jettied, the lower supporting wall being removed and the jetty underbuilt flush with the wall above. This not only extends the span of the first-floor joists but also loses any cantilever effect of the upper walls whose intended end beam loads had the effect of an upward thrust on the joists and relieving them at mid-span.

Although all these and other defects cause structural problems, because timber adapts itself gradually to these additional and varied stresses and loads, it is important only to repair and strengthen the structure, and no attempt should be made to correct distorted frames back into place unless distortion has only recently occurred and is likely to cause further structural problems. Apart from the possibility of opening up other joints, there is also a chance that new stresses may be induced into the frame.

The jointing system is an important feature of all timber-framed construction, and it is here that any movement will accumulate. The joints were secured with oak pegs and are liable to rot, becoming loose or breaking under stress, with the result that the joints may become open and unseated, and these will require to be strengthened. Any defective pegs should be hammered out and never drilled. Where wooden pegs need replacing, they should be of oak obtained from the heart wood, should be 'cleft' not 'turned' and should be tapered from a roughly square head to a point, driven in and left projecting.

Despite the distortion and structural problems caused by these defects, timber-framed structures generally suffer more from the effects of beetle infestation and fungal decay.

Infestation is ascribed to one of a number of species of wood-boring insects. First there is the common furniture beetle (*anobium punctatum*), which can destroy both softwood and hardwood, its larvae boring through the wood, digesting the cellulose. It is responsible for about three-quarters of all woodworm damage to property in Britain. The wood-boring weevil (*euophryum confine*) first became established in Britain after the last war and is already a widespread and serious threat to buildings, attacking both softwood and hardwood. It differs from other wood-boring insects in that it will only attack timber which is already decayed by wood-rotting fungi. A bettle which attacks only softwood is the house longhorn beetle (*hylotrupes bajulus*). It is found mainly in the southern home counties, particularly Surrey and Hampshire. The lyctus beetle (*lyctus brunnens*), commonly called the 'powder post beetle', came into Britain from North America many years ago. The name 'powder post' is derived from the very fine dust produced by the larvae which is quite unlike the frass of the furniture beetle. The larva is found only in the starchy sapwoods of hardwoods; the female requires a starch content of three per cent in the sapwood before she will lay her eggs. Unlike some beetles, they will attack only sound timber and are never found in timber already infected by fungus, and are therefore often associated with replacement timbers. Lastly, there is the death watch beetle (*xestobium rufovillosum*) the most damaging of all wood-boring beetles in old buildings, attacking hardwoods which have at some time maintained fungal infection, often attacking the centre of large timbers which suffered fungal heart rot when installed.

With the exception of death watch beetle, wood-boring beetles can be treated effectively by one of a number of proprietary materials classified in BS 1282, most of which contain copper, chrome and arsenic compositions in accordance with BS 7072. Prior to spraying the timbers, they must be brushed down to remove all dust and other foreign matter. Because of the particular activities of death watch beetle and its habit of attacking large structural hardwoods, normal spray treatments are less effective, and other methods have been used with some success. One system is to apply a thick paste, made up of fungicides and insecticides, liberally on the surface of affected areas. Over a period of time the paste releases its toxic chemicals deeply into the timber. Another method is the development of a special fumigation programme carried out annually when the death watch beetles emerge.

Timber structures also suffer severely from damp, which can result in devastating attacks by some wood fungi – dry and wet rot being the two most commonly known terms used to describe this fungal decay. Dampness, combined with the lack of ventilation, creates the ideal conditions for these attacks, the fungi actually being plants of a low vegetable form of the *saprophyte* family which attacks timber in buildings in order to extract food (cellulose) to maintain growth and the generation of spores.

Of these two, dry rot (*merulius lacrymans*) is the more serious and consequently a greater hazard to structural timbers. It requires moist, warm conditions with the moisture content in excess of twenty-two per cent for the spores to germinate and develop. The strands or hyphae grow from the spores to spread, producing enzymes which digest the adjacent damp timber. The cellulose, which it attacks, is broken down to carbon dioxide and water, causing the timber to lose its strength, developing cuboidal fractures (longitudinal cracks) and becoming dry and brittle, and it may be crumbled by hand. Dry rot, being malignant, will spread through brickwork, following the line of damp, in search of more timber to attack. The only treatment for dry rot is the removal of all the affected timber or, on large structural timbers, the removal of all decay and burning of all defective timbers. As the hyphae will no doubt have penetrated the walls, all plastering and rendering in the area of the outbreak should be removed and the wall sterilized, either by heating with a blow lamp or by spraying with a toxic chemical such as pentachlorophenol. When contamination of the wall by the hyphae is considerable, the joints should be cut out and a deep irrigation method should be employed, using a fungicidal solution via holes drilled in the wall. All timbers which are retained and all new timbers should be treated with a proprietary fungicide as classified in BS 1282.

Wet rot (*coniophora puteana*), sometimes known as 'cellar fungus', although not as serious as dry rot, is still a common cause of structural defects. It requires a moisture content of between forty and fifty per cent – much higher than that required by dry rot – to become active. However, when the moisture is removed, all activity of this fungal growth ceases. After attack the timber is left with small cuboidal splits and dark brown in appearance. Again it is important to remove all decayed sections of timber and in addition at least eighteen inches of sound timber. However, no treatment of brickwork or stonework is usually necessary. All new timbers should be treated with a fungicide as previously described. Although both dry and wet rot can be controlled, because of the nature and biology of the wood-rotting fungi, it is always necessary to locate and remove the cause of the outbreak. Most outbreaks are caused by the absence of an effective damp-proof course, by defective roof-covering and by leaking gutters and downpipes. These should all be repaired and kept in good order to prevent possible recurrence of the problem.

The treatment of timber against beetle infestation and fungal decay is normally carried out by specialist firms using specialist equipment and protective clothing, as many of the remedial treatment products are toxic. Care should, therefore, be taken to avoid contact with the skin and the prolonged breathing of any vapour or oral ingestion. When undertaken by specialist firms they are generally prepared to guarantee the efficiency of the completed treatment.

There are several important principles which must be observed whenever possible in repairing timber-framed buildings. First it is of paramount importance that as much of the original timber as possible is retained, and timbers should be replaced only when too much of the timber is defective to make a satisfactory repair. The timber used in repair work is also of importance and must be of the same species as that used in the original structure; when repairing an oak frame, only oak must be used, likewise where the frame is of softwood, this too should be used. When oak is used, it should be unseasoned native oak and should if at all possible be selected from timbers of the least diameter to give the required cross-section of the member.

The conversion of the timber is also important: main timbers, beams, purlins, plates and posts, larger than eight inches square should be obtained from boxed-heart logs; smaller timbers should be halved or quartered depending on size, with those with their cross-sectional dimensions less than six inches heart-sawn, the heart-face always being used for the upper or outer face of the completed building. Logs cut through and through should never be used for external work. Suitable reclaimed timbers are preferred by some, but old oak is extremely hard and difficult to work and should be avoided. Added to this the use of old timbers will tend to confuse future historians.

Timber should, whenever possible, have identical properties especially with regard to grain and moisture content; the latter is particularly important with regard to the scarfing-on or the piecing-in of new timbers, which may suffer from the results of shrinkage. When new wood is introduced into an old structure, it is always advisable to impregnate it with one of the proprietary materials previously described to discourage fungal and beetle attacks. Care should be taken to ensure that the solution is colourless so as not to detract from the appearance of any exposed work. All new oak pegs used to secure new joints or as a replacement of defective pegs should always be impregnated, as these tend to rot and as previously stated should be cleft and not turned and tapered from a roughly square head to a point to ensure a good fit. In addition all pegs should be baked in a slow oven for a day or two, so that they may expand within the hole, ensuring a snug fit. Bolts should in general be avoided when timber-to-timber repairs are undertaken. All scarf joints should, whenever possible, be skew-pegged, with each peg driven in at a different angle. The pegs should be randomly aligned and can be driven in from all sides. Above all, the repair of old timbers should be undertaken by a skilled craftsman.

As previously stated, it is recommended that timber should be used whenever possible in repair work, but it is also desirable to keep as much of the original timber as possible, and with this in mind it is often advantageous to use metal straps and plates, particularly in the strengthening of joints. Wrought iron was the traditional material used for this and should still be used whenever possible, although it is now difficult to obtain, ceasing to be manufactured commercially some years ago. As a replacement, mild steel is commonly used, but it should always be protected with an appropriate zinc-based primer or better still galvanized. It should also be remembered that all bolts and coachscrews used in conjunction with oak should also be galvanized to resist corrosion by the tannic acid in oak.

Repairs to Timber-Wall Framing

Although deterioration of timber-framing due to infestation is common, particularly in thin structural members such as braces, rot is the worst enemy. It is to be found in the sill-beams, the feet of the main posts and studs, and the upper surface of horizontal members on external walls, together with feet of braces and studs, and the joints between horizontal beams such as bridging joists, binders and girths with posts.

It is not of course a difficult matter to underpin a timber frame. Shorting can be applied to the girth or other suitable horizontal members, and the sill-beam can be disengaged from the posts and studs, removed and replaced with a new oak sill with mortices cut to engage the old tenons. At the same time, of course, the plinth, whether brick or stone, can be repaired or rebuilt and a new damp-proof course inserted beneath the sill-beam. If the sill-beam is in such poor condition that it needs to be replaced, it will probably be found that the feet of the posts and studs are also rotten, and a decision has to be made whether to cut them off to a common height and form new tenons or

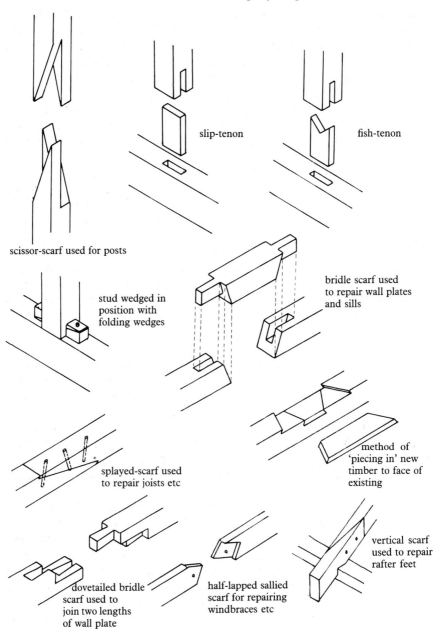

slip-tenon

fish-tenon

scissor-scarf used for posts

stud wedged in
position with
folding wedges

bridle scarf used
to repair wall plates
and sills

splayed-scarf used
to repair joists etc

method of
'piecing in' new
timber to face of
existing

dovetailed bridle
scarf used to
join two lengths
of wall plate

half-lapped sallied
scarf for repairing
windbraces etc

vertical scarf
used to repair
rafter feet

207. Joints used in repair

to repair them. When the decision is to repair them, the defective timber should be cut away until sound timber is reached and, in the case of studs, new timbers scarfed and skew-pegged. In the case of the main post, a scissor-scarf joint is recommended. In some cases only part of the sill-beam will need replacing, and in this case the defective length should be removed and replaced with new, an ideal joint in this situation being the bridle-scarf joint. Thin sections, such as struts and braces, should be half-lapped scarf joints preferably 'sallied' and pegged or bolted. New braces can be fitted with the use of wedged tenons.

A problem which often arises is when a new stud is required, either because it is defective or because it has been removed at some earlier date, but the adjoining sill-beam, girth or wall-plate is intact and is not to be replaced. This problem can be overcome by various jointing methods; the joint to the top can be formed with a tenon in the usual way and the bottom secured with a false tenon, either a slip or fish-tenon, secured with oak pegs, or with a wedged tenon. Alternatively an elongated mortice in which the bottom tenon of the stud slides into position can be used, the mortice being 'pieced-in' with new oak to match.

Repairs to Floors
Existing timber floors are often sloping or springy, and this may be due either to the failure of the bridging-joist or one or more of the common joists or to the distortion caused by the deflection of one of the joists. To replace the defective beams or in some cases even to repair the defective joists would generally entail great disruption to the whole structure, including the destruction of the ceiling beneath. If possible, repair work should therefore be undertaken *in situ*, thus avoiding serious loss to the building. Original timber should as mentioned earlier only be replaced as a last resort.

Apart from failure due to beetle infestation and rot, most structural failures in timber are caused by overloading. Fractures in beams usually occur in the bottom half of the timber, for the top half of the beam is in compression, while the bottom half is in tension. The simplest method of repairing a fracture in the bridging joist consists of placing metal plates beneath and on top of the fracture and then bolting through the joint vertically. If the joist is exposed, the plate can be painted to match the colour of the oak, helping to hide the repair.

Another likely place of failure is the joint between the bridging joist and binder or side girth. Usually the joint between the two is a double tenon, and often this joint is found to be defective due either to decay, or to shrinkage of the timbers resulting in the loss of bearing of the

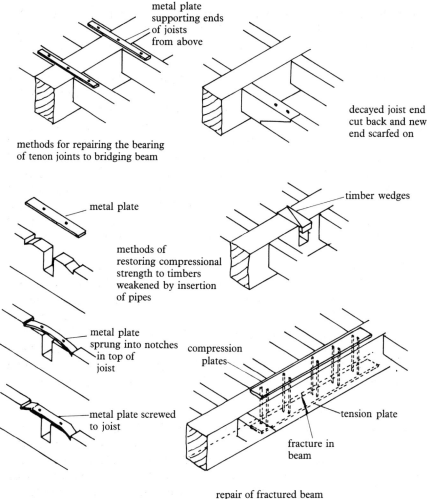

metal plate
supporting ends
of joists
from above

decayed joist end
cut back and new
end scarfed on

methods for repairing the bearing
of tenon joints to bridging beam

metal plate

timber wedges

methods of
restoring compressional
strength to timbers
weakened by insertion
of pipes

metal plate
sprung into notches
in top of
joist

compression
plates

metal plate screwed
to joist

tension plate

fracture in
beam

repair of fractured beam

208.　Repair of floors

tenon in the mortice. If the end of the joist is badly decayed, it should be cut back to sound timber and a new piece provided scarfed and bolted to the existing joist one end and the tenons re-cut the other end to suit the existing mortices. More likely, however, is that the joint has come apart and needs support, and this can be achieved by the introduction of a steel shoe or strap, the design depending largely on the position of the joists.

A similar problem arises when the joint between either the bridge joists or binder and the storey post is defective. Here, however, the end of the joist can be supported on an oak bracket bolted to the storey post. In addition, if there is any outward movement of the wall, this can be restrained with the introduction of a metal strap or in some cases a tie rod. Metal straps or shoes similar to those above can also be used.

Another common problem is caused by the insertion of service pipes notched into the top of the joists, resulting in a loss of compressionable strength. If the notches are positioned near the bearings, there is not generally any serious problem, but if they occur towards the centre of the span, the result can be disastrous. Where there is sufficient space above the pipes, the problem can be overcome by the insertion of folding timber wedges, but when, as is more often the case, there is little space between the pipes and the underside of the floorboards, it is necessary to insert a metal plate screwed to the joist across the notch. The plate can be slightly bent with the ends notched into the top of the joist, the plate being flattened as it is screwed down, with the ends thrusting outwards against the notches.

The other principal cause of failure in timber floors is the joint between the floor joists and bridging joist. When the end of a floor joist is decayed, the joists should be cut back to sound timber and a new piece scarfed and pegged in and a new joint made to the bridging joists. More often, however, the defect is caused by the lack of end bearing of the floor joists due to shrinkage of the timber. The most satisfactory method of undertaking this repair is to support the joist ends from above with a short iron plate across the bridging joist.

Repairs to Roofs
Great care should be taken in the repair of old timber roofs, the old timbers being retained as far as practicable, for roofs are generally the least altered of all in a timber-framed building. Depending on the degree of repair to be undertaken, either the roof-covering can be stripped from the portion of the roof to be repaired or, if the repair is of an extensive nature, the entire roof can be stripped. In either case the exposed timbers should be protected and never allowed to stand open to the weather, for rain and exposure are deterimental to old timbers not previously exposed to the elements, and wind can also cause severe damage. In addition, roofs should be repaired bay by bay. All joints should be carefully examined and defective pegs hammered out and renewed. Joints which have opened but are otherwise sound should be strengthened where necessary with metal straps.

Rafters normally suffer from rot in their feet and can usually be repaired with new timber scarfed and pegged to the existing with the new end shaped and jointed to the wall-plate as required to suit the original. In addition it is possible by renewing some of the rafters to repair the remainder by lengthening them with timber cut from the old rafters. The joint – again a simple scarfed and skew-pegged joint – should be located if possible above the purlin. Sometimes the bridle joint to the apex of the roof is defective, and in order not to lose the existing timber this can be strengthened by the addition of an oak collar-piece pegged on both sides of the rafter below the ridge.

The top face of the wall-plate can also be affected by rot; in some cases, where the rot is not too deep, the top surface can be repaired by 'piecing in' a new timber, the ends dovetailed and undercut and glued in position, care being taken to ensure that the new piece has matching grain. If the decay is deep, it should be made up of two or more pieces, each dovetailed and undercut to the existing. New mortices can then be cut to accommodate the ends of the existing rafters. If the wall-plate is beyond repair by this method, the defective section should be cut out and replaced with new, the ideal joint between the new and existing being the bridle-scarf joint.

Another member prone to structural failure or joint failure is the purlin. The most likely position for decay is, as in other timbers, at their ends, especially the tenon joint with the principal rafter. These can be repaired by a false tenon as previously described and strengthened by means of a straddle strap passing over the principal rafter. In some instances the back of the principal rafter is decayed as well, and this can be repaired by piecing in new timbers, dovetailed and undercut as described for wall-plates. Through purlins, either clasped or trenched, are easier to repair. The purlins are often cracked and broken, and isolated repair is often complicated by the bowed condition of the purlin, making it often difficult to scarf on a new length or even to strengthen it with plates. It is therefore probably easier to provide new lengths spanning between the trusses and jointed over the principal rafter. Another vulnerable point is the joint between the principal rafter, tie-beams, wall-plate and main-post. This can be repaired by replacing the defective timbers with new, scarfed and pegged as previously described, and new joints made as necessary.

Timber Repairs using Epoxy Resins

In the last few years there has been an increase in the use of epoxy resins in timber-framed repairs, despite some reservations by such bodies as the Society for the Protection of Ancient Buildings. Its use should be restricted to situations where traditional repairs in timber are not desirable or practicable – for instance, where it would cause undue disruption to the fabric of the building or where access is difficult or for reasons of economy. Although there is concern that the resin can deface the timber and cause condensation, with subsequent rot and insect-attack to the adjacent timber, the joint is very strong, and though one might expect any thermal or stress movement to occur here, in practice any such movement occurs with the structural joints.

Its principal use is in end-beam repairs where ends of beams or roof trusses have been subject to decay. The decayed section of timber is cut away, and glass fibre reinforcing rods are inserted into holes, drilled at an angle into the sound timber and set in position with epoxy resin paste or grouted in with low-viscosity epoxy resin and epoxy resin filler mortar. The mortar is usually composed of epoxy resin mixed with an inert material such as very fine silver sand. The cavity should be thoroughly cleaned to remove all frass and debris and brushed with a low-viscosity epoxy resin, feeding as much as possible into the areas softened by rot or excavated by beetle-infestation. Shuttering is formed to the shape of the removed section and the epoxy resin mortar poured into the shuttering and around the reinforcing rods. The mortar should be well rammed into the decayed profiles to ensure the exclusion of air pockets. When the shuttering is removed, the beam is finally shaped. Alternatively, where the repair is visible, permanent oak shutters are pieced into the surviving sound faces and glued and dowelled to finish proud of the required finished face for subsequent working back on completion of the repair. Prior to the application of the resin, the shutters and adjacent surviving timber should be protected from resin spillage and runs, with two coats of peelable rubber latex. The repair is carried out as described above but the mortar level is left below the top of the side 'shutters' to allow for cutting, fitting and pinning a timber slip on top of the repair before the mortar is cured. After curing, the latex coating is stripped off and the timber shutters are shaped and cut back as appropriate to the correct face.

Along the same lines timber joints can also be restored when they are decayed, without the aid of steel straps and bolts. However, care should be taken for it is important that joists retain their original freedom of movement, and although it is claimed that such repaired joints allow some degree of movement, in most cases the joints should be dismantled and repaired to allow for all the original movement to take place. This is achieved by building up the decayed section with resin which can then be worked freely to the original joint profile. In addition these resins can be used as hardening agents injected into partially decayed timbers, providing them with additional strength while retaining the original detail. Shakes, splits and holes can also be treated by brushing and blowing out with compressed air all loose frass and debris and treating the area with low-viscosity epoxy resin well brushed in, allowing all softened areas to absorb as much resin as possible before the void is packed with epoxy mortar finished off level and dusted with wood 'flour'.

Epoxy resin is now used in timber repairs in many European

countries, as well as Canada and USA, and long and intensive field trials have proved to be very successful. In recent years it has been used on a number of important timber-framed buildings in Britain, including those under the Directorate of Ancient Monuments and Historic Buildings. The work is generally undertaken by a specialist firm.

Replacement of Infill Panels

As we have seen previously, wattle-and-daub was the traditional infilling to the walls of a timber-framed structure but, although internally much remains in good repair, externally much is defective, for the wattle is usually infested with beetle or, because of water penetration through the daub, is rotten and needs replacement. When only an odd panel needs replacing, the wattle can be renewed using the traditional methods as previously described, with the wattle being covered by one of the methods described later. As is more often the case, however, it will be found that most of the panels are defective and in need of replacement, and a number of renewal techniques are available, the choice depending largely on the size and shape of the panels (209).

Lightweight blocks cut and fitted between the studs and jointed in mortar, in the same way as brick-nogging, rendered externally and plastered internally, are sometimes used, but they are not to be recommended for they can create problems in overloading the frame, as well as the difficulty in making a satisfactory watertight joint between the blocks and timber.

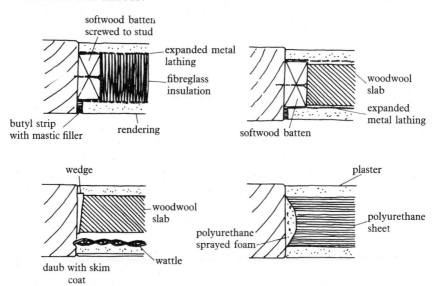

209. Replacement of wattle-and-daub

More satisfactory is the use of some form of lightweight infill panels which add little weight to the frame and which can at the same time incorporate some thermal insulation to the walls, which will certainly be desirable. A method used at the Avoncroft Museum at Bromsgrove, when re-erecting timber-framed building using both traditional techniques and modern materials, has much to recommend it. The wattle is replaced with new, formed of impregnated hazel onto which a daub (of eight parts of clay, one part lime and one part cow-dung) is applied to the face. This coat is then scratched to form a key for a skim coat consisting of equal parts of sand and lime with some cement added in the proportion 3½:3½:1, and the panel is then limewashed. The daub is applied to both sides of the wattle, but in domestic work, where increased insulation is required, it can be omitted from the inner face and replaced with a woodwool slab cut and fitted and wedged in position, care being taken to provide an adequate air space between the wattle and the woodwool slab. The woodwool slabs are then plastered and decorated in the usual way. Woodwool slabs have long been used as a replacement for wattle-and-daub. They can be obtained in various thicknesses from one inch up to four inches and in various lengths, depending on their thicknesses, from six feet up to twelve feet six inches; however, they can be obtained only in two-foot widths and so, unless the studs are closely spaced, have to be joined. The woodwool slabs are generally fixed to a treated softwood frame screwed around the openings and the panel finished off with rendering externally and expanded metal lathing fixed to the softwood frame and plastered internally. Additional insulation can be incorporated between the woodwool and the internal plaster.

Another and perhaps the simplest method is to introduce treated softwood battens of the appropriate size screwed around the opening to the timber-frame. Onto both sides of this framework, expanded metal lathing is nailed or stapled with additional treated softwood noggings introduced if the span exceeds two feet. Between the two layers of expanded metal lathing a layer of compressed fibreglass quilt insulation can be introduced and the panels then rendered externally and plastered internally in the usual way. The disadvantage with all these methods is, as with wattle-and-daub, the problem of shrinkage between the studs and panel; however, this can be overcome by the introduction of a compressible preformed butyl strip which can in addition be pointed up with a flexible waterproof mastic filler.

A modern material gaining popularity is polyurethane foam sheeting, a material which has many advantages: it can fit any size or shape of panel without joints and has the lowest thermal conductivity rate of any commercially available insulation material. It is wedged into position, the gap being filled with polyurethane sprayed foam, securely fixing the sheet in position. Because of the excellent bond of polyurethane to timber, it overcomes the problem of water-penetration at the interface of the timber. The panel is then rendered with one of the specially developed renders, such as Cemfil, and plastered internally with two coats of gypsum plaster.

A small lead flashing should be provided to form a sill at the foot of all replacement panels dressed between the rendering and infilling and projecting about an inch and turned down to form a drip. The underside of the lead should be painted to resist tannic acid attack from the oak.

Brick nogging too often needs to be replaced, because of deterioration of either the brick or more commonly the mortar. The panels should be carefully removed and rebuilt, re-using if possible the original bricks for these are often of a fine quality as regards their colour and texture, although some are somewhat porous. Galvanized or non-ferrous ties should be screwed to the face of the studs and built into the joints of the brickwork to secure the panel. The joint between the brickwork and timber frame should be raked out and the gap filled with a waterproof mastic filler to prevent the ingress of water. Even where the panels are sound, it may be necessary to remake the joint between the brick and timber; this can be remade in mortar but the problem of perimeter shrinkage still remains and it is advisable for the joints to be caulked with a compressible preformed butyl strip which gives a base for mastic filler. When rebuilding brick panels, the temptation of incorporating patterns, such as herringbone and diagonal courses, should be avoided and panels should be renewed as existing, for the custom was not devised from a desire to add interest but to encourage the bricks to exert an outward pressure against the timbers while the mortar was soft.

Repair of Daub
Although in most cases daub will need to be replaced because of the decay of the supporting wattle, often, when the wattle is still sound, the old daub can be repaired. As we have seen earlier, the specification for daub varies greatly in different areas, and one of these can be adopted in repair. We have seen that at Avoncroft a mix of clay, lime and cow-dung in the proportion of 8:1:1 is used. Another found to be serviceable is a mix of lime putty, sharp sand and cow-dung in the proportion of 4:1:1 well mixed and bound together with chopped straw or long hair. All daub should be mixed as dry as possible to reduce to a minimum any shrinkage that may occur. Any shrinkage cracks should be filled with a similar material but without the binding. In addition old wattle-and-daub panels often shrink: these should not be

removed if sound and can be wedged in position and any gap between panel and timber filled in with daub. Daub panels should always be limewashed.

Surface Treatment of Timber

As we have seen earlier, historically, exposed oak timbers were either left in their natural state or limewashed over in conjunction with the wattle-and-daub panels, and the blackening of the framing so common in the West, Lancashire and Cheshire was a later rather than an early idiom. Today there is a growing number of black-and-white buildings in these areas in which the tar-like materials are being removed, restoring the timbers to their natural state, for timbers so treated prevent them from breathing, moisture becoming trapped and decay developing.

The tar or bituminous paint can be removed in a number of ways. One satisfactory method recommended by the Society for the Protection of Ancient Buildings is an application of strong caustic soda, the surface thoroughly washed down with clean water, but a small trial area should be made in the first instance. This treatment is followed with the application of two or three coats of limewash over the oak, which after two or three days can be removed with a hard brush. A blowlamp should not, of course, be used. In those areas where traditionally timbers have been blackened, they can, for aesthetic reasons, be treated again, perhaps with a proprietary timber stain which allows the timber to breathe. Gloss paint and all tar-like products should not be used, nor should linseed oil, another common treatment, which tends to remain sticky, attracting dust and dirt as well as discolouring the timber. It is, however, probably best to leave the timbers in their natural state but, if treatment of some kind is thought to be needed, then a clear preservative fungicide can be applied after the removal of dirt. Oak can be satisfactorily cleaned with soap and water and a little household washing-soda followed by several rinses of warm, clean water.

All English oak is full of shakes, but though some appear almost alarming few are of much structural importance. It is true that in external timbers they can afford a lodgement for water but old oak is not sufficiently porous for water to soak into it to any great extent, and they should be filled only if water is being directed through the cracks to the internal face of the building. Hard fillers should be avoided, and in particular cement mortar, a material frequently seen, as these do not adhere to the timber and being inelastic do not expand and contract with the timber. A compound of oak and resin glue in the proportion of 1:1 or one of the many proprietary fillers on the market would be suitable. The filler should be kept back from the face of the timber and the base weathered to permit rain to run off. If the shake is large, oak slips should be bedded in the filler; the timber should be old but sound to avoid shrinkage.

Although oak is best left in its natural state, when repairs to the frame have been carried out, with either new or old wood, the natural weathering process can be expedited by the application of limewash over both old and new timbers, the excess being removed from the timber with a stiff wire brush the following day. Alternatively a coat of sulphate of iron can be applied, which produces a mid-grey effect. These treatments are also suitable for timber frames which have formerly been plastered.

Bibliography

Of the great number of books, booklets and articles which have contributed to the writing of this book, it is possible to mention here only those that have proved most valuable.

General Books

Addy, S. O., *The Evolution of the English House* (Allen & Unwin, 1898; revised 1933)

Alcock, N. W., *A Catalogue of Cruck Buildings* (Phillimore, 1973)

Ayres, James, *The Shell Book of The Home in Britain* (Faber & Faber, 1981)

Barley, M. W., *The English Farmhouse and Cottage* (Routledge & Paul, 1961)

Braun, H., *The Story of the English House* (Batsford, 1940); *Old English Houses* (Faber & Faber, 1962)

Briggs, M. S., *The English Farmhouse* (Batsford, 1953)

Brunskill, R. W., *Illustrated Handbook of Vernacular Architecture* (Faber & Faber, 1971; new edition 1978); *Traditional Buildings of Britain* (Gollancz, 1981)

Cave, Lyndon F., *The Smaller English House – Its History and Development* (Hale, 1981)

Clifton-Taylor, Alex, *The Pattern of English Building* (Batsford, 1962; new edition Faber & Faber, 1972)

Cook, Olive, and Smith, Edwin, *Old English Cottages and Farmhouses* (Thames & Hudson, 1954)

Crosseley, F. H., *Timber Building in England* (Batsford, 1951)

Cunnington, Pamela, *How Old is Your House?* (Alphabooks, 1980)

Harris, Richard, *Discovering Timber-Framed Buildings* (Shire Publications, 1978)

Hewett, C. A., *English Historic Carpentry* (Phillimore, 1980)

Innocent, C. F., *The Development of English Building Construction* (Cambridge University Press, 1916)

Mason, R. T., *Framed Buildings of England* (Coach Publishing House)

Mercer, Eric, *English Vernacular Houses* (Royal Commission on Historical Monuments, HMSO, 1975)

Penoyre, John and Jane, *Houses in the Landscape* (Faber & Faber, 1978)

Powys, A. R., *The Repair of Ancient Buildings* (Dent & Sons, 1929, New Edition SPAB, 1981)

Prizeman, J., *Your House – the Outside View* (Hutchinson, 1975)

Reid, Richard, *The Shell Book of Cottages* (Joseph, 1977)

Salzman, L. F., *Building in England Down to 1540* (Oxford, 1952)

West, T., *The Timber-framed House in England* (David & Charles, 1971)

Wood, M. E., *The English Medieval House* (Phoenix, 1965)

Regional Books

Davie, W. G., and Curtis Green, W., *Old Cottages and Farmhouses in Surrey* (Batsford, 1908)

Davie, W. G., and Dawber, E. G., *Old Cottages and Farmhouses in Kent & Sussex* (Batsford, 1906); *Farmhouses and other Buildings in the Cotswold District* (Batsford, 1905)

Forrester, Harry, *The Timber-framed Houses of Essex; A Short Review of the Types and Details, Fourteenth to Eighteenth Centuries* (Tindall Press, 1959)

Gravett, Kenneth, *Timber and Brick Building in Kent* (Phillimore)

Hewett, C. A., *The Development of English Carpentry 1200–1700: An Essex Study* (David & Charles, 1969)

Mason, R. T., *Framed Building of the Weald* (privately published, 1964; revised edition, 1969)

Nairn, Ian, and Pevsner, Nikolaus, *The Buildings of England – Surrey* (Penguin, 1962); *The Buildings of England – Sussex* (Penguin, 1965)

Nevill, R., *Old Cottages and Domestic Architecture in South-west Surrey* (Billing & Son, Guildford, 1889)

Newman, John, *The Buildings of England – North East and East Kent* (Penguin, 1969); *The Buildings of England – West Kent and the Weald* (Penguin, 1969)

Oliver, Basil, *Old Houses and Village Buildings in East Anglia* (Batsford, 1912)

Parkinson, J., and Ould, E. A., *Old Cottages and Farmhouses in Shropshire, Herefordshire and Cheshire* (Batsford, 1904)

Pevsner, Nikolaus, *The Buildings of England – Derbyshire* (Penguin, 1953 revised 1978 by Elizabeth Williamson); *The Buildings of England – Essex* (Penguin, 1959), revised 1965 by Enid Radcliffe); *The Buildings of England – Hertfordshire* (Penguin, 1953, revised 1977 by Bridget Cherry); *The Buildings of England – Suffolk* (Penguin, 1961); *The Buildings of England – Worcestershire* (Penguin, 1968)

Royal Commission on Historical Monuments, *Buckinghamshire; Volumes I & II* (1912–13); *Cambridgeshire; Volumes I & II* (1968–72); *Essex; Volumes I–IV* (1916–23); *Herefordshire; Volumes I–III* (1931–4); *Huntingdonshire* (1926)

Sandon, Eric, *Suffolk Houses* (Baron Publishing, 1977)

Articles etc

Baggs, A. P., 'Hook Farm, Lower Woodcut, Hampshire' (*Transactions of the Newbury District Field Club*, 11, No. 4, 1967, pp. 27–8)

Beresford, G. T. M., 'Northend Farm House, Long Crendon' (*Record of Buckinghamshire*, 18, ii, 1967, pp. 125–35)

Charles, F. W. B., 'Medieval Cruck-Building and its Derivatives' (*Society for Medieval Archaeology, Monograph Series*, No. 2, 1967)

Colman, J. G., and S. J., 'A Thirteenth Century Aisled House: Purton Green Farm, Stansfield, Suffolk' (*Proceedings of the Suffolk Institute of Archaeology*, 30, ii, 1965, 149–65)

Cordingley, R. A., 'British Historical Roof-Types and their Members; A Classification' (*Transaction of the Ancient Monuments Society* New Series 9, 1961, pp. 73–118)

Fletcher, J. M., 'Three Medieval Farmhouses in Harwell' (*Berkshire Archaeological Journal*, 62, 1965–6, pp. 45–69); 'Crucks in the West Berkshire and Oxford Region' (*Oxoniensia*, 33, 1968, pp. 71–88)

Hewett, C. A., 'Structural Carpentry in Medieval Essex' (*Medieval Archaeology*, 6–7, 1962–3, pp. 240–70); 'Jettying and Floor Framing in Medieval Essex' (*Ibid*, 1966, pp. 89–112); 'Some East Anglian Prototypes for early Timber Houses in America' (*Post Medieval Archaeology*, 3, 1969, pp. 100–21); 'Seventeenth Century Carpentry in Essex' (*Ibid*, 5, 1971, pp. 77–87); 'The Development of the Post-Medieval House' (*Ibid*, 7, 1973, pp. 60–78); 'Structural Carpentry in the Medieval House' (*Transactions of Association for Studies in the Conservation of Historic Buildings*, Vol. 1, 1973); 'The Smaller Medieval House in Essex' (*Archaeology Journal*, 130, 1973, pp. 172–81); 'Aisled Timber Halls and Related Buildings, Chiefly in Essex' (*Ancient Monuments Society's Transaction*, 1976, pp. 45–99)

Jones, S. R., and Smith, J. T., 'Manor House, Wasperton' (*Transactions of the Proceedings of the Birmingham Archaeological Society*, 76, 1958, pp. 19–28)

Mason, R. T., and Packer, G. A., 'Chennell's Brook Farm, Horsham' (*Sussex Archaeological Collections*, 101, 1963, pp. 40–7)

Mason, R. T., and Wood, R. H., 'Winkhurst Farm, Bough Beech' (*Archaeological Cantiana*, 83, 1968, pp. 33–7)

Rigold, S. E., 'The timber-framed buildings of Steventon (Berkshire) and their regional significance' (*Transactions of the Newbury District Field Club*, 10, No. 4, 1958, pp. 4–13); 'Fourteenth century halls in the East Weald' (*Archaeological Cantiana*, 82, 1967, pp. 246–56). Some Major Kentish Barns (*Ibid*, 81, 1966, pp. 1–30)

Smith, J. T., 'A 14th century aisled house; Edgar's Farm, Stowmarket' (*Proceedings of the Suffolk Institute of Archaeology*, 28, i, 1958, pp. 54–61); 'Medieval Aisled Halls and their Derivatives' (*Archaeological Journal*, 112, 1955, pp. 76–94). 'Medieval roofs: a classification' (*Ibid*, 115, 1958, pp. 111–49), 'Timber-framed Building in England; Its Development and Regional Differences' (*Ibid*, 122, 1965, pp. 133–58)

Place Index

Page numbers in italics refer to illustrations

General Index

Page numbers in italics refer to illustrations